Supporting Whole Language

Supporting Whole Language

Stories of Teacher and Institutional Change

edited by **Constance Weaver**
Western Michigan University

Linda Henke
School District of Clayton
Clayton, Missouri

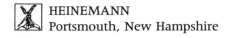 HEINEMANN
Portsmouth, New Hampshire

Heinemann Educational Books, Inc.
361 Hanover Street   Portsmouth, NH 03801-3959
Offices and agents throughout the world

© 1992 by Heinemann Educational Books, Inc. All rights reserved. No part of this book may be reproduced in any form or by electronic or mechanical means, including information storage and retrieval systems, without permission in writing from the publisher, except by a reviewer, who may quote brief passages in a review.

We would like to thank the teachers, children, and parents who have given their permission to include material in this book. Every effort has been made to contact copyright holders for permission to reprint borrowed material where necessary, but if any oversights have occurred, we would be happy to rectify them in future printings of this work.

Figure 12–1 is from *Making Connections: Teaching and the Human Brain* by Renate Nummela Caine and Geoffrey Caine. ASCD, 1991. Reprinted by permission.

Library of Congress Cataloging-in-Publication Data

Supporting whole language: stories of teacher and institutional
    change / edited by Constance Weaver, Linda Henke.
        p.   cm.
    Includes bibliographical references.
    ISBN 0-435-08704-5
    1. Language experience approach in education—United States.
2. Educational change—United States.   3. Language arts—United
States.   I. Weaver, Constance.   II. Henke, Linda.
LB1576.S895   1992
428—dc20   91-28226
                                                        CIP

Front-cover photo by Kara Nandell.
Designed by Jenny Jensen Greenleaf.
Printed in the United States of America
92 93 94 95 96 10 9 8 7 6 5 4 3 2 1

Contents

LIBRARY
ALMA COLLEGE
ALMA, MICHIGAN

Preface

This book began as a conversation at a reading conference in Toronto, where Linda made a presentation on how a whole language culture had been nurtured at Clive School in West Des Moines, Iowa. Linda explained that, as curriculum director, she had drawn upon the work of Terrence Deal and Allan Kennedy in their book *Corporate Cultures* to facilitate teacher and institutional change. In examining the most successful corporations in the country, Deal and Kennedy found that these companies gave priority to creating a culture that promoted a shared belief system. As Connie listened to Linda's presentation, bells went off and lightbulbs flashed; she remembered what she'd read of how Japanese corporations use quality circles to promote a sense of ownership and commitment among workers. Of course! What was needed to facilitate whole language teaching was an institutional culture that reflected that belief system.

Our thinking was reinforced two weeks later, when Connie talked with Peter Krause, Director General of the Lakeshore School District in the Montreal area. Peter had been reading and basing his administrative practice on books like Tom Peters's *In Search of Excellence* (coauthored with Robert H. Waterman, Jr.), which demonstrated that the most effective corporate cultures seemed to be based on whole language–like principles. Such principles include the importance of supporting collaboration and a sense of community, the importance of encouraging risk-taking and individual decision-making, and the importance of developing in all members of the corporation a sense of ownership and pride. These, of course, are characteristic of whole language classrooms, reflecting what teachers try to accomplish with children.

It became increasingly obvious that administrators and others wanting to promote whole language teaching needed to create a similar culture for nurturing teachers and, indeed, all members of the school community. What this means, in plain language, is that if whole language is to be institutionalized, the institution itself must change. Traditional bureaucratic ways of dealing with curriculum and administration must give way to an organizational structure that draws upon and develops the expertise of all those within the organization, not just those at the top.

This book grew out of that conviction. Though the individual perspectives among the articles differ, they all emphasize that whole language requires relinquishing our traditional beliefs about learning and teaching, and they all indicate—implicitly if not explicitly—that the necessary change in beliefs can be facilitated but not successfully mandated. We cannot foster a whole language belief system by means contrary to that belief system.

Introduction

* * *

1 | A Whole Language Belief System and Its Implications for Teacher and Institutional Change

Constance Weaver

In her lead article, Connie Weaver explores the principles that undergird whole language theory and practice. She suggests that in order for whole language to thrive in a school, these principles must drive not only instructional but also institutional processes. Such an accomplishment requires a major paradigm shift, a rethinking of the roles, behaviors, and activities that are deeply embedded in schooling and the administration of schools. Connie points out that mandating whole language, which has been done with surprising frequency across the country by well-meaning administrators, neglects the very principles that comprise the philosophy behind it. Successful whole language programs grow instead from a passionate regard for the learner in every child and every adult who is part of the school community.

CONNIE WEAVER is a professor of English at Western Michigan University, where she teaches courses on the reading and writing processes and a whole language approach to literacy and learning. She has recently served as Director of the Commission on Reading of the National Council of Teachers of English. Her major publications include *Understanding Whole Language: From Principles to Practice* (Heinemann 1990), *Reading Process and Practice: From Socio-psycholinguistics to Whole Language* (Heinemann 1988), and *Grammar for Teachers* (NCTE 1979). Currently she is collaborating on a book with Joel Chaston and Scott Peterson, *Growing into Whole Language: An Odyssey in Theme Exploration*, to be published by Scholastic-TAB of Canada and Heinemann.

* * *

When Lee Gunderson wrote, "There are as many manifestations of whole language instruction as there are whole language teachers"

3

(1989, p. 41), he probably did not anticipate the dilution that the term *whole language* has experienced in the last couple of years. Some teachers call themselves "whole language" teachers because they use Big Books in their classrooms—even though the way they use Big Books differs little from the way they may have traditionally used basals. Administrators think they can get their teachers to "do" whole language by bringing in an outside expert to conduct an in-service workshop or two. And commercial publishers, eager to cash in on the popularity of whole language, advertise their wares as whole language basals, whole language programs, and even whole language activity sheets—not realizing or not caring that such materials are contrary to the spirit of whole language.

Such perversions of the concept of whole language threaten its demise, for if whole language can mean anything and everything, then it in effect means nothing.

The term *whole language* seems to have grown originally from a concern for keeping language whole during instruction, from the desire to avoid fragmenting language into bits and pieces for isolated drill (Watson 1989). It reflected the understanding that the same kinds of response and encouragement that nurtured children's development of spoken language could stimulate their development as readers and writers, using whole texts with natural language patterns rather than basalese, the stilted and unnatural language characteristic of beginning reading texts. Gradually, whole language has grown into a philosophy not only of literacy development but of learning in general. Based upon a solid body of research in fields as diverse as language acquisition and emergent literacy, psycholinguistics and sociolinguistics, schema theory and literary theory, ethnography, anthropology, philosophy, and education, whole language may also be characterized as theory-in-practice, or a belief system. Figure 1–1 lists references that describe some of the research underlying and supporting whole language.

Because whole language is a belief system, it cannot simply be mandated within a school or school system. As several of the articles in this volume demonstrate, anyone wanting to "implement" whole language needs to understand and *live* this philosophy or belief system in order to develop a whole language school or school system. Or, to put it another way, a whole language philosophy will be successfully implemented to the extent that schools create a climate for change and a shared culture that reflects the whole language philosophy.

FIGURE 1–1   *References Describing Some of the Research Underlying and Supporting Whole Language*

Goodman, Kenneth S. November 1989. Whole-language research: Foundations and development. *The Elementary School Journal* 90: 208–21.

Heald-Taylor, Gail. 1989. *The Administrator's Guide to Whole Language.* Katonah, N.Y.: Richard C. Owen.

Rhodes, Lynn K., and Nancy L. Shanklin. 1989. *A Research Base for Whole Language.* Denver, Colo.: LINK.

Stephens, Diane. January 1991. Toward an understanding of whole language. Technical Report No. 524. Champaign, Ill.: Center for the Study of Reading, University of Illinois.

———. 1992. *Research on Whole Language: Support for a New Curriculum.* Katonah, N.Y.: Richard C. Owen.

Stephens, Diane, and Constance Weaver. 1990. What does the research say? Research in support of whole-to-part. In Constance Weaver, *Understanding Whole Language: From Principles to Practice.* Portsmouth, N.H.: Heinemann.

Some Basics of Whole Language

Though indeed there is no one "true" definition of whole language, there are many principles that together form a core of beliefs characterizing the essence of a whole language philosophy. Most leading and longtime whole language educators would agree upon the principles discussed below, though doubtless they would describe them somewhat differently and include other principles as well. Figure 1–2 lists some references that characterize such whole language principles.

As the following discussion will show, whole language requires not merely that teachers use new activities or materials, but also that they understand learners and learning in new ways, that they interact with students and develop curriculum in new ways, that they modify their roles as teachers, and that they hold new expectations for students and develop new means of assessment accordingly. Each of these areas has implications for administrators and other agents of change who want to see whole language actualized within classrooms.

This discussion of whole language principles is taken from a chapter in *Growing into Whole Language: An Odyssey in Theme Exploration* (Weaver, Chaston, and Peterson, forthcoming). Clearly there is some overlap among the following categories.

FIGURE 1–2   *References Characterizing Whole Language Principles*

Articles
Altwerger, Bess, Carole Edelsky, and Barbara M. Flores. November 1987. Whole language: What's new? *The Reading Teacher* 41: 144–54.

Goodman, Kenneth S. November 1989. Whole-language research: Foundations and development. *The Elementary School Journal* 90: 208–21.

Goodman, Yetta M. November 1989. Roots of the whole-language movement. *The Elementary School Journal* 90: 113–27.

Gursky, Daniel. August 1991. After the reign of Dick and Jane. *Teacher Magazine*, pp. 22–29.

Newman, Judith M., and Susan M. Church. 1990. Myths of whole language. *The Reading Teacher* 44: 20–26. September.

Watson, Dorothy J. November 1989. Defining and describing whole language. *The Elementary School Journal* 90: 130–41.

Books
Cambourne, Brian. 1988. *The Whole Story: Natural Learning and the Acquisition of Literacy in the Classroom*. Auckland, New Zealand: Scholastic.

Edelsky, Carole, Bess Altwerger, and Barbara Flores. 1991. *Whole Language: What's the Difference?* Portsmouth, N.H.: Heinemann.

Goodman, Kenneth S. 1986. *What's Whole in Whole Language?* Richmond Hill, Ontario: Scholastic-TAB. Available in the U.S. from Heinemann.

Goodman, Kenneth S., Lois Bridges Bird, and Yetta M. Goodman. 1991. *The Whole Language Catalog*. Santa Rosa, Calif.: American School Publishers.

Manning, Gary, and Debbie Manning, eds. 1989. *Whole Language: Beliefs and Practices, K–8*. Washington, D.C.: National Education Association.

Weaver, Constance. 1990. *Understanding Whole Language: From Principles to Practice*. Portsmouth, N.H.: Heinemann.

Learning and the Learner

Explicitly rejecting behaviorism as a model for significant human learning, whole language educators have been influenced by the work of cognitive psychologists and learning theorists who emphasize the roles of motivation and social interaction in learning (see Y. Goodman 1989, K. Goodman 1989). Their understanding of learning has also been strongly influenced by descriptions of learning in natural settings (for some of this research, see Stephens 1991 and 1992). Such research has given rise to the following principles:

1. Learners construct meaning for themselves, most readily in contexts where they can actively transact (or interact) with other people, with books, and with objects and materials in the external world. The most significant and enduring learning,

particularly of concepts and complex processes, is likely to be that which is constructed by the learner, not imposed from without.

2. When learning is perceived as functional to and purposeful for the learner, it is more likely to endure. That is, the most significant learning derives from that which arouses the interest, meets the needs, and furthers the purposes of the learner in the here and now.

3. In order to engage themselves wholeheartedly in learning, however, learners must be confident that they will be safe from negative repercussions. That is, the environment for learning must be risk-free.

4. Though there are developmental trends among learners, learning is fundamentally idiosyncratic, even chaotic; the nature and course of each individual's learning are unique.

5. Individual learning is promoted by social collaboration: by opportunities to work with others, to brainstorm, to try out ideas and get feedback, to obtain assistance. In short, learning is facilitated by a community of learners.

Each of these points is relevant to teachers and administrators as learners, in addition to being relevant to students. Figure 1–3 lists some of the key references for understanding this philosophy of learning and its roots.

Nature and Development of the Curriculum

Several implications for curriculum derive from the aforementioned principles of learning:

1. Since learning proceeds best when learners engage in authentic literacy and learning experiences, the curriculum should consist not of worksheets and dittos but of opportunities to engage in the myriad kinds of reading, discussion, experimentation, and research that children and adults voluntarily engage in outside of school. "Opportunities" also implies a strong element of *choice*, for learners.

2. Since choice is an important factor in facilitating learning, the curriculum is in many respects negotiated among the teacher and the students. Ultimately the teacher determines in what respects and in what instances learners may make choices, but often curricular decisions are made by the teacher and students

FIGURE 1–3   *References for Understanding the Roots of a Whole Language Philosophy of Learning*

Cambourne, Brian. 1988. *The Whole Story: Natural Learning and the Acquisition of Literacy in the Classroom.* Auckland, New Zealand: Scholastic.

Edelsky, Carole, and Karen Draper. 1989. Reading/"reading"; writing/"writing"; text/"text." *Reading-Canada-Lecture* 7: 201–16.

Edelsky, Carole, and Karen Smith. January 1984. "Is that writing—or are those marks just a figment of your curriculum?" *Language Arts* 61: 24–32.

Ferreiro, Emilia, and Ana Teberosky. 1982. *Literacy Before Schooling.* Trans. Karen Goodman Castro. Portsmouth, N.H.: Heinemann.

Goodman, Kenneth S. 1973. *Theoretically Based Studies of Patterns of Miscues in Oral Reading Performance.* Detroit: Wayne State University. Educational Resources Information Center, ED 079 708.

Goodman, Kenneth S., and Yetta M. Goodman. 1979. Learning to read is natural. *Theory and Practice of Early Reading.* Ed. Lauren B. Resnick and Phyllis A. Weaver, 1:137–54. Hillsdale, N.J.: Erlbaum.

Goodman, Yetta M. June 1978. Kid watching: An alternative to testing. *National Elementary School Principal* 57: 41–45.

Halliday, M. A. K. 1975. *Learning How to Mean.* New York: Elsevier North-Holland.

Harste, Jerome C., Virginia A. Woodward, and Carolyn L. Burke. 1984. *Language Stories and Literacy Lessons.* Portsmouth, N.H.: Heinemann.

Holdaway, Don. 1979. *Foundations of Literacy.* Sydney, Australia: Scholastic. Available in the U.S. from Heinemann.

Kelly, E., Carl Rogers, Abraham Maslow, and A. Combs. 1962. *Perceiving, Behaving, Becoming.* New York: Association for Supervision and Curriculum Development.

Rosenblatt, Louise. 1978. *The Reader, the Text, the Poem: The Transactional Theory of the Literary Work.* Carbondale, Ill.: Southern Illinois University Press.

Smith, Frank. 1975. *Comprehension and Learning: A Conceptual Framework for Teachers.* Katonah, N.Y.: Richard C. Owen.

———. January 1981a. Demonstrations, engagement, and sensitivity: A revised approach to language learning. *Language Arts* 58: 103–22.

———. September 1981b. Demonstrations, engagement, and sensitivity: The choice between people and programs. *Language Arts* 58: 634–42.

———. 1988. *Understanding Reading.* 4th ed. Hillsdale, N.J.: Erlbaum.

Vygotsky, Lev S. 1978. *Mind in Society: The Development of Higher Psychological Processes.* Ed. Michael Cole, Vera John-Steiner, Sylvia Scribner, and Ellen Souberman. Cambridge, Mass.: Harvard University Press.

———. 1986. *Thought and Language.* Trans. Alex Kozulin. Cambridge, Mass.: MIT Press.

together, during long-range planning and also in the daily give-and-take of the classroom. Often, the curriculum develops around topics and themes, with language and literacy developing through and across the curriculum.

3. Since learning opportunities need to be perceived as functional and purposeful by the learner, it follows that language itself must be kept natural and whole. This means that emergent readers will be assisted in reading rhymes, songs, and repetitive and predictable stories rather than the stilted, unnatural language known as basalese; they will read whole texts rather than the contextless bits and pieces of language that characterize worksheets and workbooks. Similarly, students will write authentic stories, poems, letters, and other pieces, not assignments like composing a story on "The day I woke up as a pencil," copying a poem from the blackboard, or filling in the blanks or lines of a workbook page.

4. Direct and indirect instruction of the "parts" of language occurs in the context of the whole and in the context of the students' need. For example, the teacher will show one or more students how to punctuate dialogue when the students have actually used dialogue in writing a story, not through an isolated skill lesson on quotation marks. Phonics skills are developed through writing and in the context of enjoying a rhyme or song, not through worksheet practice. And reading strategies are developed in the context of real reading. In a sense, instruction proceeds from whole to part and from part back to the whole.

5. Thus direct teaching occurs not according to a predetermined scope and sequence chart but in direct response to the students' interests and needs, as determined by them and by the teacher's observations. Most direct instruction occurs in response to the "teachable moment."

These principles have implications for the kinds of flexibility and support teachers need in order to become whole language teachers.

Teacher Roles and Functions in Facilitating Learning

In a whole language philosophy, the principles of learning, the characteristics of the curriculum, and teacher roles all draw heavily from research into the acquisition of language and literacy. For this reason, it is relevant to describe some of what has been observed to promote language and literacy acquisition in the home, before turning to implications for teacher roles and the learning environment in school. I will not discuss the relevant research in detail or cite the primary sources; however, a bibliography of reasonably accessible references is provided in Figure 1–4.

FIGURE 1–4   *Some Reasonably Accessible References on Language and Literacy Acquisition*

Articles

Fields, Marjorie V. May 1988. Talking and writing: Explaining the whole language approach to parents. *The Reading Teacher* 41: 898–903.

Goodman, Kenneth S., and Yetta M. Goodman. 1979. Learning to read is natural. In *Theory and Practice of Early Reading*. Ed. Lauren B. Resnick and Phyllis A. Weaver. Vol. 1: 137–54. Hillsdale, N.J.: Erlbaum.

Holdaway, Don. 1986. The structure of natural learning as a basis for literacy instruction. In *The Pursuit of Literacy: Early Reading and Writing*, pp. 56–72. Ed. Michael R. Sampson. Dubuque, Iowa: Kendall Hunt.

King, Martha L. December 1975. Language: Insights from acquisition. *Theory into Practice* 14: 293–98.

Newman, Judith M. 1985. Insights from recent reading and writing research and their implications for developing whole language curriculum. In *Whole Language: Theory in Use*, pp. 7–36. Ed. Judith M. Newman. Portsmouth, N.H.: Heinemann.

Teale, William H. September 1982. Toward a theory of how children learn to read and write naturally. *Language Arts* 59: 550–70.

Books

Clay, Marie M. 1987. *Writing Begins at Home*. Portsmouth, N.H.: Heinemann.

Doake, David. 1988. *Reading Begins at Birth*. Richmond Hill, Ontario: Scholastic-TAB.

Hall, Nigel. 1987. *The Emergence of Literacy*. Portsmouth, N.H.: Heinemann. Summarizes research.

Harste, Jerome C., Virginia A. Woodward, and Carolyn L. Burke. 1984. *Language Stories and Literacy Lessons*. Portsmouth, N.H.: Heinemann. Not easy reading, but offers a wealth of relevant detail.

Hill, Mary W. 1989. *Home: Where Reading and Writing Begin*. Portsmouth, N.H.: Heinemann.

Laminack, Lester L. 1991. *Learning with Zachary*. Richmond Hill, Ontario: Scholastic–TAB.

Newman, Judith M. 1984. *The Craft of Children's Writing*. Richmond Hill, Ontario: Scholastic-TAB. Available in the U.S. from Heinemann.

Sampson, Michael R., ed. 1986. *The Pursuit of Literacy: Early Reading and Writing*. Dubuque, Iowa: Kendall Hunt.

In acquiring our native language, what we learn are not simply words and phrases, but elements and *rules*. There are rules of various sorts: phonological (sound), morphophonological (meaning/sound), and syntactic (grammar), to mention three major kinds. One of the rules a toddler learns, for example, is the rule for forming the past tense of regular verbs, a morphophonological rule: add a /t/ sound if the verb ends in an unvoiced consonant; otherwise, add a /d/ sound (but if the verb ends in /t/ or /d/, add /ɨd/). We know that the child has learned this rule when he or she abandons *I went* for the regular but incorrect *I goed*, or discards *Mommy bought it* for the regular but equally incorrect *Mommy buyed it*. Similarly, the older child learns rules for the ordering of adjectives, such as "adjectives of number precede adjectives of age, which in turn precede adjectives of nationality," as in *the four young French girls* (Hartwell 1985, p. 111).

Of course, these and the myriad other rules governing the production of English sounds, words, and sentences are not rules the child learns consciously. Indeed, most adults do not know the rules themselves, consciously. Nevertheless, their speech is governed by these very rules that they may find hard to understand, much less to remember or teach to someone else.

However it is that children learn language, direct instruction of *rules* plays no part whatsoever.

What do we adults do, then, to facilitate children's acquisition of their native language and the rules that characterize it? Several things: First, we model, or "demonstrate," adult language structure and how meanings can be mapped onto words. Though we simplify our sentence structure and vocabulary, focusing on the here and now, we do not usually speak in unnatural language patterns. Second, we illustrate (demonstrate) a variety of language functions incidentally, by using language for various purposes as we interact with the growing child. Third, we expect success and demonstrate that expectation consistently, allowing our children to grow into language at their own rate. Fourth, we respond positively to their efforts to communicate, focusing on content and intent, rather than on the form or correctness of children's utterances. Fifth, we respond positively to children's efforts to use and control language, rewarding successive approximations to adult language rather than demanding correctness prematurely. Children receive our enthusiastic response for what they *can* do, rather than repeated criticism for what they cannot yet do.

When adults act and respond in similar ways, many children learn to read at home, in the same natural way they learned to speak and understand their language. Parents read to their children, demonstrating what it is to be a reader. They illustrate the symbolic nature of printed language as they discuss the book with the child, perhaps pointing out such features as words that stand for people and animals in the pictures, and sometimes running their finger under the words to demonstrate the link between spoken and written language. Parents often reread the story upon demand, and they encourage the child's efforts to retell the story by reading the pictures and reconstructing the meaning. They respond to the child's questions ("What does that say?" "What sound does that make?"). They exude pride as their child's efforts to read the book become increasingly tied to the words on the page. And they recognize that the child is primarily teaching him- or herself to read.

When whole language educators talk about the "natural" acquisition of literacy, what they mean is that literacy can best be fostered by using the means that parents have used, more or less naturally, to foster their preschoolers' development of literacy. Among the important implications for classroom instruction are these:

1. The teacher is, first of all, a role model. In order to foster students' development of literacy and learning, teachers must demonstrate that they themselves are passionate readers, writers, and learners. Teachers also need to demonstrate what it means to be risk-takers and decision-makers.
2. The teacher is also a mentor, collaborator, and facilitator. Often, the teacher serves as a master to whom students are apprenticed, and from whom they learn such crafts as reading and writing. The teacher shares his or her own knowledge with students while collaborating with them. The teacher offers learning experiences and choices, helps students consider and acquire the resources needed for their projects, guides students in learning valuable strategies and skills for carrying out their purposes, and responds to their needs, both those that the students articulate and those merely observed by the teacher.
3. Teachers are also responsible for creating a supportive community of learners in which everyone (including the teacher) is free to take risks and make decisions without fear of negative consequences and in which everyone is supported by others. Within this community, teachers encourage collaboration in various ways.
4. Teachers treat students as capable and developing, not as incapable or deficient. They respond positively to what their students

can do, while issuing invitations and offering challenges to stimulate students' growth.

5. Teachers share responsibility for curricular decision-making with students, thus encouraging them to take ownership of and responsibility for their own learning. By also encouraging risk-taking and decision-making without fear of negative consequences, teachers empower students to become independent, self-motivated learners and doers.

Assessment and Evaluation

It should not be surprising that in whole language classrooms, assessment and evaluation reflect many of the aforementioned principles of learning and teaching. For example:

1. Evaluation is based upon numerous assessments of various kinds, not upon a single assessment such as the score on a standardized test. Though recorded observations constitute the backbone of whole language assessment, various other means are also used, including periodic performance samples (e.g., of writing or reading), as well as data from conferences and interviews, inventories and questionnaires, dialogue journals and learning logs, and student-kept records. Self-evaluation is an important facet of whole language evaluation.
2. Assessment is ongoing and continuous, intertwined with learning and teaching. As students engage in daily learning experiences, teachers make observations about their progress and then use these observations along with other data to make decisions about how to facilitate learning and to evaluate students' learning.
3. Whatever the particular means, assessment data is gathered primarily while the learner is engaged in authentic literacy and/or learning experiences, not in an isolated test situation.
4. Assessment is primarily learner-referenced. That is, the learner's present accomplishments and stage of growth are compared more with past accomplishments than with external criteria or norms. This practice reflects the conviction that each learner's unique development should be honored.

These principles have implications for how administrators should assess teachers, and also for how administrators should be assessed.

Whole Language Requires a Paradigm Shift for Teachers

In order to act on the basis of principles and beliefs such as these, teachers must make a "paradigm shift"—they must move from the philosophy of education that underlies traditional teaching to the radically different belief system that underlies whole language. The belief system underlying traditional teaching stems primarily from behavioral psychology. Basal reading programs, for example, have traditionally reflected Edward L. Thorndike's behavioral "laws" of learning, which give rise to instruction that reduces reading to minute skills, then "teaches" reading as a matter of practicing those skills, and demonstrates reading achievement on tests that assess mastery of those skills in isolation (K. Goodman, Shannon, Freeman, and Murphy 1988).

A far different belief system underlies whole language. It derives particularly from research into the nature and course of cognitive development, the nature and facilitation of language acquisition and emergent literacy, and the nature of comprehension and the reading process (see references in Figure 1–3). These and related lines of inquiry give rise to a concept of learning that requires not practicing skills and memorizing facts so much as investigating, conceptualizing, hypothesizing, testing, and constructing knowledge.

The former paradigm or model of education is often called a "transmission" paradigm, while the paradigm underlying whole language is sometimes called a "transactional" paradigm (e.g., Weaver 1990; Monson and Pahl 1991). Figure 1–5 contrasts a transmission and a transactional paradigm or model of education.

Because such a drastic reconceptualization of education is necessary if teachers are to make the transition to whole language, it is no wonder that whole language cannot simply be mandated. Teachers need time and assistance in growing into whole language, and they need administrators who can recognize common patterns of growth and who will honor their own unique growth process (e.g., Chapter 2 of Weaver, Chaston, and Peterson, forthcoming). Teachers may adopt some new practices before actually shifting to a new way of thinking about learning and teaching; indeed, it is often the success of these new practices that eventually prompts them to adopt a transactional model of education. However, the paradigm shift must occur sooner or later if teachers' practices are increasingly to reflect a whole language philosophy.

FIGURE 1–5   *Transmission Versus Transactional Paradigm of Learning and Teaching*

Transmission	Transactional
Teacher dispenses curriculum.	Teacher negotiates curriculum with students.
Student passively practices skills, memorizes facts.	Student actively constructs concepts and meaning.
Avoiding mistakes is important.	Developing own hypotheses and taking risks are important.
Performance on tests is highly valued.	Engaging in meaningful learning experiences is valued more than test scores.
Learning is expected to be uniform; expectations are the same for all. Therefore, many students "fail."	Learning is expected to be individual; unique growth is expected. Evaluation is success oriented.

Whole Language Principles and Institutional Change

Institutional change cannot take place unless individual teachers make significant changes in both their philosophy and their practice.

Though teachers and administrators are of course more mature than children, the same principles of learning generally apply to them. In discussing the relevance of these and other whole language principles to effecting change in a school or school system, I will let *teachers* stand for both teachers and administrators who may be expected to change their beliefs and behaviors and let *administrators* stand for any agent of change trying to effect whole language teaching in the schools.

The whole language principles discussed above do not always correspond one-for-one with principles for effecting whole language education, but there is certainly a close correlation. Again, the categories interrelate and overlap.

Learning and the Learner

What clearly emerges from these principles is that whole language is based upon respect for the learner: respect for each learner's ability to make meaning from his or her experiences; respect for each learner's need and right to make choices and take responsibility for his or her own learning; respect for each learner's ability to evaluate his or her own learning; and respect for the complexity of each learner as a human being. This respect must apply equally to teachers and administrators as learners.

1. Like students, teachers must construct meaning for themselves. If they are to make the paradigm shift required by whole language, they must have ample opportunities to talk with colleagues, sharing their successes and failures and teaching ideas; ample opportunities to read and discuss professional literature with their colleagues; and ample opportunities to visit other teachers' classrooms and see how they are attempting to implement a whole language belief system.
2. Teachers too will learn most when the learning opportunities arouse their interest, meet their perceived needs, and further their purposes in the here and now. Therefore, collaboration and assistance that focus on helping teachers answer their own individual questions about teaching and learning are more likely to succeed than information dispensed to all teachers.
3. It is crucial for teachers to be able to experiment with new ways of teaching without fear of negative repercussions. For example, they may need to be explicitly told that they do not have to follow every iota of the basals or the curriculum guide. They may need to know that they will not be given a lower evaluation if their standardized test scores are somewhat lower than in previous years, as long as they can document their students' learning. Teachers will not risk making significant changes in their classrooms unless they are confident that they can do so without being penalized. Better yet, they need to know that their efforts will be approved, even if not everything they try seems to succeed.
4. Like students, teachers as learners are unique. Some teachers simply need to be encouraged and supported in the changes they are already making, while others need to be nudged into making changes.
5. Often, the best way to nudge reluctant teachers into changing their teaching is to provide many opportunities for collaborating with other teachers. Teachers' learning, like that of students', is facilitated by a community of learners. However,

administrators and teachers interested in helping their colleagues to change must do so by sharing their exciting innovations and their successes and failures in an atmosphere of
collegiality, with a sense that they too are learners, not by
preaching a new gospel or implying that they are authorities
while the other teachers are only beginners. To facilitate
teacher change, administrators need to encourage collaboration between experienced whole language teachers and those
with no understanding of this philosophy, not to polarize
them by mandating whole language.

Nature and Development of the Curriculum

For teachers, the implications of whole language principles regarding
curriculum fall into two broad areas: those related to the curriculum
of their professional development and those related to the curriculum
in the classroom.

1. Teachers need to have a say in the curriculum of their own
   professional development. That is, they need to raise their own
   questions about teaching and learning (even if someone else
   requires that they generate such questions), decide for themselves what professional materials they will read, choose what
   kinds of collaboration they will engage in, and, in short, direct
   their own professional growth.

   Administrators may find it workable to schedule faculty
   meetings in which teachers talk about how they would like to
   grow and then ask teachers to submit plans for their own
   professional growth, both within the classroom and outside it,
   as they try new ideas and interact with students in new ways.
   In this way it may be possible for administrators to mandate
   some efforts at professional growth, yet avoid dictating the
   nature of those efforts. But administrators must also be prepared to support teachers' growth by allowing time for collaboration, providing professional books as well as educational
   materials for the classroom, and demonstrating positive accep-
   tance of teachers' efforts. Requiring change without giving
   needed support seldom works.
2. Teachers also need to have considerable freedom and flexibility in determining the curriculum in their own classrooms—
   indeed, to negotiate and renegotiate the curriculum daily with
   their students. They must be freed as much as possible from

outside constraints and—as previously noted—must be confident that their efforts at innovation will be recognized and
rewarded rather than punished. Teachers and students must
be genuinely free to make many of their own choices regarding what to study and how to go about it, as well as how to
assess their learning and their progress.

Administrators' Roles and Functions in Facilitating Teachers' Learning

If administrators are to facilitate teachers' growth into whole language essentially the same way teachers facilitate students' growth in
whole language classrooms, they need to act upon many of the same
principles.

1. Administrators or other agents of change must first of all be
   role models, demonstrating what it means to grow into a
   whole language philosophy. This involves reading and discussing professional literature and, ideally, collaborating with
   others in trying to understand whole language and what it
   means to teach from a whole language philosophy. Administrators who want to implement a whole language philosophy
   should also demonstrate what it means to be a risk-taker, since
   their modeling will help teachers become risk-takers, too. Ideally, such administrators will also be passionate readers, writers, and learners: the kind of model that both teachers and
   students can emulate.
2. Administrators also need to be mentors, collaborators, and
   facilitators. They can support change by offering teachers
   varied learning experiences, helping them consider and
   acquire the resources they need for innovative teaching,
   demonstrating effective teaching practices, and responding to
   their needs, both those that teachers actually articulate and
   those the administrators observe. Administrators are often
   particularly successful in stimulating growth when they invite
   teachers to discuss their own plans for change and then ask,
   "How can I help you carry out your intentions?" At their best,
   administrators are mentors for teachers and collaborate with
   them in effecting change.
3. Administrators also need to create among teachers a supportive community of learners in which teachers are free to take
   risks and make decisions without fear of negative consequences,
   and in which they receive support from their colleagues.

Within this community, administrators must encourage collaboration, particularly in some of the same ways suggested for learners. In addition to creating a community of teacher-learners, administrators also need to develop support for learning among the wider community. Most crucially, this means involving parents in their children's schooling and, insofar as is possible, making formal education a natural extension of learning in the home and the community.

4. Administrators need to treat teachers as capable and developing, not as incapable or deficient. They should respond positively to teachers' efforts to grow into whole language, while issuing invitations and offering challenges to stimulate teachers' continued growth.

5. It is absolutely crucial that administrators who want to implement a whole language philosophy share authority and responsibility for decision-making with teachers, allowing them the freedom necessary to determine the curriculum within their own classrooms. In this way, administrators will empower teachers, and teachers will in turn empower their students as learners.

Assessment and Evaluation

The same principles that guide the assessment and evaluation of students in whole language classrooms should also guide the assessment and evaluation of teachers and administrators if the school or school system is to reflect a whole language philosophy of learning and teaching.

1. The evaluation of teachers must be based upon numerous assessments of various kinds, not upon a single assessment, such as one classroom visitation by the principal, or students' scores on standardized tests. Teachers must have opportunities to share with the principal portfolios of their students' work in order to demonstrate how their students have grown and, yes, to discuss—without fear of reprisal—their concerns about some students in particular and their teaching in general. Just as the teacher in a whole language classroom serves more as an advocate and collaborator than an adversary, so must the principal in evaluating teachers. Teachers can be invited to submit portfolios documenting their own growth and encouraged to evaluate themselves as learners and teachers.

2. Teachers' assessment of their own efforts in the classroom should become ongoing and continuous as they observe how students respond to learning opportunities they provide, assess students' needs, and promote the operation of the classroom as a community of learners. Administrators need to encourage teachers to become reflective practitioners and to include in their portfolios various kinds of data reflective of their individual growth as teachers.

3. Thus, the assessment of teacher effectiveness and growth can be based upon how successfully the teacher facilitates learning in the classroom, how the teacher otherwise demonstrates professional development, and how the teacher has grown in both—with the teacher's self-evaluation as a crucial factor.

4. The assessment of teachers, like that of students, should be primarily learner-referenced. That is, teachers' present accomplishments and stage of growth should be compared with their own past rather than with external criteria or norms, although the administrator may also share ways in which he or she would like to encourage each teacher to grow.

Whole Language Requires a Paradigm Shift for Administrators

By now it should be clear why whole language teaching cannot simply be mandated: it requires a paradigm shift, a major change in how teachers approach teaching. Furthermore, the old paradigm of instructional change (mandate it, then see that it is implemented) is contrary to the very belief system that underlies whole language education. In other words, the traditional means are inconsistent with the ends of whole language education.

Successfully implementing whole language within a school or system, then, requires that administrators understand the philosophy (which overeager administrators often don't). More than that, successful implementation requires that they *live* the philosophy. This represents a significant change in how most administrators approach institutional change: a shift from a transmission paradigm to a transactional paradigm that has obvious parallels with whole language teaching. Instead of mandating change, for example, the administrator is typically most successful when engaging with teachers in the exploration of this new philosophy and the practices it generates (see Krause, this volume). The would-be whole language administrator encourages change, rather than mandating or demanding it. And instead of being a manager, the whole language administrator is a leader, demonstrating an openness to change and sharing authority and responsibility with the teaching staff. These differences between a transmission and a transactional paradigm for effecting change are contrasted in Figure 1–6.

This description of how administrators can foster the development of whole language schools is not derived solely from the principles that underlie whole language education in the classroom. Rather, it stems from the real experiences of many administrators and teachers in a variety of schools and school systems. These experiences are documented and described in such books as *Learning Change* by Nancy Lester and Cynthia Onore (1990), and *Becoming a Whole Language School,* edited by Lois Bird (1989); they have also been articulated by the many individuals with whom I have discussed institutional change.

To develop and nurture a whole language philosophy within a school or school system, administrators and other agents of change would do well to keep in mind the following summary points, taken from my *Understanding Whole Language* (1990, pp. 285–86):

1. Realize that it will take *time* and energy and resources, both human and monetary.
2. Become a whole language educator, modeling the kinds of change you advocate: for example, become a reader and

---

FIGURE 1–6   *Role of Change Agent: Transmission Versus Transactional Paradigm for Effecting Institutional Change*

Transmission	Transactional
Manager.	Leader.
Mandates change.	Facilitates change.
Does not necessarily understand the change mandated.	Becomes a learner along with teachers.
Remains aloof from change process.	Demonstrates and participates in change.
Retains authority; dominates; demonstrates competition.	Shares authority; demonstrates collaboration.

writer of professional literature; join or start a whole language support group; take risks; empower others; discuss freely the contradictions between your own beliefs and practices and your efforts to narrow the gap between the two.

3. Recognize that whole language teaching cannot merely be mandated, nor can it be brought about merely by adopting policy statements or more holistic kinds of materials, though these can support whole language teaching and the development of a whole language philosophy.

4. Support teachers' professional growth and decision-making, and demonstrate respect for their judgment—in as many ways as possible. This may include developing a whole language climate or culture within the school. (See Linda Henke's article in this volume.)

5. Make provision for the purchase of more holistic educational materials, such as trade books that offer good quality literature and nonfiction, and a variety of materials for writing and publishing in the classroom. Money formerly used for workbooks and basal tests may often be diverted to this purpose.

6. Minimize standardized testing and downplay the results of standardized tests. Instead, encourage and help teachers develop alternative methods and means of assessment and evaluation, which can form the basis for educational decision-making.

7. Support teachers in taking risks; encourage them to move temporarily into a discomfort zone, but don't expect them to make major changes all at once.

8. Develop with teachers a policy and statement of goals that support and encourage the kind of teaching and learning environment you want to foster. This might include developing your own definition of "time on task" or "effective instruction."

9. Help parents understand what you are doing and why: enlist their support and involvement. The same holds for school board members and others in the community; they, too, need to be informed and involved.

10. Above all, perhaps, cultivate respect for one another within and among those in your school community: teachers, students, administrators, parents, school board members, and the public. When we demonstrate respect for the needs and concerns of others, it becomes natural to resolve difficulties through a problem-solving rather than a confrontational

approach. This again models the whole language, transactional philosophy of education.

Keeping these and the previously discussed points in mind will help smooth the transition from traditional to whole language teaching. Indeed, adopting a transactional model of institutional change is probably the only way to foster teaching that is "whole language" in more than name only.

References

Bird, Lois Bridges, ed. 1989. *Becoming a Whole Language School: The Fair Oaks Story*. Katonah, N.Y.: Richard C. Owen.

Goodman, Kenneth S. November 1989. Whole-language research: Foundations and development. *The Elementary School Journal* 90: 208–21.

Goodman, Kenneth S., Patrick Shannon, Yvonne Freeman, and Sharon Murphy. 1988. *Report Card on Basal Readers*. Katonah, N.Y.: Richard C. Owen.

Goodman, Yetta M. November 1989. Roots of the whole-language movement. *The Elementary School Journal* 90: 113–27.

Gunderson, Lee. 1989. *A Whole Language Primer*. Richmond Hill, Ontario: Scholastic.

Hartwell, Patrick. February 1985. Grammar, grammars, and the teaching of grammar. *College English* 47: 105–27.

Lester, Nancy B., and Cynthia S. Onore. 1990. *Learning Change: One School District Meets Language Across the Curriculum*. Portsmouth, N.H.: Boynton/Cook.

Monson, Robert J., and Michele M. Pahl. March 1991. Charting a new course with whole language. *Educational Leadership* 48: 51–53.

Stephens, Diane. January 1991. Toward an Understanding of Whole Language. Technical Report No. 524. Champaign, Ill.: Center for the Study of Reading, University of Illinois.

———. 1992. *Research on Whole Language: Support for a New Curriculum*. Katonah, N.Y.: Richard C. Owen.

Watson, Dorothy J. November 1989. Defining and describing whole language. *The Elementary School Journal* 90: 130–41.

Weaver, Constance. 1990. *Understanding Whole Language: From Principles to Practice*. Portsmouth, N.H.: Heinemann.

Weaver, Constance, Joel Chaston, and Scott Peterson. Forthcoming. *Growing into Whole Language: An Odyssey in Theme Exploration*. Richmond Hill, Ontario: Scholastic.

Focus on
Teacher Change

* * *

Focus on
Teacher Change

2 | The Constructivist Culture of Language-Centered Classrooms

Laura Fulwiler

Interested in determining whether student-centered artifacts in teachers' classrooms actually reflected a growing language-centered culture and whole language belief system, Laura Fulwiler interviewed several teachers, five of whose stories provide the basis for this article: Judy, a kindergarten teacher; Ken, a sixth-grade teacher; Carol, a middle-school teacher; Stuart, a high-school teacher of earth science; and Betty, a high-school biology teacher. From these interviews emerged common themes that serve to characterize the teachers' language-centered classrooms and their whole language belief system.

As an English teacher and a counselor, *LAURA FULWILER* has worked with students from kindergarten age through post-graduate. Both her writing and her teaching focus on the relationship between language and learning. Her research has focused on teachers talking about teaching as well as fundamental semantic and philosophical differences within the K–12 continuum on what it means to educate. She is currently Assistant Principal at Central School in Swanton, Vermont.

* * *

Over the past several years, as I worked with many teachers and visited their classrooms, I began to notice that despite their differences—in personality, subject matter, grade level, and school—many teachers inhabit remarkably similar classrooms. Certain artifacts surface repeatedly: in elementary schools, I noted charts of songs and verses hanging on racks, children's lists of classroom activities, children's catalogues of their experiences, class-dictated "News" on large pads, children's stories tacked on the board, and labels for commonly used implements—"scissors," "blocks," "crayons"—written in large letters, laminated, and pasted on the appropriate containers. I observed teachers involving children in recurrent classroom rhythms:

27

class recitations of poems and chants, individual journal writing during quiet time, taking turns sitting in the Author's Chair, pairing up to read and write to each other. In the upper grades, I watched as teachers orchestrated classroom, school-based, community-wide investigations in which students documented and reported their observations, and exchanged, discussed, and debated their interpretations of classroom experiences.

Known for their "language-centered" approach, the teachers in these classrooms build a curriculum around the personal and purposeful use of language by their students. They ask students to explore, discover, inquire, analyze, consider, discuss, debate, and revise their ideas using all modes of language—speaking and listening, reading and writing. They encourage children's own language in their stories, lists, plays, discussions, and interpretations of classroom events, and value it as the critical tool for generating and conveying thought.

The teachers I worked with made frequent reference to the Whole Language Movement and explained the artifacts in their classrooms as visible representations of "student text," which they preferred to prepackaged workbooks and basal texts. Witness to numerous educational reforms, I questioned the speed with which these classroom accoutrements had spread: was this, I mused, one more educational fad, more cosmetic than conceptual? Would this new approach to language be gone by next year's in-service, or was there something more persistent here, threaded throughout the fabric of rituals I'd observed? Did these common rituals, in fact, signify a growing "language-centered" culture within our schools? Did they reflect a whole language belief system?

Indeed, I was struck by the similar ways in which Time and Space—fundamentals of cultural anthropological study—were ritualized in the classrooms I visited. But I was also aware that I needed to transcend surface commonalities if I was really to explore the cultural dimensions of these classrooms. Lessons from ethnography had taught me that I needed to discover what these artifacts and rituals *meant* to these teachers; was there a code of meaning, a way of seeing, a *Weltanschauung*, or "world view," these teachers shared? I knew it was not enough that these teachers arranged their classrooms or engaged their students in similar ways. I needed to explore their individual perspectives, their individual lenses for viewing the world, to see if they indeed inhabited a common philosophical landscape.

To undertake this investigation, I interviewed teachers who were known for their language-centered classrooms, five of whose stories are told here. They included Judy, a kindergarten teacher in a small rural school; Ken, a sixth-grade teacher in a smaller, more rural school; Carol, a middle-school teacher in an affluent suburb; Stuart, a science teacher in a large consolidated rural high school; and Betty, a science teacher in a large suburban high school. For the purpose of this study, I have examined the language this deliberately diverse group of teachers used to describe their teaching. In doing this, echoing the teachers' approach to their students' language, I have valued their own words as critical reflections of thought. In the course of this discussion, I will sometimes quote their exact words to emphasize particular philosophical junctures.

My investigative journey began with a visit to Judy, a kindergarten teacher, in her bright, sunny classroom looking out on a mosaic of fall colors. As Judy described her approach to teaching, she spoke of change: changes she was making in her classroom, how she looked at her students, what she looked for, and, along with these, how her own role had shifted. Her words served as a foreshadowing of my findings in the rest of the study, giving name to themes that I would hear again and again from other teachers:

> Instead of assuming I knew how kids learned how to read and write, I started looking at the kids I was teaching, and seeing how they were learning. It was really scary. Each step I made, in letting go, in letting kids take hold of their learning, the quality of what they were doing was stronger.

This study of language-centered teachers focuses on and circles back to several fundamental themes noted by Judy: "looking at the kids," "seeing how kids are learning," and "letting kids take hold of their learning." Supported by other explanatory subheads, these three themes, noted casually by Judy over a cup of coffee, provide the structure of this chapter.

Looking at the Kids

As we sat in Judy's cheerful classroom, she began to describe her teaching. "The basic starting point for me is trying to understand what kids are interested in, what they're working through. . . . I try to get a handle on what is going on in their heads—what rules are they working with right now?" Judy's words immediately inform us about her fundamental beliefs. First, her students are central to her classroom; they are the "starting point" from which other decisions and directions emerge. Second, according to Judy, these five-year-olds are already independent of her, actively engaged "in their heads." Third, such "head" activity is involved with making sense of the world through "rules" they construct. Finally, there is some suggestion here of a developmental sequence, of cognitive tasks that children focus on: children are "working through" certain ideas, and Judy tries to tap into what they are "working with right now."

Though teaching at the opposite end of the school continuum, Stuart, the high school physics teacher I interviewed, "looks at kids" in a similar way, also placing them at center stage. Stuart describes his approach: "It's giving the kids a place. I mean, how did they get into the scheme of learning? I don't want them to get lost. . . . Why are we here?" Stuart "centers" his students within their own "scheme of learning" and uses metaphor (*place, get lost, get into*) to suggest a geography of personal meaning. As he speaks, he points to a sign on the wall: "I am here to learn about patterns of change happening on earth now and to learn to read earth history from patterns frozen into rock in the past." Stuart explains, "Now we've got a focus: problem-solving structured around being able to be aware of what's in the world and how to interpret it." Stuart is concerned with orienting his students to their central place as "interpreters" of the earth's text.

The way these teachers look at the kids is critical to their way of teaching. The learners in Judy's and Stuart's classes are constructivist learners. This term, coined by psychologist George Kelly (1955) and currently receiving attention among developmental and educational psychologists, depicts the learner as a scientist. Like Piaget's learner, who orders and reorders her cognitive schema, the constructivist learner continually develops and revises rules or hypotheses about the reality she experiences. As discrepancies between new observations and old rules arise, the learner revises her "theory of the world in her head" (Smith 1975).

Children are engaged in this complex conceptual work independent of school and deliberate instruction. Judy's words indicate her respect for this process:

> Before they come to school, most kids have success in directing their own learning. If we have faith in their ability to do that, the results can be amazing. Kids are fundamentally instrumental in their own learning; they're masters at making generalizations from what they experience. We just don't believe it.

Judy sees her students as independent constructors of their own knowledge, their own meaning. She respects the five-year-olds in her class as "masters" at creating conceptual frameworks from individual experiences, which they use to explain, predict, and "direct" their own learning. This is the natural process and work of the constructivist learner, yet it is a natural phenomenon that teachers, according to Judy, have difficulty trusting.

But not all teachers distrust this process. Ken, who teaches sixth grade in a small rural school, believes that each of his students engaged in this conceptual work is an authority on her own experience, and as such, is a valuable contributor to the classroom community. Ken explains:

> For their research project, students had to become expert at something and teach others. It was wonderful to watch their appreciation of each other—that "I have something to learn from everybody." For our unit in visual perception, the sixth graders taught the other classes about the eye. They need that—more independence, responsibility, freedom.

As children are prized for what they *do* know, they are also freed to explore more openly what they *want* to know. As children's autonomy and independence are nourished in this classroom, so too is a complementary respect for community.

It should be noted that the children in these teachers' classrooms are not, as a group, intrinsically or qualitatively different from children in other classrooms. But they are viewed through a different lens. As constructivists, these learners are considered competent workers who are involved in the constant and complex task of making meaning. Their "constructions" are ever-changing interpretations of their experiences, and as such, are valued in and of themselves, and not as approximations of adult standards.

Accordingly, the constructivist learner necessarily pursues a very different course of study than what most of us might think of as curriculum. Rather than a predetermined calendar of lesson plans, curriculum in these language-centered classrooms is an organic phenomenon that begins with the students.

Seeing How They're Learning

"No year's the same. It's always different and evolving through my own growth and the kids I'm working with," Ken explains. Ken's classroom curriculum appears to unfold in response to the dynamic relationship between his students and himself. Rather than a list of targeted skills and content that must be acquired, curriculum is seen more as the "totality of the learning environment" (McNeil 1986), in this case, evolving from Ken's observations of how his students are learning.

Judy, the kindergarten teacher, also watches her children carefully and notes: "Instead of having a curriculum at the beginning of each year, it evolves throughout the year . . . patterns emerge." Like an ethnographer, Judy observes the culture of her class, notes the patterns that emerge, and shapes her curriculum in response to them.

When these teachers look at how their students are learning, they embark on a nontraditional curricular path. Seeing their students as sense makers and mediators of their own knowledge, these teachers approach curriculum as an evocative and open-ended phenomenon. Carol, the middle-school teacher I interviewed, summarizes this approach: "When you get to what you think is the end and the students ask the next question . . . that's where you go next."

Knowing How Versus Knowing That

Carol defines a curriculum that focuses more on process than product, that is geared more to child-oriented experiences than to predetermined objectives. Implicitly these teachers acknowledge what Gilbert Ryle (1949) noted as the difference between "knowing how" (procedural knowledge) and "knowing that" (propositional knowledge). If we were to think of the grammar of these classrooms, we might say they are more verb than noun. Betty, one of the high school science teachers I interviewed, has her students "do as much hands-on as I can . . . instead of book reading or talking at them. I try to relate things as much as possible to their everyday lives. I try to get kids to be active in their own learning—to become involved, to make them realize, even though they may not be crazy about biology, that the process itself is important: to be able to look at things, analyze them, draw conclusions."

Rather than a canon of prescribed information, Betty's curriculum requires students' participation and mediation; note the verbs *look, analyze,* and *draw* conclusions. Betty continues: "We don't lecture. We don't give formal tests. They can't get a grade by spitting back what we tell them . . . it gets to critical thinking." The process curriculum in Betty's class necessarily challenges many of the tenets of traditional classrooms: reliance on textbooks and lectures for transmission of information and on formal tests designed to reward those students who can "spit back what we tell them."

Stuart, who teaches biology in a high school twenty miles from Betty's, also values "knowing how" over "knowing that." He explains:

> Lots of activities are cookbook activities. They know the answers. Like "Name the different kinds of rocks." If you want to know the names, take a course in rock-naming. If you want to know what they mean, come here. I can teach you how to read the earth's history.

Stuart distinguishes between *labeling* information (rock identification) and *using* information; while the first is often the focus of school courses, it is the second that Stuart values and promotes in his classroom. Learning involves *knowing how*, finding out the *meaning* of information. Stuart can teach you *how* to "read the earth's history."

Real Versus School Knowledge

When Betty tries to "relate things, as much as possible, to [students'] everyday lives," she touches on a critical aspect of curriculum as it appears in these teachers' classrooms. Rather than being an external realm of information imposed on children, curriculum takes on meaning as it emerges from and is mediated by the learner's *real* experience. Judy agrees: "The more connected everything we do is with their life, the more we make the class reflect what goes on outside as much as possible—a home, a livingroom—versus this singular phenomenon called a 'classroom,' which isn't connected with their life, their farm. . . . "

Real knowledge is viewed as the *natural* way of learning. School, by implication, is not natural for children's learning. Judy insists on integrating the learning that takes place in her kindergarten classroom: "It's not *natural* to segment 'now writing,' 'now reading,' 'now math' [italics mine]. The brain naturally integrates and is looking for connections all the time."

These teachers stress *connections* between *real life* and *school life.* Implicit in this, of course, is the tacit acknowledgment (and criticism?) that school knowledge is usually very distinct from real knowledge. *Real* knowledge is the child's knowledge, her "inner map" (Barnes 1976), constructed and reconstructed in response to her life experiences. *School* knowledge, on the other hand, which is traditionally found in textbooks and contrived "activities," is one step removed from direct and immediate experience. Stuart refers to this schism when he describes his classroom goals: "I know where I want to go. I'm playing up questions that'll get me there. If this were a real school, I'd play on kids' questions totally. I'd like to do that." *Real* schools, Stuart implies, are based on students' own questions rather than those posed by textbooks or subject guides. Real schools, Stuart also implies, are more ideal than real.

This dichotomy between *real* and *school* persists for children as well. In the real world, we are always constructing our interpretations. In school, such learning is ritualized into lesson plans, defined units, and prescribed activities. Ken, the sixth-grade teacher, tells me a story about studying the river behind his school and then reflects:

> I remember one day a couple of the boys stayed after school to plan part of it, and in the car on the way home [with me], one of them said, "I can't wait till we start this unit." And I said, "But Danny, we've been working on it for two weeks, planning it." And he said, "Oh, yeah, I guess we have!"

Despite Ken's effort to use the children's natural fascination with the river that flowed behind their school as the focal point of learning—children's real world and children's real interest—his students' school experience has taught them that learning takes place in defined units.

Thirty miles away, the river behind Stuart's school also becomes the focus of an expedition. Stuart contrasts this experience with a textbook explanation of rivers:

> The experiences my students have are *real*, not *make believe*. What I do are *real* experiments in science. We go to the Lincoln River and we measure stream velocity and its effects on rocks. The kids learn about stream energy, sorting, grain size, roundness . . .

To Stuart, *school* learning is "make believe" learning. Instead of prepackaged lab manuals and activities, Stuart wants his students to learn in an active and personal way—to discover, firsthand, for themselves, the fundamental laws of the earth. Through observing, documenting, and analyzing the rocks, Stuart's students will *invent* for themselves the fundamental laws of the universe.

Reinventing the Wheel

Stuart structures his curriculum so that in confronting fundamental questions about science, his students will need to develop their own laws about the universe. Essentially, he wants his students, through direct personal experience, to "rediscover the wheel" (Brooks 1990). He explains his plan:

> I began to see the year in terms of the big picture—first quarter was "Why is math the language of science?" Second was "How to look for different perspectives." Third was "You have to learn to do more than answer questions" or "How do we know when we're right?"

Stuart's "big picture" focuses on his students' struggle with complex scientific issues often left unexamined in the textbook approach. He wants his students to examine firsthand how they would document their observations without common mathematical symbols. He wants them to experience different points of view. Finally, when Stuart asks his students to observe and examine closely the rocks in a stream bed he is also challenging them to consider the philosophical complexities of Truth.

These teachers view curriculum as an emerging process based on, and trusting in, the student's complex role as a meaning-maker. Such a view of the learner and learning necessarily alters the traditional view of the teacher's role.

Letting Kids Take Hold of Their Learning

When Judy speaks of "letting kids take hold of their learning," she also speaks of "letting go." She is letting go of the assumption that she, as the adult teacher in the kindergarten classroom, is the sole authority on her students' learning. In letting go of this position, Judy acknowledges children as independent meaning-makers and redefines her own role in relation to them.

In her kindergarten Judy fosters children's independence. She deliberately maintains consistency and predictability: classroom materials and supplies have regular storage places; there are established favorite and private reading corners; blocks can be left up in building areas; class meeting takes place in a defined space. In addition, children experience regular daily rituals: arrival time activities, circle time, journal time, story time, and so on. Such stability is orchestrated with an eye toward children's independence. As Judy notes, "Within the predictability there's lots of freedom and newness. If every day, everything's different, students become dependent on me. In a predictable environment, they have the opportunity for more independence." "Do you mean," I asked her, "that you're deliberately placing yourself in the background?" "Definitely," she answered. "Trying to make myself as unnecessary as possible." Again, Judy puts the learner, with her own individual development needs and strengths, at the center of classroom rituals.

As teachers begin to define themselves more by their students' own learning, they alter their role as "information-giver." The teachers I interviewed all see their role as "interpretation" rather than "transmission" (Barnes and Shemilt 1974). While transmission teachers disseminate predetermined information to students, interpretation teachers see themselves as helping students in their own sense-making processes.

Carol explains, "I don't do a lot of stand-up teaching, formal talking. I try to put myself as an equal. I wouldn't do a writing class where I didn't write." A fellow-learner to her students, Carol continues:

> I'm a guide. A partner. I do feel that I'm a partner with the kids in what they're learning. Not an equal partner (after all, I'm in control, responsible, accountable). No, we're not equal, but I think I do share in their learning.

Carol has let go of the traditional role of teacher as the sole knowledge possessor in the class; she sees herself instead as the intellectual provocateur, encouraging a process already begun by the students:

> I don't think I'm the source of all knowledge. That frightens me— that any kid should think that of any teacher. My role is to help them see that I'm not the answer. That *they're* the answer, that they have within themselves how to find the answer. To be educated means to be able to find the answer. To be able to find the answer, to be able to make choices.

"Being educated" does not suggest a state of being, according to Carol, but rather a *process* of *"finding* answers" and *"making* choices" (italics mine). Carol claims that her role is "much less that of a teacher, much more that of a facilitator. . . . I don't have all the knowledge. I'm not imparting the knowledge. I'm helping kids learn, helping them figure things out."

While these teachers assess, accommodate, encourage, and exploit (in the best sense of the word) the student's learning, they are also clear that the process is in motion independent of them. "Teaching" the constructivist learner means careful and informed observation and documentation of the child's individual learning strategies, as well as provision of developmentally appropriate materials and activities. These teachers do not "operate on" students, they arrange environments where, as Judy noted, "they can't help but learn."

Contextual Assessment

Real scientists teach science, *real* writers teach writing in these classrooms. They emphasize *real* experiences in *real* contexts. It's not surprising, therefore, that they respect *real* assessments as opposed to *school* assessments. As they emphasize the need to observe and assess their constructivist students, they also look for alternatives to traditional paper and pencil classroom assessments. The real "proof," they claim, is in the "pudding," as Judy notes:

> I know they're learning when they use their learning independent of when I'm doing it with them. When a parent tells me their child has helped with the grocery list . . . when they use it and integrate it. So it's not just a classroom set of concepts they've mastered, but going in the world.

She looks to *real* events in daily life—like helping with the grocery list—as the gauge of learning. According to Judy and her language-centered colleagues, assessment cannot be restricted to one discrete activity; it is a function of how the child *uses* her learning "out in the world."

Similarly, Carol assesses her students' learning "by their interaction with others—adults, kids. If we're teaching responsibility," she says, "then I want to see if they're making good choices, being tolerant of someone else, of themselves." Like anthropologists, these teachers choose to look at their students in their "native" environment and to assess their learning through daily activities, rather than artificially and by means of externally constructed instruments. Implicit in their comments is a preference for qualitative methods of assessment as opposed to quantitative methods.

According to these teachers, quantitative assessment does not adequately address students' conceptual skills. Betty shares with me her own method of tapping into her students' learning: "One thing I try to do is ask a lot of questions . . . not necessarily to get feedback and rote answers, but to try to see if they're understanding the material. I go around and ask them 'What is it you're looking at?' 'Why is this happening?' There's a lot of science you can memorize without understanding." Like Stuart, Betty is concerned that her students be able to do more than memorize discrete facts; her students' interpretation and use of those facts is very important. Her method of assessment, while informal, is not casual. She is quite deliberate in what she values in students' learning.

The Human Teacher

Finally, these teachers see themselves as models, friends, and fellow learners. Ken shares with me an observation he made during his first year of teaching: "I had a pair of cowboy boots I used to wear. Pretty soon, I saw a couple kids wearing them, and then a couple more. I figure if they pick up on things so obvious, they must pick up on the more subliminal lessons we're teaching." Ken is clear that there is another curriculum imparted every day in his classroom, and he takes his job as role model seriously.

Stuart is equally clear and deliberate about his role as a model for his students:

> I'm trying to model a scientist—be a model of rational thought and behavior. I see myself as a scientist. I'm also a teacher. And I'm comfortable with that. I am a geologist; I'm a real scientist. [Stuart points to geological survey maps he's done with his students.] I walk through the woods and I look at rocks. I make measurements, find patterns, and try to explain the patterns.

Stuart believes that to teach science, he must be a scientist, and so models that for his students.

Their modeling is not restricted to professional roles, however. These teachers are equally clear about their own modeling of interpersonal connectedness, warmth, and caring. As Carol notes, "I share a lot with the kids about myself, my family—pictures of my cats, my kid, my home." Teachers, like curriculum and classrooms, are best when they are *real*. Ken notes that "kids stay after school a lot. They see me when I'm not the teacher. I'll have a kid up to my house in the spring . . . as they need to earn money for trips and stuff, we'll work on gardening. And I like for them to see me as a regular person." Ken is comfortable sharing his humanness and vulnerabilities with his students: "Part of my mission is to share with them my stories, my mistakes. They know you understand what they're feeling because you were there."

Teachers make personal connections with their students by tapping their own childhood experiences. Ken claims that "the best teachers are those who go back to that age when they had the best of times (to relive it) or completely miserable times (to make it better for themselves and the students). For me the middle grades were both the best and the worst times in my life . . . that's why I'm good at what I do." With Dickensian drama, Ken attributes his current pedagogical practice to his own experiences as an adolescent. Betty, too, explains her preferred teaching style by referring to her own experience as a student: "Hands-on is the way I learned best in high school, and still do. I found that most enjoyable, and the way I remembered best."

Personal connections also emerge from the particular affection these teachers have for their work. Carol believes her love of literature makes her a good teacher "because I like doing it. I like to teach it. I read all the time. They see me, above everything else, as a reader and a writer. They are my loves." In a similar vein, Betty comments: "I love science in general, and biology in particular. I hope that enthusiasm comes across to the kids. I want kids to experience it as well."

These teachers see themselves as fellow learners—Judy describes herself as "incomplete"—to the students in their classroom. "Early in the year," Ken notes, "this class seemed to be paced the same as I was. We began working together as colleagues. I'd tell them about my plans, and they'd offer suggestions." The students, respected as authorities on their own experiences and perceptions, function in a reciprocally helpful relationship with Ken, their teacher.

In many ways, the most profound similarity I found among these five teachers is their shared delight in learning. Like the students in their classrooms, they are constructivist learners, involved in making sense of their world. Stuart reflects, "I've always been excited and interested in seeing things, wondering about things I haven't seen before. As a child, my parents took me outside to look at rainbows, meteor showers . . . I've always been this way." He delights in unanswered questions, noting, "We have to have situations that create wonder and awe and excitement and promote students to ask questions. Once they've asked questions, they're ready to learn . . . and that's when I feel I'm doing my best teaching." Learning is most important when it responds to a genuine—and personal—sense of curiosity and wonder. Stuart sees this as particularly important to his discipline: "It's important to ask questions you don't know answers to—that's part of being a scientist."

In a similar way, Judy delights in the very thing she deliberately creates for her kindergartners: disequilibrium. "Having two opposite things that seem true and trying to work them out" sounds very similar to what happens when a child in her class confronts discrepancies between new information or experience and her own construction of the world. As Judy confesses, "I love the feeling of a formula. That feels good for me for a while. And then I'm uncomfortable. Getting to the disturbing point of 'Oh no, this doesn't fit' and trying to reshuffle things. I love having two opposite things that seem true and trying to work them out. . . . It's okay, we don't know; we're incomplete."

Judy acknowledges the lure of neat formulas, learning that is packaged and certain. But ultimately, she confesses, real learning happens when we are confronted with conflicting interpretations of our world, which we must resolve in some way. Although he doesn't know her, Ken describes his own delight as a learner in strikingly similar terms: "I like philosophy . . . the Big Picture. I like thinking in those ways. I like to see different patterns and systems and similarities between them."

In many ways, these teachers model the quality of *wondering*, genuinely delighting in a sense of wonder. In doing so, they speak to much of the current literature on reflective practitioners (Schon 1983) involved in classroom research (Greene 1987; Bissex 1989). As Judy notes, "One thing I love about teaching: I try something out. And step back and reflect on it."

Reflections

These five teachers really do "speak the same language" about students, the nature of learning, and their own role in the classroom. My study thus suggests that they do comprise a very real philosophical culture within our schools. Their belief in the constructivist learner, the scientist who is perpetually making and revising hypotheses about the nature of the world, lies at the center of their classrooms and shapes their expectations of, and interactions with, their students. Curriculum in their classrooms is an evolving and monitored phenomenon, colored by the conceptual development and initiative of individual students. These teachers are involved in daily assessments—primarily through careful observation—of their students' learning and in creating provocative and timely challenges for them. Finally, as constructivist learners themselves, these teachers assume a collegial relationship with their students in a context that allows for and encourages exploration.

While individually these characteristics might seem interesting, collectively, I believe, they have critical implications for education in the 1990s. Together, the beliefs expressed by these language-centered teachers challenge many of the fundamental tenets of classrooms as we know them and merit study within the current concern over educational restructuring.

Most striking, perhaps, is the shift in authority in these classrooms. As primary authors of their evolving interpretation of events, students have a voice. Their voices are encouraged, listened to, and respected in the course of classroom events. Complementing this increase in student authority are teachers who serve as fellow learners. Such factors create critically different classroom dynamics in these language-centered classrooms.

Does this development in student empowerment emerge inevitably from a classroom based on student language? Does the encouragement of student language—through recitation, interpretation, problem-solving, writing, critiquing, discussing, debating—necessarily equate *voice* with *power*? Or could it be the other way around? Does the belief in self-determination inevitably lead these teachers to a language-centered pedagogy?

Such a chicken-and-egg question is far more complex than can be answered here. I do believe, however, that this pairing—the belief in a mutually respectful and equitable teacher-student classroom and a respectful listening to students' voices—is certainly connected in fundamental ways.

If we truly listen to many voices, we must come to understand knowledge as an intensely personal as well as pluralistic phenomenon. Knowing becomes a way of seeing. Clearly, the epistemological dimensions of a language-centered culture have powerful implications for our schools.

References

Barnes, Douglas. 1976. *From Communication to Curriculum.* London: Penguin.

Barnes, Douglas, & Shemilt, Denis. 1974. Transmission and interpretation. *Educational Review* 25: 213–28.

Bissex, Glenda. April 1989. Speech delivered at Vermont Educational Research Day. Stowe, Vermont.

Brooks, Jacquelin B. February 1990. Teachers and students: Constructivists forging new connections. *Educational Leadership* 47: 66–71.

Greene, Maxine. 1987. Teaching as project: Choice, perspective, and the public space. In *Teacher Renewal: Professional Issues, Personal Choices.* Ed. F. Bolin and J. M. Falk. New York: Teachers College Press.

Kelly, George A. 1955. *The Psychology of Personal Constructs*. New York: W. W. Norton.

McNeil, Linda. 1986. *Contradictions of Control: School structure and school knowledge*. New York: Routledge and Kegan Paul.

Ryle, Gilbert. 1949. *The Concept of Mind*. London: Hutchinson.

Schon, Donald A. 1983. *The Reflective Practitioner*. New York: Basic Books.

Smith, Frank. 1975. *Comprehension and Learning*. New York: Holt, Rinehart and Winston.

3 | Learning from Teachers How to Support Their Growth

Janet Files, with Pam Shealy Wills

With delightful candor, Janet Files reveals how she came to understand more deeply that what fosters growth among children fosters growth among all learners, including classroom teachers and teacher educators. Janet demonstrates how various assumptions of her whole language theory were reflected among both the children and the adults in a Chapter 1 classroom, as she and the teacher became reflective practitioners and collaborative learners, gleaning insights from each other and from the children. Her experience emphasizes not only that whole language practices are not likely to take hold without a change in the teacher's belief system, but that a new belief system will not transform all aspects of practice overnight: it takes time for teachers to grow into new classroom practices that reflect whole language beliefs.

JANET FILES has worked extensively with teachers in her area in their efforts to develop curricula that actively involve students in reading and writing. She is the contact person for the local TAWL group and has conducted collaborative research in schools, in addition to teaching at Coastal Carolina College and presenting at professional conferences. Janet has studied with Donald Graves and Jane Hansen in their summer writing institutes and has worked with Jerry Harste and Heidi Mills while completing her doctoral degree at the University of South Carolina. Her four young children, ranging in age from one to eleven, offer her constant inspiration for creating contexts that empower all learners.

Author's Note: In the summer of 1988, I was fortunate to meet Marti Hancock, Pam Shealy Wills, and Clint Wills, who invited me to collaborate with them in applying whole language theory in their primary classrooms. I will be forever grateful for what I learned with them about the importance of a supportive community of learners who are willing to test their theory in action. This chapter highlights what I learned about the qualities of learning contexts that liberate all learners, regardless of age or position.

* * *

In the fall of 1987 I was anxious to apply all I had learned in a summer writing institute with Jane Hansen and Donald Graves to local primary classrooms. By demonstrating a writing workshop in a cooperating teacher's classroom I hoped to facilitate teacher change toward teaching writing as a process. My experience showed me I had a lot to learn about supporting teachers.

Jane Teaches Me About Facilitating Teacher Change

"Who would like to share their story with us today?" My eyes scanned the eager sea of first graders' hands waving in front of me. It was to be my last day in Jane Green's class, where I had been conducting a writing workshop three days a week for two weeks. I felt a deep sense of satisfaction as I noted that Anthony was again in the front row waving his hand animatedly.

When I had entered Jane's classroom to launch the writing workshop two weeks before, she had pointed out Anthony. "This is his second year in first grade. He also repeated kindergarten. DSS is investigating his case on suspected child abuse." Anthony's tall eight-year-old figure would have stood out in any first grade.

That first day I demonstrated writing a story about Buddy, my first dog, and then I wandered through the classroom of busily writing children nudging and supporting these budding authors in one-to-one conferences. I noticed that Anthony was busy writing; eagerly I looked over his shoulder to see his paper. At first the disconnected words *October, copy, words, Miss Green* made no sense to me. I noted that Anthony was looking past me at the blackboard and quickly found the strange source of his muse. Anthony hadn't believed me when I told the children that they all had stories to tell and that any way they could write it down was fine. They weren't to worry about spelling—just get their words down the best they could. Anthony had failed too many times to take any chances. Better play it safe and copy the words from the board.

I was rather alarmed that day to see that almost all of the ten or so high-risk children in Mrs. Green's class were following similar "safe" courses of action in the writing workshop. Germaine and Jamaal had also copied words from the bulletin board. When share time came they sat at the back of the circle not daring to raise their hands, since they felt they had nothing to share that anyone would want to hear.

After working with the class for two weeks, supporting their efforts and talking to them about their families and their after-school activities, I was delighted to see the power of hearing children's voices work its magical effects. Germaine, with his velvety eyes and shy smile, was writing about playing basketball and soccer. Jamaal had written and illustrated a wonderful story about his football hero cousin: "Boozer rasls wit me in the bed" (Boozer wrestles with me in the bed). His words reflected so much more of Jamaal than the list of color words he had painfully copied during the first writing workshop. Today, Anthony could hardly wait to share the scary story he had written about getting lost in a haunted house. He took his place proudly in the Author's Chair and had the confirmation of a rapt audience as he read, "One day I was walking in the woods behind my house and I came to a scary old place. . . . "

I left that day with the satisfied feeling that Jane would surely carry on the writing workshop after having experienced firsthand what writing can do for all children's self-confidence. After two weeks of working together I was sure Jane saw the value of such an approach to early literacy.

Upon my return from the summer institute in New Hampshire, I had approached the principal of a local primary school seeking a willing teacher in whose classroom I could demonstrate Don Graves's writing workshop. The principal had called Jane into her office and after a brief chat I was ready to begin. I had wanted Jane to be an active participant, trusting that she would see the value of the writing process and continue after I left.

When I checked with Jane two weeks following the project to see how things were going, she reported that she had continued the writing workshop, but that the children had trouble finding topics so she often gave them "story starters." My heart sank. I pictured Anthony, Germaine, and Jamaal retreating back to that safer place where you just try to guess what the teacher wants to hear. I saw them giving up searching for their own voices. I had obviously not communicated how important it is that the children—indeed, all writers—find their own topics.

Jane added that it was hard to find three hours a week to write, so she was using writing workshop once a week. I had clearly mentioned that the children needed at least three hours a week for writing in order to find their stride as writers. Good writing takes time! How had Jane missed so much of what I had stressed as important? Although I knew before I entered her classroom that Jane followed a highly structured, traditional curriculum grounded in basals and worksheets, I had naively believed that seeing process learning in action would surely convince anyone of its worth, regardless of previously held assumptions.

What's Good for the Children Is Good for the Teachers

Since my experience in Jane's class, I have had several years to reflect on how naive my notions about teacher change were.

Now I see clearly that Jane and I had completely different models for learning. My demonstration had not changed her underlying beliefs about how children learn. *If a teacher's beliefs about how children learn are not changed, explicit and implicit curriculum does not change.* Harste, Woodward, and Burke emphasize this concept:

> We have come to believe that looking at teacher behavior in terms of beliefs held and assumptions made is more cogent and powerful than looking at behavior in terms of the supposed approach being used. . . . [If the teacher] changes her approaches, but . . . does not change her beliefs, her classroom practice is unaffected (as is, in all likelihood, the outcome of her instruction . . .). (Harste, Woodward, and Burke 1984, p. 7)

Changing beliefs or making educators aware of their beliefs about learning is a key to changing educational practice. *Change* here is defined as *learning*. If I wanted to effect change, therefore, I had to maximize the potential for learning.

What I hadn't considered carefully were the assumptions I had come to believe about all good learning situations. I knew that learning occurred when the learner was *actively engaged* in experience and had *choice, time, response,* and a *willingness to take risks* in a *supportive community of learners* that encouraged *reflection* on action (Hansen 1987). I had considered these qualities and assumptions about learning in planning writing engagements for the children in Jane's class, but I had obviously failed to put my assumptions into practice in what I intended as a learning experience for the teacher-learner. I was demonstrating a teaching strategy that I hoped Jane would value and adopt. Yet if learning or inquiry stems from the learner's questions, in this case the question was mine, not Jane's. Jane's principal volunteered her, so her involvement in the learning demonstrations was peripheral at best. She was not personally invested in the writing workshop demonstrations.

I was only in Jane's classroom for two weeks. During that time I was actively reflecting on the children's response to the daily workshop and learning a great deal about supporting them in their efforts as writers, but Jane and I had only brief, "in passing" chats in the classroom about what the children needed. I had not set up time with Jane to reflect on these experiences or to generate curricular implications. We did not have time to establish a relationship of trust and shared goals. She had accepted me into her classroom because her principal had asked her to. She had not sought me out as a partner in learning and had little investment in the learning process.

Jane and I also had different perspectives on the learning process. This might have offered potential for growth, but we had no chance to discuss our perspectives. I had not even thought about inviting other voices to join our dialogue, which would have added a broader perspective to our learning. As it was, Jane and I had only limited opportunities to talk together. The responsibility to learn together had not been negotiated and made clear before the project started. I wanted to learn and I wanted Jane to learn, but I had failed to ask her if she had an equal personal commitment or if she was only "doing what she was told" by her principal.

Theory and Practice

The frustration that began after my experience with Jane continued during my work with in-service teachers as a graduate instructor teaching courses in language and literacy development from a whole language perspective. Through classroom demonstrations, discussion of current research and practice, and other reflective strategies, I had often been successful in bringing in-service teachers to the point where they had been willing to test old ways of thinking about literacy curriculum.

But what fascinated me was that, though these teachers appeared to embrace a whole language philosophy and even stated that it was the best way to facilitate literacy development, they often felt constrained about putting these beliefs into practice in their classrooms. These were the "Yes-buts." "*Yes*, I believe that using real literature is most effective in creating lifelong readers, *but* the district mandates that we use basals." "*Yes*, I want to implement reading and writing workshop, *but* how can I find time for it and the mandated curriculum." "*Yes-but. . . .* "

A few teachers were willing to put their beliefs into practice, regardless of district mandates or administrators who did not openly support a whole language philosophy. Some of these teachers chose to do so by closing their doors and following a policy that seemed to say "What they don't know won't hurt me!"

What Makes the Difference?

As Carolyn Burke has said, "You can't sidle up to whole language. You have to take a leap!" (1990). What makes the difference? How could I encourage teachers to take this leap?

In the summer of 1988 my doctoral research gave me the opportunity to try again. This time I was going to do my best to make my research consonant with my assumptions about learning. I did not want to repeat the mistakes I had made with Jane. I hoped to learn how to help teachers develop a personal action theory of learning based on their own classroom research within the context of a supportive learning community.

The Research Project Begins

My theoretical model had a strong start when Pam Shealy Wills and two other primary teachers invited me into their classrooms. These were teachers who *chose* to conduct collaborative research in their classrooms and who *embraced the chance* to be a part of a supportive research team in which each of us would be equal and no one would be considered the outside expert. We felt responsible to each other to learn all we could together and planned to have weekly meetings with any interested teachers and administrators to increase our opportunities for sharing diverse perspectives. Our main goal was to learn all we could together.

My Evolution as an Agent of Change: A Tentative Beginning

August 30, 1988—12:05 P.M.

I tried to enter Pam Wills's Chapter 1 classroom as unobtrusively as I could while carrying a clipboard and a tape recorder. I was five minutes late for her first meeting with the reading class I would be a part of for the next eight months. I didn't want to miss the first day, since I knew Pam would be setting the tone for the rest of the year. I took a seat at the back of the circle of children and uncertainly tried to record whatever a researcher is supposed to record and to do or not do whatever a collaborative researcher is supposed to. My main aim was to let the children, Pam, her assistant Debbie Conder, and myself get comfortable with each other. I also wanted to observe how Pam, on day one, would translate into practice her hopes to create a reading-writing classroom with a whole language philosophy into practice on day one.

In my interview with Pam about her plans for the year she had said, "Last year I was very happy with writing workshop and using the authoring cycle in my writing curriculum. This year I want to handle reading like I do the writing."

The previous summer Pam had written in her curricular wishbook: "Begin the year with family stories theme. Read Cynthia Rylant's books to the class to begin a unit on 'Memories.' " I loved watching Pam's wishes take shape. Pam was seated on a child's chair in the middle of a group of eight second-grade children, who surrounded her on the rug. She was in the process of reading Rylant's *When I Was Young in the Mountains*. I watched the children's faces as Rylant caught them in the storyteller's web:

> When I was young in the mountains, we listened to frogs sing at dusk and awoke to cowbells outside our windows. Sometimes a black snake came into the yard, and my Grandmother would threaten it with a hoe. If it did not leave, she used the hoe to kill it. Four of us once draped a very long snake, dead of course, across our necks for a photograph. (Rylant 1982)

Eddie declared, "I wouldn't have my picture taken with no dead snake!" Many of the children voiced their agreement. Children in South Carolina know about snakes.

At the end of the story Pam talked to the children about the author. "Cynthia Rylant wrote this from memories that really happened. We all have memories." The children began to make connections to the story. Jonathan noted, "I went to the Smoky Mountains." Christy added, "Once a snake crawled across our feet in the mountains."

"Maybe you have a memory about something you like to do with your family," Pam suggested. Hands shot up. Jonathan offered, "I took a trip to Ohio with my family." Kim, a delicate blonde in a white karate outfit, said, "We went to Canada. We drove and drove for days." We chatted about our memories. I shared a story about making hay tunnels in my grandmother's barn. Debbie Conder talked about growing up in the West Virginia mountains and going to a johnny house before there were such inventions as indoor plumbing.

At the children's request Pam read them another book, this one by Miriam Cohen and titled *Best Friends*. During the reading the children asked if they could join in. Pam got down on the rug so the children could be closer to the print, and they finished the book in a makeshift choral reading.

"We have only ten minutes left before you have to go back to your regular classroom. Let's take this time to find a book from our reading corner or the table to look at."

I was happy to put down my clipboard and join blonde, pig-tailed Kim, who had selected *Friends* by Helme Heine. "Kim, I'm Janet Files. Would you mind if I shared your book?"

Our first hour was at an end and already distinct faces and stories had emerged among the former group of strangers. We were on our way to becoming a community of readers and writers with more than a year of stories to share.

I felt comfortable interacting with the children. Pam welcomed my presence and seemed to trust my level of participation. But I didn't feel very comfortable at all in my new role as collaborative researcher. I wanted to nudge Pam on certain issues and actions, but at the same time I wanted her to lead with her questions and concerns.

I didn't know how to proceed, but I went forward with the faith that "doing" collaborative research and reflecting on doing would show me the way as Pam and I pulled our chairs closer together to talk about our observations of our first day and what curricular news we had generated. Through our conversation we would begin developing a trust in each other's judgment and a confidence that what we had to say was being heard by someone who was genuinely interested. This reciprocity in and of itself generated the potential for new thoughts.

I entered Pam's class with a well-developed theory about how children learn language and evolve into competent language users. For three years, however, while I worked as a graduate instructor with in-service teachers, I had not had the opportunity to put my assumptions into practice in a classroom. I approached this chance to put beliefs into reflective practice with excitement and some trepidation. I knew this experience would also transform some of these assumptions as they were reformed in new contexts.

Assumption 1: We learn from active engagement in authentic demonstrations, and we learn what is personally salient.

I was not going to be a passive observer in Pam's class, because I knew that we only learn from active engagement and from reflecting on that experience in light of current theory. From the first day, I participated in the classroom, thereby sharing vulnerability and visibility in risking "getting caught with my assumptions showing" as I attempted to put my theory into action in demonstrations of classroom strategies. Pam and I provided authentic teaching demonstrations for each other as we alternated between teacher and observer roles and allowed each other the mutual opportunity to learn from these demonstrations what was personally salient.

Assumption 2: Learners must have choice. We must generate our own questions and actively seek our own answers.

I wanted to help Pam make curricular changes. I also wanted to help the children learn new strategies that would enable them to be more effective readers and writers. But change cannot be imposed from without. I believed from the outset that change only occurs when an individual has the opportunity to reflect on experiences that are in some way related to the questions he or she is asking.

Believing that good collaborative research has to start with the teacher's own inquiry, I had asked Pam to let me know her current questions regarding literacy learning. Her concern, she reported, was how to bring her reading curriculum more in line with what she believed about how children learned to write. I was delighted with her focus, since I believed that reading and writing were intimately connected, and I thoroughly supported her goals.

My own challenge was how to "lead from behind" (Newman 1985). I wanted to stand next to Pam in an equal position. I felt it my responsibility to share with her all that I had come to know about creating literacy environments that enhance the child's learning potential. Yet I would never have insisted that she simply adopt my perspective. As we shared co-teaching and research responsibilities, Pam was able to reflect on my teaching demonstrations and extract those characteristics she considered relevant and make corresponding curricular changes. This is open-entry, open-exit learning (Stephens 1986). The choice of what is learned is in the learner's hands.

Assumption 3: All learning involves risk-taking, and risk-taking requires trust. Therefore, learning involves developing trust among the members of the learning community. This takes time.

Pam and I had to negotiate what my role in her classroom would be and how we would learn together. I began the research project with respect for Pam and her approach to a literacy curriculum. Trust had to come with time—among all members of the learning community. The more we trusted each other and ourselves, the greater the potential for our learning together. My tentative approach to my role left me open to learning more than if I thought I had all the answers to start with.

Pam and I were not operating from a preconceived curriculum with a list of instructional objectives. We were collaboratively generating the curriculum as we tried to understand what the children were attempting to do and then to help them do it (Smith 1983). Frank Smith describes this as the one difficult way to make learning to read and write easy. Pam and I were equally vulnerable as we tried to find our way together. We needed each other's trust to take the necessary steps toward learning.

Putting Assumptions 1–3 into Practice: Action and Reflection

As I have learned over and over again, it is one thing to have beliefs about learning but quite another to put them into practice in contexts that are unique and unexplored. It is like walking on a bog

(Skagestaad 1981). We have to negotiate and renegotiate each step carefully as we test the ability of our theory to hold our weight and keep us afloat while we move into new territory. It is important to know the learner in order to fine-tune our demonstrations in terms of the learner's needs.

It was the second week of our work together. The children were all deeply involved in writing workshop. I wanted to work with Eddie on some of his writing. I was intrigued by his idiosyncratic spelling. He had just written "My Daddy is a ranticnaitf maine. I like my Daddy." (My Daddy is a Horry Rescue member. I like my Daddy.) (See Figure 3–1.) I had observed from this and from his previous writing samples that when he didn't know the conventional spelling of a word he employed only the barest of graphophonemic strategies for spelling it, seemingly adding as many extra letters to placehold his meaning as seemed adequate for the length of the word. I had been reading Marie Clay's *Early Detection of Reading Difficulties* (1988) and had tried using

---

FIGURE 3–1   *Eddie's Writing*

the Elkonin technique with some children who had trouble hearing sounds in words. I wondered if such a strategy would help Eddie.

I sat down next to him and suggested that we "play a game" in which he would listen to the phonetic sounds in some words he had tried to spell and try to write the sounds he heard in boxes I would provide for him. I had assumed that he needed a strategy for hearing the sounds in words, since he seemed to have few strategies available to him. He enjoyed the "game" and did fairly well, showing me that he had more graphophonemic knowledge than he typically applied in his writing. But as he continued writing that day he did not rely on the strategy but spelled unknown words with what seemed to be random choices of letter strings.

After class each day, Pam and I usually "debriefed" each other, highlighting interesting observations about the children. In retrospect, I realize that as a novice researcher, I felt somewhat responsible for "earning my keep" in the classroom by demonstrating new strategies and ideas. This, coupled with my enthusiasm about finally being back in the classroom, made me a little overzealous at first. I was eager to share the Elkonin technique with Pam but was also eager to talk about why it hadn't been effective with Eddie.

Pam explained that Eddie was a very reluctant writer at the beginning of the year. Eddie's mother had reported to Pam in their first conference that he even doubted his ability to draw pictures. Pam's main goal for Eddie, therefore, was fluency. He needed to feel confident as a writer before he was ready to focus on spelling conventions. She wanted him to feel successful.

We both agreed that pointing out strategies to Eddie in too obvious a way might cause him to doubt himself again and to retreat from his current willingness to take risks with his writing. We decided that we could demonstrate strategies for the whole group, and those Eddie needed he would be able to use without feeling on the spot.

This story stands out for me because it transformed my understanding of several important aspects of the research. I found that I didn't have to feel responsible in order to be an "expert"—I had a lot of theoretical information to draw on, but I could learn the most by stepping back and reflecting on what was most important. Pam always saw the children in a broader context than I did, and I had to rely on her to "fill me in," since I wasn't with them every day. Collaboration relies on mutual respect for the members of the group. From the outset I had great respect for Pam's professionalism, but instances like this helped me become conscious of why I respected her teaching so much. She knew how to step back and wait for the child to show her the way. She knew how to trust the learner.

Those of us who wish to understand teacher practice likewise need to learn to trust that the teacher-learner knows why she is making certain curricular decisions. Typical evaluation formats are based on one or two hours of noninteractive observation that reduces teaching to a decontextualized checklist of disembodied activities. We who only visit classrooms occasionally must know that the teacher will always have a more complete context within which to evaluate and interpret individual actions and curricular experiences. We must respect this knowledge and learn to take time to ask teachers why they are enacting certain curricular practices and what their priorities are in making particular decisions in their classrooms.

In my research journal entry for October 5, I wrote about the Eddie story: "I am finding myself more eager to know what the teacher's questions and thoughts are and how to support them. I am less 'pushed' to show demonstrations or nudge them in the direction I think makes sense. I have learned I need to slow down and listen and look more closely, both in terms of the teacher's learning and the students' learning."

I had learned that Pam and I could grow together in important ways simply by taking time to share insights. Frederick Erickson tells us that

> collaboration means working together in ways that exchange mutual help [to solve dilemmas]. The help exchanged must be genuine, not just action that looks like help. (1989, p. 431)

Pam and I were collaborators focusing on a shared interest and an authentic question: how to help Eddie become a more efficient speller. We brought different knowledge and experience to the dialogue, and because we shared it with the hope of learning new information that would help Eddie, we both gained. We began a dialogue that day about how to help Eddie based on his personal needs, a dialogue that continued throughout the year.

I had knowledge about the conventions of spelling that I tried to share with Eddie, but he saw no immediate need for my demonstrations. He was satisfied with his spelling. He could remember what it said and read it just fine. There was little in the context of this experience to encourage him to seek other strategies.

In response to our continued dialogue about Eddie's spelling, Pam and I tried periodically to demonstrate the strategy of spelling by sounds to the whole group, validating different spellings by reading all approximations and highlighting other children's spelling strategies. Eddie's writing became more fluent, but he still didn't seem to be

motivated to bring his spelling closer to conventionality. In October
he wrote:

> My Daddy is youniz naiyz [very nice]
> Dale is yauniz naiyz to. [Dale is very nice too.]
> Dale and I and my Daddy go fishing and niyuting to. [Dale and I and
> my Daddy go fishing and hunting too.]

In December he wrote about his Christmas presents from his dad
(Figure 3–2):

> the pasngis [the presents]
> My Dadd is geting it. It is dig and fat. I do not knot [know] wilth
> [what] it is. There are littlys [little ones] to. I like the dig on [big one]
> I and the liuttys [little ones] too. They are pair np [wrapped up]. I
> will oponi [open] them on Chirstmas. Eddie

FIGURE 3–2   *Eddie's Writing, December*

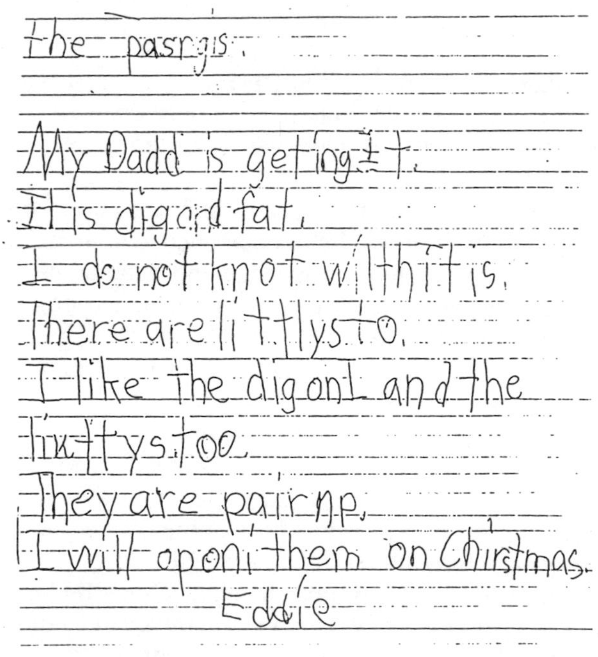

Because Pam and I were engaged in continuous reflection on our curricular strategies, we had the opportunity to learn from Eddie's response. When the curriculum doesn't engage the learner we need to change the curriculum, not the learner. In this case, we gave Eddie a *reason* to be more concerned about conventional spelling.

Assumption 4: Learning always occurs within the context of use.

Pam and I had decided to ask my graduate students to be pen pals with her class for a semester on a weekly basis. In late January Eddie received his first adult pen pal letter from Linda.

Jan. 21, 1989

Dear Eddie,

    Hi! My name is Linda and I am going to be your pen pal. I am a teacher in North Carolina. My students are in the 5th grade. I love to paint. Do you? My hobbies are drawing, skiing, chess and read- ing. What do you like to do? I am looking forward to getting a letter from you.

Your Pal,
Linda

We were amazed by how many of the strategies and conventions of letter writing Eddie demonstrated in his reply (Figure 3–3):

Jan 31, 1989

Dear Linda

    Hi! My name is Eddie and Iam going to be your pen pal. I am 8 years old. I am in 2th grade. I likeed your letter. My hobbies arc hunting an fishingan reading an drawing an skiing.
    I am going to the mountains.
    How old are you?

from Eddie

The context of the situation was clear to Eddie. He was writing to an adult who wasn't immediately accessible if he needed to clarify what he had written. Eddie readily transferred Linda's form to his own letter and used many of her words to express his meaning. He also made use of other spelling strategies like spelling by sounds and referring to printed texts in the room, such as the book *When I Was*

FIGURE 3–3   *Eddie's Letter*

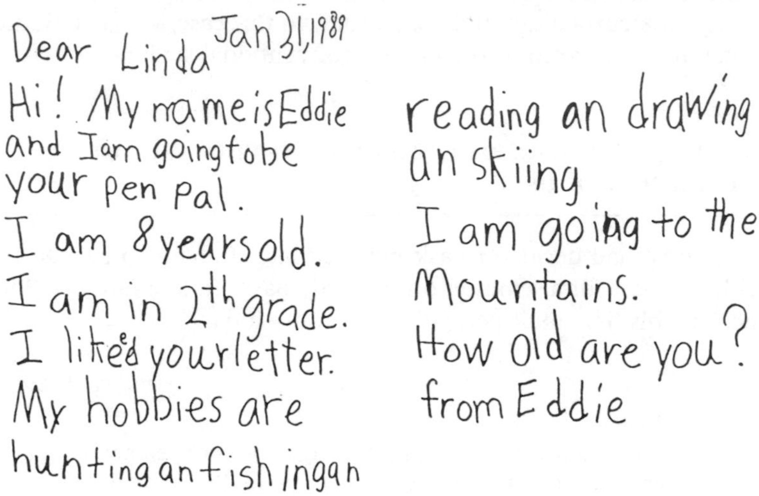

Dear Linda Jan 31,1989

Hi! My name is Eddie
and I am going to be
your pen pal.

I am 8 years old.

I am in 2th grade.

I liked your letter.

My hobbies are

hunting an fishing an

reading an drawing
an skiing

I am going to the
Mountains.

How old are you?

from Eddie

Young in the Mountains, to clarify the spelling of words such as "mountain." He chose to use strategies that enabled him to spell conventionally because the social context of the situation demanded clarity and he was a sophisticated enough language user to recognize this. He used Linda's strategies and others along with his own content to generate new possibilities for communication.

Pam and I not only learned from each other, we truly collaborated in our learning with the children, and in this case with pen pal Linda too. We found that Eddie needed wider audiences to communicate with in order to be motivated to use the social knowledge of conventional spelling for his personal meaning making.

Neither Pam nor I believed in a skills model for language learning. In my early demonstrations to Eddie of Elkonin spelling strategies, however, I had failed to consider another tenet of my language learning theory: all language learning is embedded within the context of use. Spelling is not a skill, it is a social convention that conveys personal meaning. When the context of use for spelling demanded better control of the convention of spelling so that his pen pal could understand his meaning, Eddie exercised greater control over that convention and drew on the demonstrations of spelling strategies that were available to him.

When the context of use of my literacy theory demanded that I look more deeply at how I believe spelling can be supported, I gained a deeper understanding of my theoretical beliefs. In effect, my theory became three dimensional as I saw it in action.

Eddie's story highlights my deepened understanding that learning takes *time*, and that the appropriate time is determined by the learner. Eddie and Pam also taught me that, yes, we learn from *demonstrations* of language in use, but it is the personal need for such a demonstration that determines whether the learner is sensitive to the demonstration and becomes engaged in it enough to make it his own (Smith 1981). What is learned is the learner's *choice*. Eddie's story illustrates the importance of these learning tenets from the child's perspective.

Assumption 5: Not only will learners learn what is personally salient in a demonstration, but they will learn it in their own good time. Learning from demonstrations may take time to mature.

Reflection on our research emphasized that we as teacher-researchers learn most effectively through the same supportive context as the children. The learning process is the same regardless of the age of the learner (Harste, Woodward, and Burke 1984). In her curricular wishes for the research year, Pam had commented that she wanted to bring her reading curriculum more in line with her writing curriculum. The way she chose to do this in September was to have writing workshop on Monday, Tuesday, and Wednesday and reading workshop or reading-related activities on Thursday and Friday. I had observed reading-writing classrooms in New Hampshire, where the children had a block of language arts time and could choose whether to read or write during this time. I strongly believe that reading and writing are intimately related. If we enhance their connection in our curriculums this can *enhance* the potential of creating readers who know how to "read like writers" and writers who can write like authors of the excellent books they have read (see Hansen 1987). I was eager to nudge Pam to let the children choose whether to read or write during their workshop period. Two weeks into the research study I was given a natural opportunity in class to demonstrate to Pam that the children might get ideas about writing from their reading.

I noted that Derrick had finished one piece but was stuck on what to write about next. I had brought in several of my Wright Group

read-together books, and Derrick had enjoyed great success with
them during reading time the previous week. I suggested to Derrick,
"Why don't you read one of those orange books you like so much and
you can share it after you share your writing during Author's Chair
time." Derrick took my suggestion. He eagerly shared reading his
book *Silly Old Possum* (Cowley 1990) during writing share time. Pam
complimented him on his efforts but noted, "This is writing sharing.
We won't share any more books today."

Following class I informed Pam that it had been my idea to have
Derrick read during writing class and explained my theoretical reasons for doing so. Pam acknowledged that writing and reading are
two sides of the same coin but added that she was afraid that if she let
the Chapter 1 children choose to read or write, they might never
choose to write, since they were not as familiar with this form of
communication and might not take the risk if given a choice. Even
though I was still in favor of letting the children decide, I was
impressed with the fact that Pam was such a reflective teacher. She
did not make her curricular decisions willy-nilly but after careful
reflection on what she felt would create the best learning context for
her Chapter 1 students. I learned always to ask for the reasons Pam
had chosen to enact certain curricular decisions. I also learned that
demonstrations have a way of maturing over time. When learners are
ready for the demonstration they will learn from it, but not before.

As the year progressed, Pam struggled with the problem of not
having enough time in five fifty-minute segments each week to fit in
all she wanted to cover in her reading-writing curriculum. She tried
different approaches to include more reading. In her curriculum journal entry on October 3, Pam wrote: "I am not having writing workshop this week to allow more time for reading activities." At this point
she had decided that every four weeks she might take one week to
devote just to reading. In her journal on January 2, Pam wrote: "The
last two weeks before Christmas I gave the students the choice to have
reading or writing workshop. The two going on at once worked fine.
Some students did not choose to do reading at all. Others chose only
reading." Again, on February 20: "Today I gave the children the
choice of reading or writing workshop. Maurice Sendak is our new
text set. The children were especially taken with my Maurice Sendak
poster book."

Pam and I continued to talk about the reading-writing connection
throughout the year. We were both noting with delight how much the
children's writing reflected the authors she was introducing them to.
At the end of the research year in our final interview (June 19), Pam
talked about her evolution to using more literature in the classroom:

PAM: At the beginning of the year one of my goals was to include more literature—more reading. I had done a pretty good job with writing and I wanted to do a better job with reading. One of the things that I was so glad that I did, and I did even more of as the year went on because I saw how much it was affecting what we were doing in our classroom, was just reading to the children during those mini-lesson times rather than just doing strategies, which I still think are important. . . .

JANET: What kinds of things were you seeing?

PAM: That the children were developing such a great background in literature. Becoming familiar with authors and why they liked certain authors. I saw it in their stories and I saw it in the comments they made while I would be reading a story—the things that they noticed and picked up on to want to comment on. I don't know that we ever really set the structure for that—I always loved it when they would notice something and just say it.

JANET: They'd make connections with other pieces of literature. I would love to look more closely sometime at what kinds of literature connections the children made in their writing. Like Christy, Jonathan, and Kimberly—they would use little themes, techniques, pictures. . . .

PAM: You know, a first-grade teacher in our weekly meeting group was saying she was having a hard time getting her children to write fiction, and I was thinking that was almost all my children wrote about now—toward the end of the year. I realized it really is because they would use that as a jumping off point. Some of them might just use the title and it might not have anything to do with the story—they would just use that as a title and that would make them think of it in a different way and they would go ahead and write their own story. Others would try to make a story that was similar but change it somehow.

That wasn't something I really encouraged them to do, though I did highlight the fact that you could write your own story about the *Napping House*—I think I just mentioned it one day and one person did it and her story was really good so others got the idea. . . .

Pam had a year of accumulated insights into the power of literature to affect children's writing. The changes in her theory and practice regarding how children learn to read and write are reminiscent of the old Ukrainian folktale called "The Mitten." In this ancient tale, a little boy loses his new white wool mitten in the snow. The cozy mitten appears to be a perfect home to several wild animals. Its bulging seams resist bursting as a mole, rabbit, hedgehog, owl, badger, fox, and bear squeeze in to keep warm. Finally an ant crawls in and the seam bursts with great force. Similarly, our theories must accumulate many tested hypotheses and reflective experiences until at last the old theoretical seams burst and we are pushed to reconstruct our perspective and act differently.

In this case, Pam's experience came to fruition in the year following the research. She was again teaching Chapter 1 language arts and decided to combine reading and writing workshop, letting the children choose. She commented: "I don't know why I waited so long to do this. It is working beautifully. The children are teaching themselves so much about writing with the books they choose, and they do a much better job of deciding when to read or write than I could do for them. One little girl who has a great deal of difficulty reading chose to read the same book over and over again. Finally she asked if she could read it to the class. Debbie and I were so impressed with how fluently she read it. She had taken the time she needed to learn how to read that book well! If I had interfered I might have messed up this learning opportunity for her."

Pam's story taught me an important lesson: teachers need time to "try on" and "revise" new strategies and curricular structures before incorporating them in their "final draft" form. Pam's particular learning style was very thoughtful. She carefully thought through how she structured her curriculum and why she included what she did. She was not impulsive in adopting new strategies. She took her time in trying out new ideas in her classroom and analyzed why she found them useful. Since Pam only had her children for fifty minutes five times a week, she felt that how she structured that time was very important.

The reflective nature of our research together allowed Pam to note the literature connections the children were showing in their writing. As she struggled to find more time for reading, she was free to try out new formats, or "rough drafts," and to reflect in her journal and in her conversations with the research team about how this went. Because she saw how powerful her literature demonstrations were and because I was able to encourage her and assure her that it "worked in New Hampshire," she was ready to try out her current "final draft" for writing-reading workshop the following year. The research year gave her the *time* and *support* to think through her experimental structures. This enabled her to decide with conviction how she would change her curricular structure in the year following

the research. Like Pam, all teachers need to be given *respect as curricular decision-makers*. Part of that respect involves letting them *choose
their own timing* for adopting new curricular ideas. Demonstrations of
new curricular strategies often need the support of accumulated
reflective experience before they become personally salient enough to
propel us to transform our theory and actions. We need to trust the
process, the learner, and the time it takes for learning demonstrations
to mature.

Conclusions

I rely on the fact that whole language is a *"professional theory,* an
explicit theory *in* practice. That is, it is neither theory divorced from
practice nor practice that is blind to its own theory. . . . It is the
teacher's stated beliefs, . . . the *deliberately* theory-driven practice—
not simply the behaviors—that make a classroom whole language"
(Edelsky, Altwerger, and Flores 1991, p. 7). My research attempted to
put my whole language theory into practice in supporting teachers
through my own learning. As Carolyn Burke (1990) points out, "We
have been pretty successful in beginning to liberate the learning lives
of our children. . . . We need to step back and give ourselves the
opportunity to really find out what it feels like to be inquirers. . . . We
need to create learning engagements and learning contexts for
ourselves that allow us to live inquiry in the same way we are encouraging our children to live."

   When asked to reflect on what we learned through the research,
we all agreed that the year was the most productive and exhilarating of our professional and, in many ways, our personal lives. As
Pam said:

> I wouldn't take anything for this experience because it made me
> reflect on everything that I do in my classroom—why am I doing
> this? It made me do a better job of not just reflecting but doing
> something about what I reflected on. . . . Now, even if I am not
> involved in a research project I will continue to do that. Doing the
> research together helped me to get there.

   Learning together in supportive contexts not only felt wonderful,
it also helped imbue us with the courage of our now very conscious
convictions. We all changed some of our beliefs and refined others,
but perhaps the most significant change was that we had become

conscious of what these beliefs were and how they looked across varying contexts.

Whole language—whole learning—cannot be a set of predetermined actions because our theory will look different depending on the context within which it is enacted. We must constantly seek ways to put our theory into action. The opportunity to bring my theoretical creation to life in the classroom empowered me with a deeper conviction that whole language is the most promising theory for transforming learning environments, no matter what the age or educational position of the learner.

Finding our way may be like walking on a bog as we renegotiate our footing with each step. Yet there is real substance in the classroom to help us: the learner's response. As Robert Pollock (cited in Sebranek, Meyer, & Kemper 1990) tells us, "Somehow, if you really attend to the real, it tells you everything." Reflecting on theory in action is the only way to keep moving forward.

References

Burke, Carolyn. 1990. Liberating the learner. Keynote address given at the Whole Language Conference on Empowering Teachers and Learners at USC Coastal Carolina College, Conway, S.C.

Clay, Marie. 1988. *The Early Detection of Reading Difficulties.* 4th ed. Portsmouth, N.H.: Heinemann.

Cohen, Miriam. 1976. *Best Friends.* New York: Macmillan.

Cowley, Joy. 1990. *Silly Old Possum.* San Diego, Calif.: The Wright Group.

Edelsky, Carole, Bess Altwerger, and Barbara Flores. 1991. *Whole Language: What's the Difference?* Portsmouth, N.H.: Heinemann.

Erickson, Frederick. 1989. Research currents: Learning and collaboration in teaching. *Language Arts* 66: 430–41.

Hansen, Jane. 1987. *When Writers Read.* Portsmouth, N.H.: Heinemann.

Harste, Jerome C., Virginia A. Woodward, and Carolyn L. Burke. 1984. *Language Stories and Literacy Lessons.* Portsmouth, N.H.: Heinemann.

Heine, David. 1988. A sociosemiotic perspective of learning: Teacher learning and curriculum exploration through collaboration. Unpublished doctoral dissertation, Indiana University, Bloomington.

Heine, Helme. 1986. *Friends.* New York: Macmillan.

Newman, Judith, ed. 1985. *Whole Language: Theory in Use.* Portsmouth, N.H.: Heinemann.

―――. 1990. *Finding Our Own Way: Teachers Exploring Their Assumptions.* Portsmouth, N.H.: Heinemann.

Rylant, Cynthia. 1982. *When I Was Young in the Mountains.* New York: Dutton.

Sebranek, Patrick, Verne Meyer, and Dave Kemper. 1990. *Write Source 2000: A Guide to Writing, Thinking and Learning.* Burlington, Wis.: Write Source.

Skagestaad, Peter. 1981. *The Road of Inquiry.* New York: Columbia University Press.

Smith, Frank. 1981. Demonstrations, engagement and sensitivity: The choice between people and programs. *Language Arts* 58: 634–42.

———. 1983. *Essays into Literacy.* Portsmouth, N.H.: Heinemann.

Stephens, Diane. 1986. Research and theory as practice: A collaborative study. Unpublished doctoral dissertation, Indiana University, Bloomington.

Wood, Don, and Audrey Wood. 1984. *The Napping House.* Orlando, Fla.: Harcourt Brace Jovanovich.

4 | Supporting Teacher Growth

Yvonne Siu-Runyan

Drawing upon her experiences as a consultant in the schools, Yvonne Siu-Runyan discusses many of the factors important in supporting teachers as they grow into whole language teaching. She explains the importance of making a "paradigm shift" from traditional beliefs about teaching to the significantly different beliefs held by whole language teachers, and suggests how this paradigm shift can be facilitated. As Yvonne's experiences indicate, clearly a school or district cannot simply mandate whole language; administrators must themselves effect a paradigm shift, and be guided in their own actions by a whole language belief system.

YVONNE SIU-RUNYAN has been an elementary, junior high, and high school teacher in the states of Hawaii, Michigan, Ohio, California, and Colorado. Her most recent classroom experience has been teaching children in grades 3–6 in a small mountain schoolhouse. Besides working as a consultant in schools, she has worked as a district reading specialist and language arts coordinator. Currently, she is an associate professor at the University of Northern Colorado (Greeley), where she teaches undergraduate and graduate courses in the reading process, the writing process, and children's and adolescent literature.

* * *

A basic principle of successful whole language teachers is that they are not and will never be finished products—that this journey toward becoming expert holistic literacy teachers is a process, like all learning, which needs continual support and encouragement. Unfortunately, many staff development programs aimed at helping teachers apply holistic literacy principles do not operate on the notion that teachers need more than "a myriad of one-day, 'hit and run' workshops" (Loucks and Zigarmi 1981). To learn how to teach in a holistic way, teachers need much more than a few new teaching ideas given during an in-service workshop.

Because whole language is not a method but a philosophy of learning and teaching, becoming a whole language teacher involves changing one's basic beliefs about children's learning and the teacher's role in this process. In order to make these changes, teachers need opportunities to question and modify their concepts of teacher, learner, and classroom community member—all very difficult without long-term support and encouragement. For example, as teachers who want to teach in a holistic way move away from using basal readers and toward literature-based literacy instruction, they need different teaching skills. No longer can they rely on the scripted lesson plans in the basal text. Instead, teachers must take their lead from their students and at the same time provide authentic literacy experiences that are child-centered, are integrated with the other language arts and content areas, use real literature, and are evaluated using techniques other than traditional standardized tests. In other words, helping teachers make the change from a more traditional skill-based approach to a process-oriented, literature-based, holistic philosophy involves making the long-term commitment to support teachers as they change and develop a new culture and belief system—a new paradigm of learning and teaching.

In order for any staff development program to work, the administration as well as the teachers must be involved. Newman and Church (1990) agree that helping teachers move toward holistic literacy instruction requires much more than giving them a few whole language tips in a few in-service sessions. But they also propose that school administrators examine their own pedagogical beliefs and instructional practices, involve themselves in the change process, and create a supportive environment so that teachers feel safe taking risks, making mistakes, and experimenting. As Newman and Church write,

> Because whole language is not a program to be defined and mandated but a belief system that is in a constant process of evolution and implementation, everyone involved in implementing whole language philosophy has to become a learner. Administrators need to recognize that changing one's philosophical stance involves the same learning processes that teachers are trying to establish for students in the classroom. . . . And that cannot happen unless administrators are working from the same philosophical position they are attempting to help teachers implement. Therefore, principals and district-level administrators must also examine their beliefs about learning and teaching and about teacher development. (p. 24)

My experiences in working as a consultant with teachers in a medium-sized school district that serves approximately 21,500 students in grades K–12 confirm these notions. I have learned that in varying degrees the following are essential requirements if teachers are to take risks and grow in the process, since each reflects a philosophical position or pedagogical stance toward teaching and learning:

1. Changing teacher and administrator paradigms of reading and writing.
2. Receiving support from the school administrator.
3. Having tangible district support for change.
4. Having the time to learn.
5. Having support from the district to use literature.
6. Reflecting process learning/teaching in the district testing program.
7. Working with a skillful consultant.

I will discuss each of these in turn in the following sections.

The Paradigm Shift

In response to my frustration about not being able to help teachers change their paradigm of teaching reading from a skills and basal reader approach to one that reflects a holistic, process-oriented, literature-based philosophy, Donald Graves suggested during the fall of 1983 that I start with writing. His insight proved to be significant. As teachers experienced success involving students in the writing process, many (not all) naturally began to question what they were doing in reading. They began to question the value of centering their reading lessons primarily around the basal text and doing the accompanying workbook pages. They began to see the value of involving the students in reading more literature. They started to understand that if they wanted their students to write quality pieces, the students needed to read quality literature. And because students were busily working on their developing pieces of writing, teachers no longer needed to rely on workbook pages and worksheets to keep students busy while they were involved with reading or writing conferences. In addition, understanding the writing process helped the teachers see the many connections between reading and writing. In the end, I was glad that I had not encouraged teachers to focus on reading first. The decision to follow the teachers' inclination to focus on writing was an important one in helping them shift their writing paradigm and move toward becoming more holistic literacy teachers.

As the teachers became more holistic in their literacy lessons, their students flourished. Students became excited about reading and writing, and were doing more of it. As this happened, more and more of the principals began to see the value of holistic literacy instruction. Most principals, however, did not find it easy to shift from a skills approach to one that reflects a holistic philosophy. Although a few already had a holistic philosophy, many did not. Those who didn't felt the pressure of standardized tests and approached teacher evaluation and student learning from the clinical supervision or mastery teaching perspective in which they were schooled. What I saw was a rather schizophrenic perspective presented by many administrators. On the one hand, they liked the fact that kids were writing and reading and taking a real interest in these activities; on the other hand, they still emphasized student performance on standardized tests and the elements of a good lesson from Madeline Hunter's mastery model (1976).

Even though principals were invited to participate in the courses and workshops developed for the teachers, most did not, or attended only sporadically. Thus, many administrators did not have a clear idea of what the teachers were learning or struggling with. Of course, the consultants who worked with teachers kept the principals abreast of what was happening within their respective buildings, but unless they had already internalized the philosophy of holistic instruction, most principals were not active participants in the culture or new belief system being built in the school. I found the administrative aspect of the staff development program to be a shortcoming.

As I work with administrators, I have discovered that the same conditions that facilitate teacher change must exist for principals too. Clearly it would have been helpful if the district had some kind of ongoing in-service activities just for administrators. Two topics to explore in these administrative in-service activities would be, first, principles of holistic literacy learning and, second, literacy issues such as skills, testing, teaching, and so on. In addition, part of the time during these administrative in-service workshops should be spent on having the participants experience the writing and reading processes and their connections. I have found that principals, like teachers, need experiences that encourage them to examine their current ways of thinking, and someone to support them as they make the change to a new paradigm. The following section illustrates what happened in two different schools—one in which the principal was supportive and the other in which the principal was not. As I hope to show, the principal is significant in effecting or retarding the change process.

Support from the School Administrator

Schools have different atmospheres. I noticed that teachers in some schools willingly tried out new ideas without fear, while others (though they may have felt uncomfortable with what they had long been doing) made little movement toward changing their instruction. When I thought about the various teachers, schools, and principals with whom I had worked and considered the instructional changes that were made, I realized that the differences were not primarily related to the student population or even to the teachers themselves. The differences primarily reflected differences in the school principals (Wood, Thompson, and Russell 1981). But what, I wondered, did principals do that made such a difference? Why were the teachers in some buildings excited about what they were learning and others not? Why was it that in some buildings teachers openly shared their failures as well as their successes with one another while in others, silence prevailed?

My examination of the behavior and attitudes of principals with whom I have worked has led me to three conclusions. The first is obvious. It concerns whether or not the principal explicitly supports the program. The following list outlines how some principals lent support:

1. Actively participated in learning and modeled learning by
   a. Asking teachers what they were learning.
   b. Attending the in-service workshop sessions and actively participating in them.
   c. Reading at least some of the articles and books that the teachers were reading and chatting with the teachers about them when the opportunity arose.
   d. Asking consultants what features to look for in an effective literacy development program and reinforcing teachers for including them.
2. Focused on the learning of students by
   a. Making positive comments to teachers at faculty meetings about the authentic literacy events in which children engaged.

  b. Sharing, at faculty meetings, pieces the children wrote and
     stories the children read.
3. Coordinated other school activities with the staff development
   program by
  a. Having consultants speak to parent groups about the read-
     ing and writing processes.
  b. Having consultants share information about literacy devel-
     opment with classroom aides and volunteers.
  c. Encouraging teachers to integrate curricular areas.
  d. Writing the annual goals by which the principals them-
     selves would be evaluated in light of the literacy develop-
     ment emphasis of the school.

A principal did not have to do all these things for teachers to feel
supported. I did observe, however, that four of these activities in
particular had a tremendous impact: if the principal 1) read some of
the articles and books the teachers were reading and chatted with the
teachers about them; 2) reinforced teachers when they provided
authentic literacy events for their students; 3) made positive comments to teachers at faculty meetings about the holistic literacy activities that were going on in classrooms; and 4) shared stories children
wrote and commented on some of the books they noticed children
reading at faculty meetings. These were significant gestures, since
they highlighted not only the learning the teachers did and the
changes they had made in their teaching, but also the effects that the
teachers' learning and their changes were having on students.

   For example: at a faculty meeting, John, who was then principal
of a school with four classrooms at each level (grades K–6), shared his
observations of the kinds of authentic literacy activities he saw in the
building. At this same meeting he also read to the teachers some of the
stories the children had written. As he told me later, he was amazed
at the results. That day and throughout the week, teachers either
came into his office or stopped him in the hall with their students'
writings in hand to show him. They also described their reading and
writing programs to him and said such things as, "Come into my
classroom. I want you to see how I am teaching reading and writing,"
or "Here are some things my class wrote. Would you like to take a
look at them?" After that, John said he noticed even more reading
and writing occurring in classrooms. Besides sharing student reading
and writing and commenting on them at faculty meetings, John also
responded to student reading and writing when he visited classrooms.

Then he would talk to the classroom teacher about all the wonderful things he noticed.

My second and third conclusions about the behavior and attitudes of principals are distinct but related. One concerns whether or not the principal overemphasizes student results on the district's standardized testing program, the other whether or not the principal encourages teachers to find and refine the artistry of their own teaching. Both demonstrate the need for principals to internalize the philosophy they want teachers to reflect. To illustrate these points, here are two different scenarios and my interpretations of them.

Jeannie's Class (Grades K–3)

In Jeannie's class the students wrote daily. They didn't write for the teacher. Instead, they wrote for each other and themselves. Mike was working on a joke book. Geoff was rehearsing by drawing a picture to figure out what he wanted to write about. Naomi and Jessica were sitting on the floor next to a chalkboard brainstorming ideas for the next episode in their story. Jenni was sitting quietly at her desk copying a picture book. As I glanced around the room, I saw all the children were busily at work composing.

I asked Jeannie, "Does this happen all the time?"

Enthusiastically, she replied, "Yes! The children have taken control of their own writing. I'm just here to help them when they get stuck. Look over there! See Mike and Matt. They're doing some research so that they can coauthor a book about submarines. And then there's D.J. His parents were told that he'd always have trouble learning to read and write. But you ought to listen to him read! He's terrific. He's reading a big fat informational book from the library about early man. His reading has improved dramatically ever since I started this approach to writing instruction. My students ask to write. Whenever they have free time they want to work on their pieces."

Jeannie showed their writing folders to me. I compared their writings over the past months and saw improvements in spelling, punctuation, and thinking.

Jeannie used the drafts as diagnostic information to document her students' development in writing. She noticed which skills and spelling words her students were struggling with, and simply taught them what they needed to make their writing better.

Literature was also a key component in her writing program. When she was concerned about the quality of her students' pieces, she started to read quality literature to her students. She would discuss with her students how the author used design and carefully crafted words to paint pictures with words. She said that once she started doing this, her students' reading and writing improved.

Jeannie worked for Mark, a principal who encouraged experimentation and valued creativity. He understood that not all teachers teach alike, that each must find the artistry of his or her own teaching. Mark was also able to put student results on standardized tests in proper perspective; he understood that they are only one measure of students' achievement and have their limitations. Most important, he shared his excitement about what he noticed with the teachers and encouraged them to find and use alternatives to basal texts.

Not all principals feel as Mark does. In contrast, Mary (not her real name) worked for Wynn (not his real name), a rather strict, "by the book" person who believes in ability grouping and numerical scores on standardized tests, and who wasn't able to internalize the whole language philosophy.

Mary's Class (Grade 2)

The students in Mary's class wrote, but they did not write daily. They wrote at the most twice a week at the teacher's request and on teacher-selected topics. Concern for correctness permeated the class. Mary wanted to focus more on the writing process and use literature books instead of the basal, but felt torn. She felt she had to teach the expected grade-level skills as outlined in the basal text because she was concerned about her students' performance in the district's standardized testing program.

So instead of learning to write by writing and read by reading quality literature, students completed workbook pages and skill sheets, wrote on teacher-selected topics, read stories from the basal text, and were rewarded for neatness and correctness. In addition, reading and writing time was broken into discrete units. There was a time for handwriting, a time for spelling, a time for punctuation skills, a time for reading round-robin style, and a time for free writing and reading.

Wynn believed that there are certain mechanical writing skills students should learn at various grade levels, with little regard for where they are developmentally. So instead of encouraging teachers to discover their own artistry, he preferred that they be given a formula for teaching. To Wynn, student performance on standardized tests and the school's ranking in comparison to other schools in the district were strong measures of teacher effectiveness.

The Differences

These scenarios depict two very different primary classrooms because Jeannie and Mary worked with two principals with vastly different leadership styles and goals. The in-service sessions at Mark's school were exciting, yet relaxed. Teachers openly shared failures and asked each other for suggestions and support. Some teachers felt comfortable enough to challenge me openly and share their thinking when grappling with new ideas. In contrast, the in-service sessions at Wynn's school were subdued. At times, there was an undercurrent of hostility, and teachers were quick to defend what they were doing. Little sharing occurred, and teachers did not ask each other for assistance. They were concerned primarily with doing what Wynn expected them to do: making sure they covered the basals. So instead of taking their lead from the children, they relied on scripted lesson plans and felt uncomfortable diverting from the basals. They were not kidwatchers, nor did they evaluate their own teaching. Little growth, if any, occurred.

Why the difference? When I think about these two principals and why they differed in their ability to support their teachers, several things come to mind. Mark read some of the articles distributed to teachers on holistic literacy learning and conferred with the consultant about them. At these meetings with the consultant, Mark asked many questions as he began shifting his thinking. In addition, Mark believed in process learning in science, so he already understood the strengths of having a process paradigm for learning. All the consultant had to do was help him understand the need for process learning in reading and writing. Wynn, on the other hand, saw his role very differently. For him, a strong indicator of teacher success was how well the students at his school performed on standardized tests. Because his students scored consistently high, he had no reason to encourage his teachers to rethink what they were doing. In addition, Wynn actively supported grouping students according to ability levels and believed that only through the direct teaching of skills would students improve (as measured by standardized test scores). He did encourage his teachers to engage children in literature-based instruction, but only after the basics were covered. In other words, Mark was able to internalize the philosophy of holistic literacy instruction and Wynn was not.

District Support for Change

Each teacher involved in in-service workshops on the writing process was released during the school day to attend. Even though the number of release days reflected only a small portion of the time teachers actually spent in in-service activities, this support demonstrated, in a concrete way, the district's commitment to teachers. When districts honor teachers as professionals through tangible support such as release time, teachers actually give more of themselves than what they receive. And the big winners are students.

In addition to providing teachers with time on the job to explore, examine, and learn, the district brought in guest speakers to talk with teachers about the writing process and its connections with reading. These outside experts usually spoke during afterschool hours, because the district leadership thought it wiser to use release days to involve teachers in such things as watching and discussing demonstration lessons, conferring with other teachers in small groups, and attending district-planned in-service activities. It is interesting that at each presentation by an outside speaker, approximately two hundred teachers were in attendance even though it was optional.

To help teachers network with other teachers in schools, after-school grade-level meetings were conducted. At these meetings, teachers shared teaching and organizational ideas, talked about their successes and failures, and considered new materials. These meetings not only gave teachers support but provided useful information to the district leadership about teacher concerns and the kinds of assistance teachers wanted.

Besides having time during the school day to learn, listening to outside speakers and networking with others, teachers also wanted books to read. I found that giving teachers titles of books, while helpful, was not enough. Teachers wanted these professional materials right away and often did not have time to hunt them down. They wanted to take the books home to read immediately so that they could begin thinking of strategies to implement these new ways of thinking in their classrooms. To meet this need, I ordered books from the local university's bookstore on consignment. Then at in-service workshops, during cross-school grade-level meetings, and working with teachers one-on-one or in small groups, I shared these professional resources, and teachers purchased them. Some of the resources that teachers found helpful were *Towards a Reading/Writing Classroom* by Butler and Turbill (1984); *The Art of Teaching Writing* by Calkins

(1986); *Lessons from a Child* by Calkins (1983); *In the Middle* by Atwell (1987); *A Writer Teaches Writing* by Murray (1985); *Writing: Teachers and Children at Work* by Graves (1983); *Breaking Ground: Teachers Relate Reading and Writing in the Elementary School,* edited by Hansen, Newkirk, and Graves (1985); *When Writers Read* by Hansen (1987); *What's Whole in Whole Language?* by Goodman (1986); *The Craft of Children's Writing* by Newman (1984); *Whole Language: Theory in Use,* edited by Newman (1985); *Spel . . . Is a Four-Letter Word* by Gentry (1987); *Reading, Writing and Caring* by Cochrane, Cochrane, Scalena, and Buchanan (1984); *Read On: A Conference Approach to Reading* by Hornsby and Sukarna with Parry (1986); *Write On: A Conference Approach to Writing* by Parry and Hornsby (1985); *Reading Without Nonsense* by Smith (1985); *The Child as Critic* by Sloan (1984).

Time to Learn

As those experienced in fostering educational change are well aware, "significant improvement in educational practice takes considerable time and long-term inservice programs" (Wood, McQuarrie, and Thompson 1982, p. 28).

After twelve years of working with teachers, I have developed a way to provide enough time for long-term in-service programs that support change, especially when I am working with several schools during an academic year. The following schedule is flexible and can be adapted to individual situations.

1. Initial contact with a school: one week. Provide release time for teachers to attend either an all-day or a half-day in-service workshop. After the workshop, have teachers decide how they want to spend the rest of the week. In my experience, teachers may request any of the following kinds of services from the consultant:
   a. Meet in grade-level teams to discuss questions, concerns, and goals.
   b. Meet in cross grade-level teams to discuss questions, concerns, and goals.
   c. Meet one-on-one to discuss questions, concerns, and goals with consultant.
   d. Meet in grade-level teams, cross grade-level teams, or one-on-one to watch consultant work with children. Debrief

after the demonstration to discuss what was observed and set goals.

2. Then no visit for about six weeks. During this time consultant is working with other schools.
3. Go back to school after six-week period. During this time, teachers meet with consultant in grade-level teams, cross grade-level teams, or one-on-one to discuss questions and concerns that have arisen during the previous six weeks, to set new goals, and/or to have the consultant demonstrate teaching techniques with students. Consultant is in building for three to five days.
4. No visit for another six-week period. Consultant works with other schools.
5. Repeat steps 3 and 4 for as long as school year permits.

Since the consultant returns only every six weeks or so, teachers have time to try out new ideas, read and reflect, and decide for themselves the kind of additional support they need. As Newman and Church state, "Curriculum leaders need to create many different kinds of learning situations so that everyone is supported in a long-term exploration of learning and teaching" (1990, p. 24). At the end of the first school year of implementation, many teachers felt they needed another year of support. So teachers were given the opportunity to continue working on implementing holistic literacy principles during the next school year, and in some instances during the next two years.

I found that it usually took about three years of intensive work in one building to help teachers make and sustain changes. The first year, teachers began the process of change and had many, many questions. The second year, teachers made radical changes in their literacy programs. With supportive principals, teachers moved away from scripted lesson plans and basal texts and observed students in order to learn what to teach next. The third year, teachers refined their teaching and became more confident. After this third year, many teachers became teacher experts and worked in leadership roles with others.

Support for Using Literature

As teachers move away from basal texts, they need other kinds of materials—more quality literature books, paper, pens, binding machines, and so forth. Without the support of the building principal and district administrators, teachers find moving away from using basal texts and workbooks difficult. So, it's important for all administrators to understand the need for new resources and materials and to provide them.

In the school district where I worked, most administrators at both the school and district level agreed that teachers who wanted to move away from using basal texts and workbooks could do so. To facilitate this process and to help teachers choose from among the many materials on the market, they developed certain guidelines:

1. Only basal materials on the district's approved list could be purchased. No others were allowed.
2. Original trade books, not stories rewritten to match readability levels, could be purchased. When selecting original trade books, however, teachers needed to consider their communities and take into account such things as sexual overtones, the preaching of religious doctrines or related moral judgments, the depiction of blatant defiance of authority, the excessive use of violence and the occult, the excessive use of profanity, a too didactic style of writing, the accuracy of the subject matter in nonfiction materials, and the relationship of the book to the developmental levels of the students.
3. Packaged literature programs could be used, providing the books in these packaged programs adhered to the criteria used to select quality literature books. Teachers found it helpful if these packaged materials were listed and described on a handout distributed along with publishers' catalogs to the school, since they did not have the time to do the searching themselves.

In addition, a cadre of teachers, working together with the district's literacy specialists and the children's librarian for the city, put together a list of over three thousand books to guide teachers in selecting materials. For each book listed, the committee included information about appropriate grade level(s), genre, plot structure or design, topic(s) of study, and any other information teachers might find useful, such as strong lead, dialect, interesting use of language, and predictability of text. After this project was completed, which took the better part of a semester, each elementary school received a hard copy and a computer disk of the list so teachers could select for themselves the books they wanted to use. Teachers have found this list extremely helpful. They have been asked to keep the list current by submitting information pertinent to the books they recommend to the district office.

The District's New Testing Program

A paradigm shift toward holistic instruction involves reexamining the evaluative techniques and instruments used to assess reading and writing. Even though there has been and continues to be pressure from various constituent groups throughout the community to raise test scores, the district decided to implement a process approach in evaluating writing. During the 1988–89 school year, I was part of the district committee that developed this plan.

Because the assessment technique needed to be an authentic student task, the procedure provided several things: 1) sufficient time; 2) a supportive environment; 3) resources students could use; and 4) an opportunity to use the writing process. Briefly, here is the assessment plan we developed:

1. Classroom teachers in grades 3, 5, 8, and 10 share a letter from the school librarian in which the librarian asks for the students' help in planning his or her purchases for the next school year.
2. Students are asked to write a letter in response that tells who their favorite authors are and the topics in which they are interested. They are also told that it would be helpful if they included titles of books in their letters. And finally, students are informed that decisions about which books to purchase will be based on how well they are able to convince the librarian that their choice is best and on how well their letter is presented.
3. Teachers can provide resources, such as dictionaries, *Children's Books in Print*, writing implements, and so forth, but they cannot give students direct assistance in rehearsing, revising, or editing. Of course, students may use each other as resources in conferences, but no help outside of school can be given. In other words, all writing must be done in school.
4. The timeline for the completion of this writing assessment is between two and three weeks, depending on how frequently and for how long students write.
5. For scoring this letter, an anonymous random sample of papers from each grade tested is selected. All papers from this

sample, regardless of grade level, are scored together. Scorings are made on several levels. First, a holistic score, which reflects a general, overall impression rather than specific details, is given to each paper by two trained scorers using a scale of performance ranging from 1 to 7 (7 is high). Prototype papers for each of the seven levels are used. Then statistical correlations are performed to see the relationships between scores on this type of assessment and on standardized achievement tests.

6. The unit of analysis is the entire district. Individual scores are not reported. Because only an anonymous random sample of papers is used, unscored papers are returned to teachers so that they can evaluate the writing development of their own students.

Although this procedure was developed primarily for district office use, teachers involved in this process are finding it extremely helpful. As they review their students' persuasive letters from rehearsal to final copy, they are able to collect information about how well their students use the writing process, what their students know about books and authors, and whether their students enjoy reading. In addition, they are able to see firsthand how the students use the resources around them as they revise and edit their letters.

Because this technique is new to the district, only time will tell if this assessment procedure proves to be helpful. Nevertheless, the value of this particular approach is that it not only taps into the writing ability of students and the process they use from rehearsal to final copy, but it also provides information about how students view reading and books, and moves everyone toward looking at literacy as a holistic process rather than a fragmented one.

The Skills of the Consultant

It is particularly difficult to describe the skills necessary to be an effective consultant. Of course, the consultant must be knowledgeable. But working with teachers and sharing information involves forming partnerships—a human encounter as varied as people are—based on mutual trust and respect.

I have learned that one of the best ways for a consultant to form partnerships with teachers is to shift perspective. Instead of focusing on what the teacher does, that is, scrutinizing the teacher's plans, her words, and so forth, it is advantageous if the consultant focuses on the children and what they are doing (Siu-Runyan 1990). Most teachers don't feel entirely comfortable when they are being watched and evaluated. By focusing on the children, both the teacher and consultant can learn a lot about instruction and have something common to talk about. Given this focus, teachers more readily accept a consultant's suggestions about how a teacher can modify teaching strategies to help the children.

I have also realized that the teacher must be in charge (Siu-Runyan 1990). Consultants must put aside their own agendas for the kinds of instructional improvements they would like teachers to make. Instead, consultants must listen, be sensitive to the needs of teachers and where they want help, and provide them with what they want, not what a consultant thinks they need. Taking this approach with teachers is no different from taking our lead from children. Just as teachers must be able to take their lead from students in order to do a good job, so consultants too must be able to put their own agendas aside and take their lead from teachers.

And last, consultants must be willing to share their mistakes with teachers. When consultants share the mistakes they have made in working with children, teachers learn a lot about what not to do. In addition, teachers who see the consultant as fallibly human are more willing to take risks and less afraid to try out ideas. Only through risk-taking do we improve, even if it involves making a mistake. As one teacher said to me, "I like working with you. You make the kind of mistakes I make and yet you're able to laugh about it with me. Thanks for being human. It makes it easier for me to take risks."

Conclusion

Supporting teacher growth does not happen in a one-shot, dog and pony show workshop setting. It takes time, commitment, and resources from *all* the various levels in a school district, and it develops from successful human encounters. Everyone involved in the process of change needs to respect learners, whether they are students, teachers, or administrators. In both the short and the long term, a staff development program aimed at helping teachers become holistic literacy teachers will be successful to the degree that it respects teachers, encourages risk-taking, and provides time for reflection and thinking.

The results of the staff development program where I worked came to fruition four years after it began. On the evening of February 26, 1987, the district's Board of Education approved using literature for literacy instruction. As the *Daily Camera* reported the next day:

Board Approves Reading Plan

Should students learn to read by reading good books or by reading the stories in a basal textbook? Should they learn by semantics and syntax and comprehension or by the phonetic approach?

Reading good books is a more natural and better way of learning how to read than the phonetic, basal-reader approach, most, but not all, education researchers say.

The . . . Board of Education Thursday night approved new fiction and non-fiction books that can be used in lieu of, or in addition to, basal readers.

Many teachers already have been using a literature approach to reading, but the approval marks a change in emphasis away from basal readers.

"This is a very powerful statement," board member Dale Vigil said after the meeting. "This is reading in a natural setting as opposed to a contrived setting."

Vigil said he was a slow reader as a child. "This is how I should have learned to read." (Section B, p. 1)

Because in real life no story really ends, I feel that it is important to mention two final reflections. First, because the board of any school district wields tremendous power in making policy for educational programs, having informed and knowledgeable board members is critical. Former school board member Dr. Dale Vigil went into classrooms, saw the benefits of holistic literacy instruction firsthand, and was instrumental in helping form this policy.

Second, times change and so do personnel, board members, and budget constraints. During the 1990–91 academic year, this district has moved forward with site-based management, and there is no longer a district-level staff development program for literacy development. Because of this change at the district office, those who had been involved in this seven-year staff development effort have either retired, left the district, or taken classroom positions. In addition, as in any other district, over time there have been changes within the teacher and administrative ranks—some have retired, left the district, or changed schools. Change can be exciting, but also disconcerting. With each change, there is a ripple effect that has consequences for what happens in classrooms and for the kind of learning experiences in which students are engaged. Thus, my concern at this point for the teachers in this particular district is whether or not they will receive the continuous, long-term human support for risk-taking and learning at the building level in order to continue the movement toward holistic literacy instruction. As Newman and Church state in discussing change:

> Real change involves a critical appraisal of our instructional practices, trying to identify contradictions within our theoretical assumptions and their impact on our students. There is no safe middle ground, no convenient compromise. We won't make much progress toward developing a whole language stance, or toward discrediting the myths, unless we are willing to make ourselves vulnerable and become learners too. (1990, p. 26)

Site-based management, the current focus of the district with which I worked, does indeed have the potential for maximizing teachers' opportunities to take charge of their own professional growth. But as in any educational movement, there are also limitations. Such potential and such limitations are related to the degree to which parents are involved and helped to understand, and teachers and administrators are able to honor and support each other, hear the voices of children, examine issues thoughtfully and openly, reflect critically upon the actions taken, and do the hard job of implementing long-term professional development in a variety of ways. Learning, a collaborative and cooperative venture, involves courage, commitment, and communication from everyone, since it is always more difficult to build than to destroy or remain the same. Because progress toward holistic learning and teaching means changing deeply ingrained paradigms, it will never be an easy feat, but one requiring the continuous effort of knowledgeable, committed people.

References

Atwell, Nancie. 1987. *In the Middle: Writing, Reading, and Learning with Adolescents*. Portsmouth, N.H.: Boynton/Cook.

Butler, Andrea, and Jan Turbill. 1984. *Towards a Reading/Writing Classroom*. Portsmouth, N.H.: Heinemann.

Calkins, Lucy McCormick. 1983. *Lessons from a Child*. Portsmouth, N.H.: Heinemann.

————. 1986. *The Art of Teaching Writing*. Portsmouth, N.H.: Heinemann.

Classroom report: Board approves reading plan. 1987. *Boulder Daily Camera*, Feb. 27, B–1.

Cochrane, Orin, Donna Cochrane, Sharon Scalena, and Ethel Buchanan. 1984. *Reading, Writing, and Caring*. Winnipeg, Manitoba, Canada: Whole Language Consultants.

Gentry, J. Richard. 1987. *Spel . . . Is a Four-Letter Word*. Portsmouth, N.H.: Heinemann.

Goodman, Kenneth S. 1986. *What's Whole in Whole Language?* Portsmouth, N.H.: Heinemann.

Graves, Donald H. 1983. *Writing: Teachers and Children at Work*. Portsmouth, N.H.: Heinemann.

Hansen, Jane. 1987. *When Writers Read*. Portsmouth, N.H.: Heinemann.

Hansen, Jane, Tom Newkirk, and Donald Graves, ed. 1985. *Breaking Ground: Teachers Relate Reading and Writing in the Elementary School*. Portsmouth, N.H.: Heinemann.

Hornsby, David, and Deborah Sukarna with Jo-Ann Parry. 1986. *Read On: A Conference Approach to Reading*. Portsmouth, N.H.: Heinemann.

Hunter, Madeline. 1976. *Improved Instruction*. Segundo, Calif.: TIP Publications.

Loucks, Susan F., and Patricia Zigarmi. 1981. Effective staff development. *Educational Considerations* 8: 4–8.

Murray, Donald M. 1985. *A Writer Teaches Writing*. Boston, Mass.: Houghton Mifflin.

Newman, Judith M. 1984. *The Craft of Children's Writing*. Portsmouth, N.H.: Heinemann.

————, ed. 1985. *Whole Language: Theory in Use*. Portsmouth, N.H.: Heinemann.

Newman, Judith, and Susan Church. 1990. Myths of whole language. *The Reading Teacher* 44(1): 20–26.

Parry, Jo-Ann, and David Hornsby. 1985. *Write On: A Conference Approach to Writing*. Portsmouth, NH: Heinemann.

Siu-Runyan, Yvonne. 1990. Forming partnerships. *Journal of Reading* 33: 458–59.

Sloan, Glenna Davis. 1984. *The Child as Critic*. New York: Teachers College Press.

Smith, Frank. 1985. *Reading Without Nonsense*. New York: Teachers College Press.

Wood, Fred H., Frank O. McQuarrie, Jr., and Steven R. Thompson. October 1982. Practitioners and professors agree on effective staff development practices. *Educational Leadership* 40: 28–31.

Wood, Fred H., Steven R. Thompson, and Sr. Francis Russell. 1981. Design-
    ing effective staff development programs. In *Staff Development/Organiza-
    tion Development*, ed. Betty Dillon-Peterson. Alexandria, Va.: Association
    for Supervision and Curriculum Development, 59–91.

5 | Collaborating in Coursework and in Classrooms: An Alternative for Strengthening Whole Language Teacher Preparation Cultures

Jean Anne Clyde and Mark W. F. Condon

Jean Anne Clyde and Mark Condon begin their chapter by describing the frustrations felt by undergraduate preservice teachers, practicing teachers, and university professors when they try to teach according to a whole language belief system in an educational environment that does not support teacher growth. After discussing the belief system that characterizes whole language contexts and cultures, the authors describe how they created supportive contexts in which they as well as preservice and in-service teachers worked collaboratively. In sharing their experiences, the authors provide a valuable model for collaboration between preservice and in-service teachers within university coursework and school settings. The discussion is enriched by the reflections of three pairs of preservice and in-service teachers.

JEAN ANNE CLYDE is Assistant Professor of Language Arts at the University of Louisville, where she works with both graduate and undergraduate students. In addition to her interests in promoting collaboration between preservice and in-service teachers, she is involved in her own collaborative project, co-teaching with a first-grade teacher. Together they are exploring the links between print literacy and alternate communication systems such as art, music, drama, and dance. Jean Anne's recent book, *Portraits of Whole Language Classrooms*, with coeditor Heidi Mills (Heinemann, 1990) provides detailed descriptions of whole language classrooms from preschool to college.

MARK W. F. CONDON is Associate Professor of Elementary and Secondary Reading at the University of Louisville, where he teaches courses in literacy and computers for graduate students. He also directs a graduate program that recruits second career students with academic strengths in areas other than teaching and prepares them for kindergarten-to-fourth-grade certification. In addition to his work in creating a holistic teacher education program, Mark is currently focusing on the development of teachers throughout their careers in education and on collaborative writing among elementary and middle-school students.

* * *

A Preservice Dilemma

Paula has taught for just a few years since her graduation from our university's teacher-preparation program. This semester she has volunteered to become a "cooperating teacher" for an undergraduate who needs a field placement in an elementary classroom. But Paula soon realizes that her assigned undergraduate, Jan, is required to teach lessons that run counter to Paula's beliefs about what constitutes effective teaching. An advocate of basal readers and quiet classrooms, Paula finds the social nature of the "strategy lessons" Jan is conducting to be very disruptive. In her distress, she insists that Jan take her first graders someplace outside of the classroom to teach her required lessons.

An excerpt from Jan's field journal expresses the frustration and discouragement she has endured in spending an entire semester searching for a place to teach.

> . . . I was in hopes that [my cooperating teacher and I] would work close together and be a help for each other. It hasn't really been like that. Paula has let me know that things are to be the way she wants them since it is her classroom and I am a guest in it.
>
> She told me right out that her classroom is to be quiet and has let me know if it was too noisy. Sometimes it's my fault because I like to talk to the kids and there is very little time during the day for that. Paula is extremely structured, totally unbending. . . .
>
> I feel like a second-class citizen. . . . I'm like Rodney Dangerfield—I get no respect! The vibes I get from Paula are that my work doesn't matter. There is no respect for the time I took to prepare the lesson. I've taught on the stairs, in the hall and the supply closet, in the kindergarten room, in the computer room, and now outside. Guess you might say I'm versatile!!
>
> I worked hard on my lessons. I didn't do any slipshod lessons. I thought they were well thought out and a good learning experience for the students. It's a shame they weren't treated that way. . . .

Maybe I should have spoken up, but it's like a catch-22. The cooperating teacher has to evaluate me. If I make her mad because it isn't what she wants, will that affect my evaluation?

I'm going to save this journal. Someday if I ever have a[n undergraduate] student, I'm going to get this journal out to remind me not to do the same thing to someone else. I really think I could have been more of an asset to Paula in her class. Oh, well, the best way to look at this is that it's her loss.

The problem isn't just Paula's. What Jan is experiencing is not uncommon in teacher education. Because of the number of student placements that the university must secure, preservice teachers often find themselves in hostile or counterproductive contexts working with teachers who are unable or unwilling to "cooperate." As a result, students like Jan can find it impossible to experiment with the new concepts they are encountering in their university coursework.

At the heart of this dilemma is an apparent disconnectedness between the teacher-educator's expectations and those of the classroom teacher. What Jan's cooperating teacher expected from her teaching and what her university professor had required represented conflicting cultures of teaching and learning. Although the intent of the field placement was to promote her growth and development, she ended up working in a hostile context, isolated from the support the system was designed to create for her.

It is not surprising that experiences such as these, which place preservice teachers "in the middle," trying to come to grips with what they see as two competing sets of goals, often convince them that what is well grounded in theory may also be impossible in practice.

An In-Service Dilemma

Although Susan is a veteran teacher, she is in a position very similar to Jan's. She teaches in what her school district calls a "traditional school," created in response to the expressed desire of many of its constituent families for a school setting similar to those current parents remember—quiet and controlled, emphasizing high standards, grades, and "basic skills."

Recently, in the coursework Susan has been taking at our university, she has accepted the challenges her professors have issued to reflect on her teaching. Intrigued by stories of whole language teaching, she has begun to investigate its appropriateness for her and her students; in doing so, she has begun to take instructional risks in her own classroom. This endeavor, however, has often proved to be a lonely one. Like Jan, Susan suffers from the lack of connection between the university's support for her developing abilities as a whole language teacher and the "traditional" kinds of support her school was created to provide. Like Jan, Susan is working in isolation from other teachers who are learning to become more learner-centered. In this traditional school setting, she has found little support for the ideas about learning and literacy she finds compelling. Her decision to embrace whole language has caused her to come up against one of the political liabilities of diverging from the local norms of practice: as she struggles to operate in a context that is wary of, if not antagonistic to, holistic teaching, she has simultaneously suffered the loss of her social support system (Harman and Edelsky 1989).

A University Dilemma

The frustration experienced by these two professionals is also characteristic of the feelings of university professors like us. As a new professor, one of the authors demonstrated, studied, and advocated whole language teaching. She invested her energies in "sowing the seeds" of holistic and learner-centered instruction, only to see teachers who might otherwise have adopted these approaches wither in inhospitable environments in the classrooms of other professors in her university. Like Jan and Susan, she felt isolated from like-minded colleagues who could support her professional growth and development.

Students in our programs take courses from professors with a wide range of orientations, which is as it should be in a university. But many of our colleagues hold different views of what effective college teaching looks like, the kinds of university experiences that can be educative, and what kinds of professional behavior indicate success in our students. This can naturally divert the attention of emerging whole language teachers. The demonstrations and support of whole language teaching that university professors provide can get lost, be thwarted, or even be rebuked in the university context.

Three Dilemmas—One Common Problem

Such experiences lead us to believe that our successes at promoting whole language to date are a function of the traditional weaknesses in all educational cultures. As Lortie has noted, the conditions we generally associate with a rich subculture do not prevail for classroom teaching:

> Structures affecting entry have been kept loose to ease recruitment; the occupation does not filter candidates through a fine selection screen or subject them to a powerful induction sequence. Cellular organization retards rather than enhances colleagueship. . . . [T]he workplace of the teacher—the school—is not organized to promote inquiry or to build the intellectual capital of the occupation. (1975, p. 56)

At the same time, "a predominant barrier to the spread of change throughout a school is the independence of staff members and the lack of opportunity for them to interact" (Corbett 1982, p. 34). Ironically, when every teacher functions independently, paying only lip service to administrative belief systems and policies, then even if the school "cultures" are not directly supportive of students' growth it is possible to operate freely enough to develop as whole language teachers. In the school's culture, it is when there is antagonism toward whole language or when the consideration of change implies a confession of inadequacy on the part of the teacher that such freedom is not possible. When preservice teachers come up against teachers like Paula, when an in-service teacher finds him- or herself in "traditional" schools, or when we share our students with more traditionally oriented university colleagues, the limitations in our own culture seem particularly striking.

Examining Strong Whole Language Cultures

In considering solutions to what seemed to be a matched set of "whole language dilemmas," we began to reflect upon other contexts in which developing teachers have felt supported and successful as risk-takers. For her dissertation, one of the authors became involved in field research at a day-care facility for three-, four-, and five-year-olds (Clyde 1987). In this collaborative study, the director and two classroom teachers were invited to participate actively as researchers while the author participated actively as a classroom teacher. It was not the purpose of that study to focus on staff development, but rather, to work collaboratively to find ways to create literate environments for the children. But as professionals who trust one another will do, the four relied on each other's support in taking risks with the literacy curriculum, sharing the results of those risks, reflecting upon the curricular implications of those results, and altering instruction to reflect the insights gleaned from this collaborative effort. Among the many pleasant outcomes of this endeavor was our realization that when children are trusted as curricular collaborators, teachers can become learners and learners can become teachers. When there is genuine collaboration, the experience helps everyone involved to grow.

In the end, working together we were able to create a context that served all learners—adults and children. It was a context that expressed a set of rules characteristic of whole language cultures. These rules, commonly referred to by whole language advocates as "assumptions," provide for a commonality across whole language contexts that enables us to identify them as such. Our assumptions are presented in Figure 5–1. In short, these contexts are learner-centered and inquiry-based.

Strengthening Whole Language Cultures

A discussion with the teacher-researchers from the preschool study led us to consider how to apply what we had learned there to the dilemmas that our three groups of educators—preservice, in-service, and university teachers—were experiencing. How different it would be if we could work together as professionals, taking risks together, talking through our successes, and analyzing our less successful moments.

FIGURE 5–1 *Assumptions (from Mills and Clyde 1990)*

A whole language context is one that:
1. Highlights authentic speech and literacy events.
2. Encourages risk-taking by recognizing error as a natural part of the learning process.
3. Provides choices for learners.
4. Is developed with a sense of trust in learners.
5. Is collaboratively established.
6. Casts teachers in a variety of supportive roles, from participant to guide to learner.
7. Capitalizes on the social nature of learning.
8. Encourages reflection.
9. Empowers all participants as teachers and learners.

Our conversation inspired the idea for a class that would combine two separate courses into one and unite preservice, in-service, and university teachers in two contexts: at the university and in elementary school classrooms. "Introduction to Reading and Language Arts" is a course required for all preservice teachers seeking K–4 certification from our state. "Reading and Writing with Young Children" is a graduate elective commonly taken by practicing teachers who have come to realize the need for a professional "boost" in their practice in language arts. In the fall of 1988, we sought a small number of teacher volunteers from the graduate class who would be willing to accept preservice partners from the undergraduate class. Each in-service teacher would "adopt" a preservice partner for whom she would serve as cooperating teacher. We also interviewed preservice teachers who were interested in this arrangement and who would be agreeable to attending the graduate course in lieu of its undergraduate equivalent.

To comply with the administrative requirements of our university's degree and certification programs, each student registered under the usual course numbers. Requirements for each course remained the same, but we arranged for both preservice and in-service groups to meet in one classroom.

Having paired our "experienced" teachers with our "less experienced" teachers, we attempted to structure this combined course so that participants would feel secure as risk-takers—feel sufficiently challenged, and yet feel successful as learners. We were searching, too, for ways to capitalize on the social nature of learning by inviting the participants to share their strengths and insights in supporting one another as learners. (Note: From this point, we will use the term "teachers" in referring to the group as a whole. It reflects our belief that we were all teachers and learners.)

We designed assignments to encourage the teachers to adopt a teacher-researcher stance. They maintained response journals in which they recorded their own personal reflections about readings, class discussions, and field observations. In order to involve them directly in action research, we required that each of them focus a case study report on one child in her elementary classroom in a way that highlighted that child's literacy strengths and needs. We also encouraged partners to collaborate with one another in compiling and determining the significance of the data they had collected in their individual case studies.

While undergraduates were assigned a collaborative take-home midterm exam, graduate students were required to implement an "I've always wanted to do that with my kids but was afraid to" project in which they pursued a curricular "wish" of their own choosing. Throughout the project, they were to keep track of their decision-making and their students' responses to their project. They were also invited to decide upon a format for sharing their research findings.

Preservice teachers were encouraged to provide assistance to their in-service partners in whatever ways that they could. They were also assigned to teach strategy lessons in their classrooms. Based on a socio-psycholinguistic model of reading, these student-centered and discovery-oriented lessons "are different both procedurally and theoretically from the skills lessons which transpire daily during most reading instruction" (Atwell and Rhodes 1984). A total of four of these lessons were formally evaluated, two by their classroom partner and two by the university teacher, for their records at the university. Essentially, the course was reflective of all whole language contexts: experiences and assignments were developed to allow both graduate and undergraduate students to "choose curricular areas to explore, negotiate activities with the teacher, collaborate with other students, take risks and chances with the structure and the content of their projects, and work with and create authentic texts" (Harman and Edelsky 1989, p. 397).

What made this class unique, however, was the potential that existed for importing beliefs and assumptions from the whole language university classroom into the elementary classroom. We hoped that the shared university coursework and experience would provide some common ground, a point of departure for graduate and undergraduate partners as they worked together in the elementary classroom. Having long ago recognized our own need for supportive colleagues with whom to consider professional issues, we felt certain that having another like-minded adult nearby would offer a degree of security lacking in most preservice and in-service fieldwork.

This pilot course was very well received by both preservice and in-service teachers. The in-service teachers came to view themselves less as experts and more as learners, while the students seemed to feel accepted as teachers. Their work together in class was enthusiastic and focused. Pleased with this promising arrangement, we have continued the program, each semester inviting a maximum of ten graduate students who are registered for the course "Reading and Writing with Young Children" to adopt an undergraduate partner. In order to demonstrate the potential benefits of this rather unique collaboration we have selected two pairs from the thirty graduate and undergraduate participants to date as the focus of our discussion here.

Susan and Page, and Cathy and Renee participated in this course as partners in the spring semester of 1989. Their successes as teams were quite impressive, yet their points of departure were remarkably different. Would it be possible for one class to address the needs of students with such diverse experiences, objectives, and beliefs?

The Collaborators and Their Stories

Susan, Classroom Teacher

Susan has already been introduced; she was the whole language teacher trying to operate in a "traditional" context that focused on a "back to basics" approach to education. She entered this course in January to continue her pursuit of whole language, which she had begun to implement while taking another university class, eagerly searching for more support for the changes she had begun to initiate in her classroom.

Page, Susan's Preservice Partner

Page had spent more than ten years working in schools in a support capacity. Quiet and reserved, she was well organized and convincingly professional. She trusted Susan implicitly, but this trust did not extend to herself. Aware that Susan was experimenting with the strategies presented in class, Page carefully attended to Susan's demonstrations of effective teaching. She was somewhat hesitant, however, to initiate changes or ideas independently.

Cathy, Classroom Teacher

Unlike Susan, Cathy had registered for the class because she needed university coursework to update her teaching certificate, and a Wednesday evening class fit perfectly into her busy schedule. A satisfied basal reader advocate, she accepted an undergraduate partner, completely unsuspecting of the fact that their relationship could have much of an impact on her *own* teaching, much less lead her to a critical juncture in her professional career.

Renee, Cathy's Preservice Partner

Renee was a confident young woman who easily accepted the learner-centered nature of whole language and the potential that it held for her and her teaching. A headstrong risk-taker, she was initially taken aback by Cathy's reliance on published materials and expressed frustration to her professor about Cathy's reluctance to experiment with the ideas that both she and Renee had been hearing and reading about at the university.

Two very different classroom teachers with two very different agendas. Two equally different preservice teachers. Conversations with these four individuals provide insight into their experience and the impact that it has had on their professional development.

Success in a Traditional School

Like a majority of the in-service teachers who have taken the course, Susan commented that working with Page provided the impetus for her to take some risks as a teacher. Knowing that Page was aware of the whole language concepts she had been exposed to, Susan felt compelled to try some of them for Page's sake. "It helped because Page was there," Susan said. "It was encouragement to try new things. She would understand why I did what I did, and how it differed from other things we had talked about in class. By taking the class together, the teacher and the student teacher were focused more on ideas. Ordinarily, I think the focus is on management and teaching hints. . . . The strategy lessons were a jumping off point for us. We'd all participate in them at the university. Then we'd [members of the class] go to school and try them out, and come back to class and share. Even if you hadn't tried them with your kids, it made you wonder, 'Why *didn't* that work?' That's where I was at that time. I was trying to figure out why kids weren't succeeding."

Page concurred. "Basically, that's what I was wondering, too. Why? Why did kids get one thing and not another?"

"I believe that if a child keeps trying, eventually he can learn anything," Susan told us. "But I'd seen too many kids quit in the traditional program. [The kids] wouldn't play by the rules. Everyone was supposed to be on the same lesson, but there was to be no interaction. They would all be working at their desks, all doing their own work, and they'd better not talk! The teacher was supposed to know everything, and the kids were to do what she said. . . . But with Page and me, I felt that we were learning *with* the kids."

Page nodded. "The way the kids responded would make you want to keep trying strategy lessons. You'd think, 'Hey! They *want* to know more!' So you'd keep trying. If Susan was doing a strategy lesson, or I was, and we saw how a child was responding, we would look at each other and understand."

The two went on to discuss one of their second graders, a student who, by many teachers' standards, would have been classified as a "problem": "Joey was a bright kid, and he wasn't that much of a discipline problem. He just wanted to do what he wanted to do," Page told us.

Susan talked of the benefits of working together in their handling of Joey. "I think it helped because we looked at Joey and thought, 'Why is he doing this?,' instead of seeing him as acting out. When Page would see something that I wouldn't see, we could talk about it. We were coming from the same background." Later she noted, "There are some teachers at my school I can't talk with because we can't get past our different perspectives."

Susan and Page also talked at length about the numerous occasions when they communicated simply by exchanging knowing looks with one another. One of their university experiences, for instance, had involved them as readers in a basal reader lesson that had been presented in an "alternate alphabet" or code (Burke 1982). That class had had a powerful impact on both of them and had left them with common convictions about the impact of packaged reading programs on children. Page recalled one particular lunch hour when she and Susan had joined an "in progress" conversation in the teachers' lounge at their school. "The teachers were all complaining about how their kids were reacting to basal stories," Page said. "They were expecting certain behavior from their students." But having gone through the "reading group" experience in class, "We knew *they* would have behaved the same as the kids," Susan explained.

"We just looked at each other and knew what the other was thinking," Page smiled.

Susan and Page are now teaching in buildings that are miles apart. They readily admit that they miss each other deeply.

Success with Shared Leadership

As we have seen, Cathy, unlike Susan, entered the course as a skeptic. She was secure with her reading program and fairly satisfied with its results. As she recalls, "I did everything the publisher said to do, and the principal said I did it well." She admits that she did have students who weren't "making it," but she rationalized that what they needed was more of the same thing, more time, a special tutor . . . but *not* a different approach.

Early in the semester, her preservice partner, Renee, expressed frustration at being unable simply to set aside Cathy's notions of literacy and implement her own. It seemed to help when we gently reminded her that a teacher who had invested nine years in a particular approach to teaching deserved time to rethink her beliefs. That teacher would also require some evidence that the new ideas she was encountering were actually worth considering. Given Renee's relatively sophisticated understanding of whole language, she responded to our encouragement to be strategic in approaching Cathy, to provide her with demonstrations of the effectiveness of the ideas she was so excited about, and to use Cathy's materials to do so. It took little more. Renee was off and running, looking for ways to convert basal lessons into strategy lessons (Atwell and Rhodes, 1984).

Renee described how she got started. "I took the stories out of the basal, and I began to do different things with them." This was very comforting to Cathy, who was extremely concerned about her accountability for her students' mastery of district-mandated skills.

The challenge of finding alternate ways to accomplish Cathy's goals really united these partners. "It worked out well for us because we sat down together to see how we could get the skills done. That made me realize that the kids were not completely losing ground," Cathy said.

In reflecting upon the factors that encouraged her to take some risks, we were surprised to hear that Renee became Cathy's "scapegoat" while she was rethinking her ideas about teaching and learning. We laughed to hear Cathy describing several episodes in which she and Renee were in the teachers' workroom photocopying pages from the basal reader for the lessons they were devising. Their activity elicited many raised eyebrows and questions from other teachers, who were suspicious of what the two were up to. "I'd say, 'Well, you know, I have this . . . student from U. of L.,' " Cathy reported, somewhat embarrassed. We discovered, however, that this was an important "keep going" strategy that enabled her to take risks among a faculty she perceived to be unaccepting of the ideas she was exploring. "It was safe . . . I didn't have the background knowledge to say, 'Well, I'm trying some things to see how they work.' I think my biggest fear was that I was really not familiar with whole language. What would I do if the ideas didn't work? I had to see that everything that needed to be accomplished was accomplished."

In the end, it was Cathy's willingness to experiment with the strategy lessons presented at the university that got her started and helped her understand the benefits of actively engaging the learner. "Some things were obvious to Susan and Page," Cathy told us. "But I needed more than Jean Anne telling me things would work. I really didn't get it until I sat in on Renee's lessons." She recalled her prediction of what would happen when Renee approached her "at risk" readers with a challenge: sequencing a collection of illustrations from a basal reader story they had not yet read and writing their own texts to accompany them. "I expected that my kids wouldn't get as much from this, but they did. They got the sequencing, the main idea . . . everything! They got it easily, without struggling."

Over time, with mounting evidence that even her "lowest" readers could handle sophisticated meaning-based challenges, Cathy had to confront one of her most cherished assumptions.

"One thing I had to get over was that my kids didn't need me quite as much as I thought they did," she told us. "I've always been a stickler. I've always read the story and interpreted for the kids what it meant. I felt that it was help for them. . . . When doing whole language, you have to learn to accept your kids' ideas. That's not what you're used to. But I can let go now. Now if my kids can justify their answers, I can accept that. Before it had to be in black and white." Pausing for a moment, she admitted, "There are times when I still feel that maybe I'm giving them too much responsibility. I think that before you can completely accept whole language, you have to give that up."

In reflecting on the transitions she and Cathy had experienced together, Renee seemed to have gained a new perspective on the developmental nature of teaching. "I learned that change really takes time. Going in as an undergraduate, I thought it all ought to be there. But anytime you do something, and you know you do it well, change is hard. It doesn't happen overnight. You just take it one step at a time."

Successes of the Individuals

How did Susan, Page, Cathy, and Renee come to experience the advantages of the new arrangement? How did it strengthen their commitment to the values of the whole language culture?

The balance of Susan's master's program was very traditional. Only one class, which she had taken the previous semester, had fit well with her own developing philosophy of whole language teaching. With this minimal support from the university, she had decided to begin moving her classroom to a much more child-centered orientation. Susan's story provides evidence that growth in the direction of whole language is possible even within the larger context of a traditional graduate teacher-preparation program. These efforts were intensified and strengthened through her collaboration with Page during this course.

Page found it all fascinating—watching Susan lead the children rather than dictate to them and allowing the children to choose their working mode or product. Page could easily begin to develop a vision of what whole language instruction must be like. Her attempts to emulate or to elaborate upon the kind of teaching she saw Susan demonstrate were naturally supported by Susan. In fact, Susan indicated that it was unfair that she was asked to fill out a form evaluating Page, when Page never had the opportunity to do the same thing for her. In saying this, Susan had naturally made the connection between her whole language literacy instruction and the holistic teacher education the course was designed to offer.

Cathy's is perhaps the most delightful story because she had entered the class with such different expectations than the others. Buoyed by the confidence that Renee exhibited, and intrepid enough to sit in as a student in Renee's lessons, Cathy began to experience directly the benefits of being supported as a learner in a learner-centered lesson. Her efforts to protect herself and Renee from the scrutiny of her traditional peers were a bold statement about the security she and Renee both needed as they explored new ways to teach.

Renee had come to the university class as a learner. Given her general attitude about the importance of actually engaging the concepts discussed in her classroom, however, there was never a question that she would want to explore the kinds of teaching she experienced and discussed during class. She offered another connection between whole language teaching and holistic teacher preparation. With the support she received from Cathy, she showed the kind of leadership that is possible from any "low group" student when faced with working with a "high group" student. Her demonstrations for Cathy were not polished products of teaching craft; rather they were deliberate free-flowing explorations of the potential classroom applications of the research they had read at the university.

Exceptions to the "Rules"

Naturally, there were exceptions to the successes that Susan, Page, Cathy, and Renee experienced. The culture that developed in this combined course—with its transportable support system—was not perfect by any means. The social context that afforded growth for these four professionals did not work its magic on everyone. It is perhaps of interest that two of the teachers mentioned earlier, Jan, the disillusioned and desperate undergraduate who just wanted some respect, and Paula, the teacher who exiled Jan from the quiet, no-nonsense class, were also partners in this experimental university class. In fact, not only did Paula prohibit Jan from completing assignments in her classroom; we later discovered that Paula had coerced Jan into completing university course assignments for her as well. In doing so, she neatly avoided generating any evidence, either in her own classroom or at the university, that might have led her to challenge her own values and create new assumptions about teaching and learning.

Luckily for Jan, and yet perhaps ironically, she and Paula were in the same school as Renee and Cathy. Renee, the other undergraduate in the school, and Cathy, the "doubting Thomas," went beyond the structures of the class and became Jan's support group. Since that support group only functioned outside the classroom, it lost much of the impact it might have had, yet it was enough to give Jan the courage to continue to explore and to learn about her own teaching. Even in these less than ideal circumstances, Jan was able to become part of the whole language culture.

But what about Paula? How is it that within the same building three very different teachers could learn to support each other in their newly developing culture while this single teacher was left behind? Our answers to that question are fairly speculative, but those of her school peer, Cathy, are powerful. They are also important because they reveal that Cathy is becoming a member of the whole language culture of the course.

In discussing Paula, Cathy used the language that others in the culture have come to share in talking about young learners, and it works equally well in considering learners within the profession. Cathy recalled that, like Paula, she had been uncomfortable trying out new ideas for herself; she chose, instead, to do so vicariously through Renee. But "Paula wouldn't give Jan a chance. It was *her* classroom. . . . My children never felt that. The kids looked at both [Renee and me] as teachers. That was the way we approached it. *We* shared everything. *We* shared lessons. . . . We never felt teacher-student; we felt teacher-teacher."

The interpretations we received from all three of the "successes" in that school seemed to focus upon the necessity for an initiate to "engage" the new culture, to take the risk of trying something that might just prove wrong (or right), to allow another learner to become involved enough in one's successes and failures to be able to learn from that person. This is one of the rules of whole language classrooms and of the course in which Paula was enrolled. But she did not follow it.

Paula seemed to play by the rules of a different culture, one that she knew better and felt more comfortable with: that of the traditional teacher-preparation program, in which success is measured by high grades, not necessarily by changes in one's approach to teaching. In this traditional culture, success can be earned by learning how to please the professor and courses are taken not necessarily to advance one's professional practice but to earn advanced certification or a pay raise.

Lack of engagement, mistrust of teachers, misunderstanding the central purpose of the tasks one is asked to perform—these are some of the same qualities found in children who fail to accept the invitations to literacy that are proffered by whole language teachers. This is the experience of children like Susan and Page's Michael, who do not learn to read and write despite the rich community of readers and writers available in whole language settings to support them. In retrospect, it seems clear to us that for all our efforts to create a special supportive context for learning to teach, we have still not been completely successful at convincing all class members to adopt—or even to consider—the beliefs of our whole language culture. As Renee so aptly observed, development takes time. Abilities such as reading, writing—and teaching—are developmental, the products of the aggregated experience and reflection of the learner. For those who will in time become part of the culture, such experience may take months, even years, to affect their beliefs and responses to the culture in which they find themselves. This course lasted only one semester.

We are holding out for Paula. The culture in which she has grown professionally has supported the teaching she has embraced. That she has been placed in the new *context* afforded by the combined class for one semester can no more guarantee that she will become a whole language teacher than surrounding a child with books for one year guarantees that that child will become literate. Immersion in a language community is still the best way to learn a language, but subsequent isolation will see the decay of that capability. For Michael, the youngster in Susan and Page's room, to come to learn the authentic benefits of literacy and to become a member of the literacy club (Smith 1988), a continuing supportive *culture* is needed. All the natural supports and rewards for literacy will have to be available all the time. This experience is quite different from one that starts in August and ends the next June, never to be experienced again. Similarly, for us to feel confident that Paula might someday begin to pay more attention to her children than to the teacher's manual, the kind of encouragement, understanding, and support available from the course and from her peers must be in place in one form or another continuously, not for a mere semester. Only when a strong whole language culture is available throughout a teacher's program of study and arena of practice are teachers like Paula likely to become members of that culture, accepting and acting upon its belief system. Only when more teachers (like Cathy), or the principal, demonstrate the processes, products, and values of whole language in her school can we predict Paula's move into the incipient whole language culture within the schools in our community. There is hope for Paula. We believe that when faced with the preponderance of evidence that supports the impact of authentic communication and child-centered instruction, she will become a more holistic teacher of literacy.

References

Atwell, Margaret A., and Lynn K. Rhodes. 1984. Strategy lessons as alternatives to skill lessons in reading. *Journal of Reading* 27: 700–705.

Burke, Carolyn L. 1982. Personal communication.

Clyde, Jean Anne. 1987. Creating literate environments for preschool children: Teachers as participants, demonstrators, researchers and learners. Unpublished doctoral dissertation, Indiana University, Bloomington.

Corbett, H. Dickson. 1982. To make an omelette you have to break the egg crate. *Educational Leadership* 40: 34–35.

Harman, Susan, and Carol Edelsky. 1989. The risks of whole language literacy: Alienation and connection. *Language Arts* 66: 392–406.

Lortie, Dan. 1975. *Schoolteacher: A Sociological Study.* Chicago: University of Chicago Press.

Mills, Heidi, and Jean Anne Clyde, eds. 1990. *Portraits of Whole Language Classrooms: Learning for all Ages*. Portsmouth, N.H.: Heinemann.

Smith, Frank. 1988. *Joining the Literacy Club: Further Essays into Education*. Portsmouth, N.H.: Heinemann.

Wilson, Everett K. 1971. *Sociology: Rules, Roles, and Relationships*. Homewood, Ill.: Dorsey Press.

6 | Whole Language Support Groups: A Grassroots Movement

Nancy Mack and Ella Moore

As Nancy Mack and Ella Moore point out, top-down educational reforms seldom amount to much. Whole language, however, has originated as a grassroots movement among classroom teachers, even though these teachers may be supported by administrators and university educators. In this article, Mack and Moore describe how and why teacher support groups are crucial to the whole language movement, empowering teachers to develop, through reflective practice, an evolving theory and belief system that in turn sustains and informs their practice. The rise of teacher support groups in Ohio forms the basis for the authors' observations and reflections, and rich descriptions of these support groups provide models for organizing and conducting such groups.

NANCY MACK has taught middle school students, prison inmates, and college students. She teaches in the English department at Wright State University. Her current projects are teacher outreach programs such as the annual summer institute, Writing and Its Teaching, and forthcoming essays in *Composition and Resistance* (Boynton/Cook), *Social Issues in the English Classroom* (NCTE), and *PRE/TEXT: A Journal of Rhetorical Theory*. This year the Ohio Council of Teachers of English Language Arts named Nancy Mack one of Ohio's Outstanding College English Language Arts Educators.

ELLA MOORE has been an elementary teacher, gifted coordinator, curriculum and special projects director, and adjunct university professor. Formerly she was a member of the Ohio Department of Education as a consultant on staff development. Currently, she is a coordinator for special projects and grants for Pickerington Local Schools. She continues to advise the Ohio Future Educators of America Association. In the future, she plans to publish several children's books about geography and global concepts.

* * *

Educational innovations spread in interesting ways. Far too many innovations come to teachers from the top down. An alert administrator might start the process of change after reading the handwriting on the state legislature's wall. Or perhaps, a curriculum director sees a flashy new curriculum model in a conference showroom and brings it home for a test drive. Many such innovations amount to little more than transient fads that come and go, leaving only a few clever buzzwords behind.

In Ohio, the change to whole language has not been a top-down movement—although many principals, curriculum supervisors, university professors, and state department personnel have assumed leadership roles. The critical difference has been the teachers' commitment to whole language support groups, which now number around fifty and include thousands of active members. These support groups play an important part in empowering teachers to become active professionals who build theory through their reflective practice. This essay will address why and how these support groups are crucial to the whole language movement.

Why a Grassroots Movement?

Forced curriculum changes disenfranchise teachers of the very improvements from which they are supposed to benefit. For example, an ambitious curriculum supervisor in a suburban school district created a new remedial reading program for the district's elementary teachers. Each teacher received a curriculum package at the beginning of the school year that included textbooks, tests, a timer, lesson plans, and a script complete with every word the teacher was supposed to speak to the class—with specific instructions forbidding the teacher to utter one word that was not written down in the script. Although this is an extreme example, it illustrates the passive role that teachers are frequently asked to assume in regard to classroom innovations. Whether it is a new approach to discipline, a new test required by a state mandate, or a new curriculum update, the majority of teachers have often been excluded from the very process that develops the policies they are asked to implement. In a few cases, a democratically minded district supervisor may involve department chairs or building representatives in writing the actual courses of study, but for the most part, someone higher up decides what changes will be made, which grade levels will be involved, and when the changes will go into effect. Most teachers are informed of decisions that will have a dramatic impact on their classrooms after the fact, leaving them to put into practice on a daily basis policies to which they have, at best, no commitment or, at worst, direct opposition.

Without the necessary grassroots support, teachers may become alienated from their work. Perhaps alienation is not such an unusual thing in this culture, since many Americans who work on assembly lines or behind counters and desks feel that what they do is just a job—that what they do doesn't really matter in the larger scheme of things. But teachers are a very idealistic lot: many have forsaken more lucrative careers for what they consider a more fulfilling one that offers them the opportunity to help people and improve society. Collecting a paycheck is an important reality of any job, but feeling that what one does is meaningful may be just as necessary—especially for teachers. William Glasser discusses the importance of meaningful work in a new book, *The Quality School* (1990). Although Glasser concerns himself mainly with students, he also acknowledges that teachers suffer from the same kinds of boss-management tactics. Changes in the classroom often come about because teachers are coerced into making them rather than because they are encouraged to become self-motivated innovators authorized to initiate improvements. Teachers are not alienated from the idea of change itself. In fact, teachers may actually agree with the motives underlying many school district changes; however, it is the means through which these changes are actualized—the coercion—that take away the teachers' sense of integrity.

Regrettably, even whole language itself has the potential to alienate if it is forced upon teachers. In one school district in Ohio where the elementary teachers were very interested in experimenting with whole language, the curriculum director decided to expand the scope of whole language to include the middle-school teachers. In a meeting, the middle-school teachers were informed that soon they too would be required to "do whole language." A veteran teacher leaned forward and informed the curriculum supervisor in no uncertain terms that she was not "doing whole-language anything," that she had six years until retirement and they would just have to work around her. Interestingly enough, this teacher has already made some changes in her classroom and uses teaching strategies that would be classified as whole language. The point is that she resisted change not because it involved whole language but because it was forced upon her.

Many curriculum directors are aware of how important grassroots support can be to the success of a new program but feel that they do not have the time or the means to elicit such support. Instead, school districts truck in outside experts for quick in-service presentations sometimes referred to as "dog and pony shows." Teachers are herded into the school auditorium in order to listen to a lecture about the latest hot topic lasting from one hour to a full day. It is not surprising that they resent the time spent away from their classrooms. Many teachers display open contempt for the whole situation by not showing up, cutting out early, talking, making negative comments, or bringing papers to grade. It is common knowledge among most administrators that classroom teachers either have to be given time off or paid to come. This kind of hostility gives the outward appearance that teachers do not care about improving classroom instruction.

The above scenario need not be the case. For the past seven years, teachers across Ohio have been gathering on their own time and paying money out of their own pockets in order to attend whole language support group meetings. The number of groups and the number of regularly scheduled meetings per group is amazing. Total attendance figures exceed anything that the authors have seen in a lifetime of involvement in education. On a large scale: a teacher from New Zealand drew huge crowds at support group meetings all over the state; in audiences of over three hundred, teachers came on a weeknight, a Friday night, and a Saturday morning in order to hear about whole language instruction; over 1,600 teachers listened to Leana Trail, and one group in Marion, Ohio, even braved a traveler's advisory for ice and snow in order to attend. On a small scale: teachers meet informally once a month to share whole language teaching ideas. Keeping track of these small groups is not easy, because many new groups are forming all the time. Teachers are assuming the authority to form these groups themselves since there is no need to gain permission from some larger organization in order to begin.

These grassroots meetings serve many functions. Teachers need the support of other colleagues so they do not feel as if they are all alone in their efforts to teach reading and writing through an integrated language arts approach. Others seek successful classroom ideas recommended by fellow teachers. Many are hungry for more information about whole language, which can be gained from attending workshops or purchasing professional publications. Some come to be inspired by a big name expert in the field so they can return to their classrooms with renewed enthusiasm and vigor. Still others wish to share their own classroom strategies and problems with a caring group who wants to listen. Repeated attendance by teachers at both large and small support group meetings attests to the success of these support groups in meeting teachers' needs.

The benefits are more emotional than tangible. Certainly, many companies offer classroom materials and books full of teaching ideas that can be ordered from the comfort of a reclining chair, and there are several other strong local teacher organizations that emphasize a particular content area or grade level. Whole language support groups succeed in Ohio because they offer more than slick publications and prepackaged lesson plans; they offer empowering support for teachers who find themselves alienated from teaching. It is no coincidence that these support groups are growing at the same time that pressure from external sources is increasing: standardized testing, sweeping legislative changes, district funding inequities, and attacks in national reports about education. Such external pressures make it crucial for teachers to find ways to reclaim their dignity and renew their belief systems. Unlike the mastery of a few discrete skills, teaching is a complex profession that requires continuous personal growth and commitment. In much the same way that student growth takes place in the whole language classroom, teacher growth is most possible in a context that is whole and meaningful to the participants. Meaningfulness isn't something that can be purchased or imparted from someone else; it has to be developed personally on the local level.

Grassroots support groups provide an environment in which teachers can develop a personal commitment to what they do—to the classroom practices that they create. In Ohio, teachers actually feel that they are creating whole language from the ground up rather than just mastering someone else's version of it. This means that they come to local meetings in order to become better producers of knowledge rather than mere consumers of it. Teachers are not passively being indoctrinated with the "right" way to "do" whole language; they are actively authoring new practices that must be continually redesigned to suit each teacher's unique and changing classroom situation. Few educational movements acknowledge the complexity of the classroom community. Teachers know that what works for one teacher in one context on one particular day may not be immediately transferable to another person, place, or time. Local whole language groups provide the ongoing support teachers need to adapt to a constantly changing reality.

Why Support Groups?

Teachers often feel that they stand alone. They believe that they must individually weather personal attacks from government, business, industry, parents, administrators, and students. Becoming part of a profession should make it possible for teachers to face these problems as members of a learned group. Teachers, however, belong to an odd career group that has not had the opportunity to develop its own professionalism. In a famous study of the teaching profession, Dan Lortie (1975), a sociologist, discusses how teachers, unlike other professionals, tend to personalize failure. Doctors face their failures as members of a group, working with a limited body of knowledge, who may currently be unable to do certain things, such as extending the life of a patient with a particular disease. Unlike doctors, teachers are constantly blamed as individuals for the failures of their students. The notion of accountability has recently fueled a movement in education that emphasizes standardized test scores as the indication of success or failure. But it isn't just test scores that teachers are being held accountable for; today they must answer for a myriad of social problems as well, ranging from appropriate classroom behavior to AIDS. More important than just the need to defend themselves against outside attacks is the need to develop their expertise as members of a professional group.

Unfortunately, a teacher's workday is structured in ways that discourage collegiality and collaboration. For the most part, teachers are isolated in individual classrooms and spend less than an hour in the company of other teachers. Being able to develop meaningful dialogue during a few moments in the hallway or the teacher's lounge is doubtful. Student teachers usually report that their first trip to the teacher's lounge is an eye-opening experience; these preservice teachers are shocked to hear the negative complaints of their role models, who take their few moments of privacy in the lounge to vent their feelings about their students, the parents, other teachers, or the principal. Likewise, teacher's meetings are not generally occasions for meaningful dialogue. These meetings are usually called by the principal in order to inform the staff about a new policy or procedure. Problems may be discussed, but generally the problems and procedures are more concerned with controlling students and teachers than with improving instruction. Without the opportunity for meaningful dialogue, teachers cannot develop a sense of collegiality, nor can they improve their professionalism.

Most of the dialogue at support group meetings involves teachers sharing with other teachers. Since even teachers from the same school district do not know one another, support group meetings give them the opportunity to talk about mutual concerns. Although support groups tend to attract people from one geographic area, they usually bring together people from several different school districts. But territoriality means very little; these teachers tend to relate to one another as colleagues rather than as representatives of one particular school district. In addition, there is no effort to identify participants according to amounts or types of expertise. The number of degrees or the years of experience are not a cause of division among group members. All participants are viewed as knowledgeable. Through informal sharing or formal presentations, group members are asked to talk about what they do in their classrooms. In the same way, published authors, university professors, and state department personnel are treated more as colleagues than as experts. Teachers want to hear what these people have to say, but they feel no obligation to adopt a speaker's practices or philosophy. Teachers come to support group meetings in order to give and receive help rather than to control one another. Groups generally operate without bylaws or parliamentary procedure. Little effort is made to keep track of attendance, since most members come because they want to and not because they feel they have to attend.

Within any single support group there is much diversity. Some teachers may be teaching almost exclusively from a basal textbook, while others may be teaching totally from individual trade books. Teachers accept one another as members without first checking to see how knowledgeable the other person is about whole language. In fact, many of the support groups do not use the words *whole language* in their organizational names because they do not wish to offend the teachers who may not consider themselves to be whole language teachers or who may disagree with certain whole language practices.

Virtually anyone is accepted at the meetings, even if the person is hostile to the idea of whole language itself. At one meeting during the first year of a new support group, for example, a number of teachers who were adamantly against whole language and who felt polarized during discussions about district textbook adoption were invited to come. No mention was made of the outsiders' hostility. When people broke up into grade-level subgroups in order to share classroom strategies and problems, the subgroup containing the hostile visitors spontaneously went down to one teacher's classroom to see some of her teaching ideas. The visitors were immersed in a whole language classroom. Within fifteen minutes everyone was happily chatting: the previously anti-whole-language teachers were sharing similar classroom practices and accepting new ideas from the regular members. This was primarily due to the fact that no one forced the idea of whole language on anyone else. The teachers simply shared what they found to be successful in their own classrooms, thus finding common ground in a nonthreatening way.

Of course, it would be inaccurate to portray support groups as all sweetness and light. Teachers often disagree and learn a great deal from these differences in opinion. During a meeting of the Beaver-creek Literacy Network, members in the first-grade subgroup got into a heated discussion about whether spelling could be taught without a spelling textbook's weekly list. Teachers confronted one another with angry "That-wouldn't-work" comments every time a new idea was suggested. A university professor was called over as a colleague for added input. Finally, a group member asserted, "Look, this is how I tried it in my classroom and it does so work." When the meeting finally ended, with no pat answers, the group members were left to continue pondering just how to teach spelling in an integrated language arts classroom. This support group meeting gave teachers a safe environment in which to start rethinking how they taught spelling. Teachers in whole language support groups are linked together because of similar experiences and interests; they are not chained together demanding that everyone subscribe to one particular set of procedures or practices.

The History of Whole Language Support Groups in Ohio

The whole language or integrated language arts support groups in Ohio have all sprung up independently. A state or parent organization does not exist, although the Ohio Department of Education has encouraged the development of these groups. In the spring of 1989, Ella Moore, a consultant in the Division of Inservice, created a list of the existing support groups. She came up with nineteen, and just one year later the number had grown to forty. It remains difficult to document exactly how many groups there are because many do not seek to be listed until they have been meeting for two or more years. A current list of support groups can be obtained by writing to the Ohio Department of Education, Division of Inservice, Room 611, 65 South Front Street, Columbus, OH 43266-0308.

The two oldest support groups in Ohio are The Literacy Connection in Columbus and the Cincinnati TAWL (Teachers Applying Whole Language). The people who would later find themselves beginning these groups met at an International Reading Association conference where whole language interest groups were given time to share ideas and philosophies. Coming back to Ohio, they saw the need, as did teachers from other states they had heard about, for gathering people with similar interests together. With the help of university personnel, they organized.

The Literacy Connection began in 1983. Three teachers, a school district administrator, and a professor from Ohio State University called the first meeting. This meeting featured Don Holdaway, an international expert on whole language, as a guest speaker. Similarly, the Cincinnati TAWL formed in 1984 with the help of a dozen or more regular and special education teachers, principals, supervisors, graduate students, and professors. This group has been assisted by a professor from the University of Cincinnati and featured Donald Graves as a conference speaker. For the first few years, the groups averaged between thirty-five and forty members except when major speakers were advertised. Both groups have experienced rapid growth, and now each has a total membership of about eight hundred. The Literacy Connection has been closely associated with the Upper Arlington School District. Recently, two teachers from this district and a professor from Ohio Wesleyan have published a book about reading and writing poetry. Cincinnati now has several "small TAWL's," which are geographically organized groups of teachers who live near each other. The Cincinnati group is currently working on a pilot community service project that will collect used reading material and make it available to parents and children in its own free store.

Many of the support groups throughout Ohio, like the two just mentioned, have become quite large and offer a full schedule of meetings. The South Dayton Whole Language Support Group has an active membership of around four hundred. Last year this group had five large meetings, which focused primarily upon locally and nationally known speakers. This group also has at least one meeting a year offering several smaller sessions led by local classroom teachers, and an administrators' group has recently been organized. The Akron area group is now so large that smaller groups have begun to meet on their own.

In addition to these larger groups, there are many more smaller groups that generally have an active membership of under forty and may meet in someone's home. Sometimes these groups are spinoffs whose organizers have regularly attended larger groups and have returned to their own area to start a smaller group. These groups center more on sharing ideas and problems of group members, although many will try to have a guest speaker one or more times a year. One activity that several groups have become involved in is gathering books together in order to make complete classroom sets available. Simple things such as not having enough copies of a book like *Charlotte's Web* can be a big hurdle for a teacher who wants to supplement a basal reader for the first time.

The next step for some of these groups seems to be networking. In the fall of 1989 at a writing conference jointly sponsored by the Ohio Department of Education and the Ohio Council of Teachers of English Language Arts, leaders from whole language support groups across Ohio met for the first time at a recognition reception. This was an exciting meeting because veteran leaders could offer ideas to new support group leaders. A volunteer coordinator, Mabel Cheetham, has created a large wall map pinpointing existing groups throughout Ohio so that teachers inquiring about membership can be referred to the nearest support group. Several teachers have reported that just seeing the map or the list of existing support groups has given them the courage to try to organize a new group in their area. At this same conference, a full day was devoted to helping administrators learn how to foster this teacher movement.

In the future, support groups are planning to reach out to parents and undergraduate education majors. In addition, work has been progressing on a new statewide electronic network that would put teachers in the more rural areas of Ohio in touch with other teachers who wish to share resources and information. There also seems to be an increased political awareness among Ohio teachers, since much recent legislation is having an adverse effect upon the classroom. Groups like the Ohio Testing Consortium and the Ohio Coalition of Literacy Advocates have organized efforts to educate legislators about the impact of proposed House bills and to encourage teachers to become more politically active.

What Organizational Features Make for Successful Whole Language Support Groups?

Like mushrooms, support groups seem to appear overnight all over Ohio. The groups are formed primarily by people who want to attend support group meetings locally. Initial organizing efforts may be assisted by an outside person, such as a university professor, a school district administrator, or a representative from the state International Reading Association. Groups often spring up after a particularly great in-service workshop or curriculum revision, or as a spin-off from another support group. Most groups have minimal dues to cover postage where necessary. The exception seems to be when large fees are needed for nationally known speakers. Sometimes these speakers can be obtained through contact with a nearby university that is funding an on-campus visit. Otherwise, funds are generated by charging the large number of teachers who attend a fee of a few dollars.

For regular meetings of the support groups, teachers meet either in a school, a home, or a public library and often take turns serving light refreshments. Groups tend to meet no more than once a month during the school year, with smaller groups meeting after school and larger groups generally meeting on a Saturday morning. Some publish newsletters and fliers with notices about coming meetings and other sources of information, such as local workshops or university classes. Membership seems to grow by word of mouth; there is no need or desire to have membership drives. Teachers come primarily because they are interested in the topic and in meeting with one another.

The large groups are very successful. Their main appeal seems to be the nationally recognized speakers they invite. Through the efforts of these groups, teachers in Ohio have been fortunate enough to hear Nancie Atwell, Lucy Calkins, Marie Clay, Marjorie Frank, Mary Ellen Giacobbe, Yetta and Ken Goodman, Donald Graves, Don Holdaway, Judy Newman, Frank Smith, and Rob Tierney. These groups also sponsor conferences featuring several sessions with local teachers as speakers. Through these experiences, many local teachers become speakers at other support groups, district in-services, and state conferences. Support groups are helping teachers to see themselves as experts.

The small groups are successful in a different way. Their goal is not to foster the growth of membership but to foster the personal growth of group members. These groups want to stay small in order to encourage sharing and group solidarity. Members need to feel that they can trust one another in order to share their problems and disappointments freely. Some teachers are very timid at first and need to be encouraged to share even the smallest classroom ideas. Because teachers need to speak candidly about district policies, such as textbook adoptions, they sometimes feel most comfortable when administrators are not present. Generally, the administrators who find the time to come to these meetings tend to be those who are very supportive of teacher-initiated changes and are therefore accepted as nonthreatening. Such administrators are rarely experts about whole language. At a recent administrator's conference, one principal remarked, "I don't know how to do this, but I'm willing to learn with the teachers. The children teach us as we observe their success." Administrators like this one encourage a collaborative spirit. In this type of educational community, the first concern is what is best for children.

No matter what the size of the group, there is a strong effort to keep attention focused on teacher needs. Groups are more concerned with selecting common meeting times and places than with creating bylaws or rules for membership. Although a curriculum supervisor may have helped to start the group, great care is taken to see that the format of the meetings encourages teachers to feel comfortable talking and sharing. The official contact person for the group may be an administrator, but this is usually just because the administrator has a phone and the means to distribute notices about meetings. Teachers establish strong ownership and control over their support groups.

Teachers have also developed supportive relationships with others who are interested in whole language. Just as they are linked to district administrators, support groups may work with university personnel, although university people do not control the group. A university may provide a place to meet, mailing services, or contact with a big-name speaker, but the university is not viewed as the owner of the group. Individual professors may be strong guiding forces in such groups, but they try to take a backseat to teacher needs. A professor may organize and attend meetings but she attends to support the teachers, not to teach them. State department curriculum people offer assistance as speakers and facilitate contacts among groups, but they do not control the groups. Even whole language materials companies offer support. Many times companies are invited to set up displays or to provide a speaker, but they do not give sales pitches for their materials. These outsiders work with teachers and respect them, yet they do not take over the group. Working with individuals other than teachers helps teachers to initiate changes on several levels. Whole language groups in Ohio have initiated change in their buildings, their districts, their counties, and the state.

The following are possible programs a support group might have:

- Teachers bring classroom activities and books about a particular teaching theme to share.

- A librarian, bookstore owner, or classroom teacher shares new and favorite children's literature titles.
- Teachers share favorite professional books, periodicals, and conferences.
- A whole language teacher is invited to share specific teaching ideas from his or her classroom.
- A teacher leads a hands-on workshop where teachers learn how to create classroom materials or make books.
- A presenter is invited to speak whom other teachers have heard speak at another support group meeting or a state conference.
- Those in attendance divide into grade-level groups and share teaching ideas that work and/or troubleshoot classroom problems.
- Teachers discuss a book or article about whole language.
- Teachers investigate new sources of funding or the reallocating of funds for more books in the classroom.
- Teachers bring favorite teaching lessons to share, such as songs, chants, class-made big books, etc.
- Teachers bring examples of student work to share and discuss.
- Teachers brainstorm thematic unit ideas.
- A textbook salesperson does a workshop or sponsors a classroom teacher to do a workshop on a specific classroom practice.
- Teachers discuss issues of professional concern, such as textbook adoptions, standardized testing, new legislative mandates, etc.
- Teachers discuss community and family problems of their students.
- Teachers share problems and brainstorm solutions for working with individual students.

Personal and Professional Growth

As an educational movement, whole language is much more difficult to implement in the classroom than such things as assertive discipline or sentence combining. Whole language classroom practices are not touted as easily reproducible or universally applicable. They often require extensive study and experimentation. Perhaps what whole language lacks in simplicity, it gains in significance. After making the transition to whole language, many teachers proclaim that they have made major changes in their classrooms. Some even report that they have made changes in their whole philosophy of education: one teacher remarked that she found it "harder than ever to be a teacher, but a million times more fun!" Her principal described her as "a new person, someone who was often smiling" when previously he had thought of her as solemn and withdrawn. Both the principal and the teacher attribute her revitalization to the support group she regularly attended. This teacher is just one of many who credit whole language with improving their careers as educators.

As miraculous as these changes seem, they do not occur overnight. They are the result of a long process of growing awareness, a commitment to change, extensive classroom experimentation, and transformative action. Paulo Freire (1972) describes this process as "conscientization," or developing a critical consciousness. Freire developed his understanding of critical consciousness through his literacy work with oppressed groups in several countries. The concept of critical consciousness can provide insights into how learning to read and write can be empowering for both teachers and students. It is a process of reflective growth and change.

Teachers can use whole language support groups as a means for developing their own critical consciousness. This process may begin by the simple act of discussing new classroom practices at a support group meeting. One teacher may at first be uncritically attracted to the newness or popularity of one method, such as Big Books or journal writing. Another teacher may be dissatisfied with traditional teaching practices and may start to seek out more effective approaches.

Yet just trying out a new teaching practice would not account for the dramatic changes our colleagues have reported. Teachers in support groups become more reflective about their actions and begin to critique many aspects of what they do in the classroom. As teachers become more reflective about their classrooms, they may be willing to make changes that are directly motivated by this critical reflection. New practices or changes will continue to require reflection and perhaps additional adjustments. Critical consciousness is developed through an ongoing interaction between action and reflection, and whole language support groups offer a safe environment where teachers can critique their own practices and reconsider what they have been doing in the classroom.

It is the critical reflection that makes all the difference. Simply making a change here or there is not significant enough to cause a teacher to reconsider entrenched assumptions about learning. In other words, just using children's literature in the classroom is not the same thing as rethinking how to select reading material, how to sequence reading lessons, how to teach skills, or how to group students. One teacher explained that her whole life changed through her interaction with children's literature. "I had always been too busy teaching from basals and raising my own children to read children's literature. . . . I now find myself reading nightly and living a childhood I never had in a nonreader household, not even with my children. Now that we are writing every day, I might even write a story myself!" Not only has this teacher reflected about her classroom, she has also reconsidered her own literacy. Now she views herself as a reader and a writer, not just someone who teaches reading and writing as a content area. Her own practices of reading and writing are informing her theory of teaching reading and writing.

As a teacher becomes more reflective, this critical reflection doesn't just happen during the safety of the support group meeting, it happens in the classroom as the teacher has to create spontaneous midcourse corrections. What has been started is a process of critical reflection and transformative action. Teachers begin to take full responsibility for the changes in their classrooms. Perhaps the most interesting feature of this process of action and reflection is that it is continual. Teachers use their reflective critical consciousness to critique all of their classroom practices again and again, even the newest whole language ones.

In a way, the classroom becomes a research site where the teacher is a researcher experimenting with new methodologies, which in return promote the development of new theories of language learning. Whole language teachers do not learn to teach in a whole language way; they actually create a theory of whole language in their own classroom, individually and from the ground up. All teachers of reading and writing already operate from a theory of learning, even if that theory is largely implicit and unconscious. The whole language teacher uses the daily events in the classroom as an active means to construct theory. The whole language teacher may be informed by other teachers, other teacher researchers, and even university researchers, but the whole language teacher takes on the role of primary researcher in his or her own classroom.

Classrooms should not be directed by the work of theory builders who are absent from the room. Classrooms should be directed by teacher-researchers who continually make sense out of their own classrooms. As Ann Berthoff suggests in her often-cited essay "The Teacher as REsearcher" (1981), theory becomes the heuristic to help us reformulate new questions and answers about our classrooms. Theory can help us to make meaning out of what we do—to consider what has happened and explain why certain practices do or do not work.

Being a classroom researcher isn't a graduate project; it's a daily course of action. Through their research, whole language teachers are learning from their students. This process creates a new relationship between theory and practice: unlike old notions of theory and practice in which theory precedes practice and practice is informed by theory, these teachers create a dialectical relationship between theory and practice.

Because the teacher takes control of the transformation process in the classroom, this process can be viewed as praxis, a political decision on the teacher's part to transform his or her classroom to make it a better place for learning. Such a decision is a highly ethical one that often touches the teacher's deepest values. Teachers who use critical reflection to create transformative action are not merely more effective teachers, they are people who have gained a new sense of integrity about their actions as teachers. They have begun to forge a stronger connection between what they experience in their classroom and what they believe about education.

This new sense of wholeness may be shared by other teachers who are also struggling to transform their classrooms. Transformative teachers need to come together in support groups to become a true community of learners. An important part of the individual teacher's growing critical consciousness is the realization that he or she is a member of a professional group that can cause change through collective action.

Far too often teachers conclude that it is emotionally easier to learn how to survive rather than to continue being frustrated by things they cannot change. One twenty-eight-year veteran said that she was counting the years until retirement when she was invited to a support group meeting by a colleague. Now, a year later, she is excited and renewed, and never even thinks about retiring. As she remarked, "I'm just finally getting started." She had been disillusioned and angry with those who had been controlling her classroom—district administrators, state department of education mandates, and board members—but now, she reported, "I finally know how to teach kids reading and I'm going to do it right for my last few years! I had never believed in basal readers and always felt guilty for skipping workbook pages." Now the workbooks are gone and her room is filled with real reading and writing. Whole language support groups offer teachers, new and old, the opportunity to believe in what they do.

References

Berthoff, Ann E. 1981. The Teacher as REsearcher. In *The Making of Meaning: Metaphors, Models, and Maxims for Writing Teachers*. Portsmouth, N.H.: Boynton/Cook.

Freire, Paulo. 1972. *Pedagogy of the Oppressed*. New York: Herder and Herder.

———. 1985. *The Politics of Education*. South Hadley, Mass.: Bergin and Garvey.

Glasser, William. 1990. *The Quality School: Managing Students Without Coercion*. New York: Harper and Row.

Lortie, Dan C. 1975. *Schoolteacher*. Chicago: University of Chicago Press.

Shor, Ira, and Paulo Freire. 1987. *A Pedagogy for Liberation: Dialogues on Transforming Education*. South Hadley, Mass.: Bergin and Garvey.

Focus on
Institutional Change

* * *

7 | The Evolution of Whole Language at the Smith College Campus School

Margaret Yatsevitch Phinney and Martha Alpert Batten

Written in a dialogue format, this discussion between Margaret Phinney and Martha Batten describes how whole language theory and practice have evolved at the Smith College Campus School in Northampton, Massachusetts. They highlight how reflective practice informs theory, as well as vice versa; how consultants, principals, and other agents of change can assist teacher growth; why whole language cannot be mandated; and why it is crucial for the culture of a school as a whole to reflect a whole language belief system, in order to encourage teachers' growth into whole language teaching and learning.

MARGARET YATSEVITCH PHINNEY has taught elementary school in Canada as well as at the Smith College Campus School, where she collected the data to complete her doctoral work through the University of Massachusetts/Amherst. Her research interest is in children's social interactions in relation to their school engagement in writing. Her years as a reading resource teacher led to the publication of her holistically oriented teacher's handbook, *Reading with the Troubled Reader* (Heinemann, 1988). She is currently an assistant professor at the University of Minnesota, Minneapolis.

MARTHA ALPERT BATTEN, Supervising Principal of the Smith College Campus School and mother of two Campus School students, taught in local elementary schools before coming to the Campus School as a fifth- and sixth-grade teacher in 1972. In addition to her work as principal, Martha is a lecturer in the Department of Education and Child Study at Smith College and Supervisor of the Graduate Fellows in Education. She is also a consultant in language arts.

* * *

MARGARET: So . . . Dr. Weaver wants us to tell the story of the Campus School's evolution in whole language, eh?

MARTHA: Eh? Eh? You still have your Nova Scotian "Eh," don't you!

MARGARET: True! I guess it'll always be a part of me. And my Canadian experience is very much a part of the story. But that's not where it started at the Campus School, is it? Didn't it really start with Jan Szymaszek attending a workshop on whole language with Don Holdaway?

MARTHA: Yes and no. The enthusiasm that the Cambridge Literacy Project kindled in her was certainly the spark that brought the whole language philosophy into view for us, but it was really our history as a laboratory school that led us naturally into the movement.

As the laboratory school for the college's Department of Education and Child Study, our underlying purpose is to provide a model site for the observation and research activities of education and psychology students and for the training of intern teachers. Because of this, we seek and generally attract supervising teachers who are thoughtful and articulate as well as interested in being mentors.

MARGARET: Yes, there is no doubt that working with student teachers keeps us on our toes! If it isn't because they are sponges, wanting their "Why?" questions answered all the time, it's because they don't ask *enough* questions and we have to work to help them see why they need to be seeking and searching. In either case, if *we* haven't thought through what we're doing—and why—we are caught with our pants down.

MARTHA: Also, I think the way the administration is structured at our school reinforces a connection between current theory and practice. It sounds disjointed when people first hear that I'm the Supervising Principal three-fifths time and a member of the faculty two-fifths time, but it makes it easy to integrate the work. I teach the language arts curriculum and methods course and supervise the graduate teaching fellows that work with you in the afternoons.

MARGARET: So you can see how your presentation of theory is coming out in practice on a day-to-day basis.

MARTHA: The position allows me to catch misconceptions and highlight true understandings immediately. I also see classroom practice through the eyes of the student teachers in their class discussions and journal entries, which helps me keep in touch with the theory-and-practice connections as they actually operate. So given the fact that our school is a laboratory, the move toward whole language didn't represent a radical change. It's expected that a school of our type would move in directions suggested by current research and literature.

MARGARET: So what exactly did happen to inspire Jan so?

MARTHA: Jan heard Don Holdaway speak in Cambridge in 1984. She came to me overflowing with new energy, and I quickly encouraged her to try out some of the things she had heard and read about. Her five-year-olds began to write and use invented spelling. And every time she and I talked, our observations began to spin off each other, leading to further changes. She carried this enthusiasm to the other kindergarten teacher, and the two of them developed a series of routine lessons that expanded on a technique using enlarged text called "the morning message."

MARGARET: And how did process writing come into the plan? When I arrived, that was just getting under way, too.

MARTHA: Actually, several things came together in that respect. I guess my own background as an undergraduate English major contributed to my interest in seeing literature study and writing as related. Susan Etheredge took a course in 1980 in which she was inspired by the work of Peter Elbow's *Writing Without Teachers* to loosen up her approach to the teaching of writing with her second graders. Watching her work with children and their writing made me reflect upon my own approach to writing as a teacher in the seventies—anything goes, all writing as first draft, little criticism, no revision, writing as process only, the belief that the act of writing alone led to improvement. Susan had the children write more than I thought seven-year-olds could. They obviously saw themselves as writers, and Susan was one of those teachers who could weave in both a kind of "freeing up" and a structure.

MARGARET: Were any of the other teachers interested in changing their curriculum, too?

MARTHA: Yes. Independently of Susan's interest in writing, the teachers of grades 3–6 had begun to get interested in writing. I had responded to a question about writing from one of my more traditional teachers by giving her a copy of Lucy Calkins's *Lessons from a Child* (1983). She got really excited and started to fire up the other intermediate teachers. They decided they wanted to spend our Wednesday afternoon curriculum time during the next year exploring the process of writing. The primary-grade teachers wanted to use their time to develop their understanding and practice of whole language. I am not sure that at that time we clearly saw the connection between the primary and intermediate work!

MARGARET: One of the characteristics of teachers at our school is that they keep in touch with what's coming out in the literature and are accustomed to watching for, and attending, interesting-looking workshop and conference offerings. I think that's a credit to the administrative structure, too. In some systems, asking to go to a conference is regarded as a request for a vacation from work. You and Ray [Ducharme, the director of the school and a professor in the Department of Education and Child Studies] are always putting conference notices and book reviews in our boxes! Speaking of books, you all agreed to do some reading over that summer, didn't you?

MARTHA: Yes, the school purchased and circulated copies of Lucy Calkins's *Lessons from a Child* (1983) and Holdaway's *Stability and Change in Literacy Learning* (1984). We thought they would give us a common reference point for discussions. We saw this changeover as a really important move in our growth as a school for a couple of reasons. In addition to our feeling that the whole language philosophy made such common sense, we wanted a powerful focus for the coming year to ease the transition into a new administration. Concentrating on an exciting new approach to teaching and learning would contribute to academic and social cohesion in the school.

MARGARET: It was during that summer that the Campus School and I discovered we needed each other!

MARTHA: You said it! What serendipity that was! Tell that one.

MARGARET: My family and I were moving back to the States after twelve years in Nova Scotia. I had been trained there as a whole language teacher under the rigorous and watchful eye of a New Zealander, David Doake, at Acadia University. I had been working for six years as a whole language teacher—and as somewhat of a low-key agent of change—in a rural public school. When we decided for family reasons to return Stateside, I wanted to continue my master's program, so I transferred to the University of Massachusetts. I needed part-time work.

MARTHA: Yes, and we realized we needed extra help if we were to give the teachers the support we anticipated they would need. Since Smith College was conscious of the need to get more women into administration, we were allowed to hire an "administrative intern" for the year. We arranged with the university to offer a part-time position to a woman student in school administration in exchange for a stipend and a tuition waiver.

MARGARET: I saw your ad in the bulletin of the School of Education and even though I was in the Division of Instructional Leadership, not Administration, the position looked so exciting, I decided to take a chance and apply.

MARTHA: We couldn't believe someone with a background in whole language and process writing could be falling into our laps at such a moment in our development! It was very unlikely we would have found someone locally at that time—whole language was a very new concept at the practitioner level in this region. (Of course the fact that you were the only one who applied for the job had nothing to do with our hiring you!)

MARGARET: Now don't rub it in. You didn't tell me that until much later, thank goodness! Anyway, that was one tough year—studying full time and working with your dynamic and thoughtful group of teachers. I guess if I were to offer advice to whole language consultants working in a school that's just getting started with the transition, I would suggest they not have anything else going on in their lives that first year. The teachers needed *lots* of support, not just in the form of information, resources, and problem-solving discussions, but in the form of morale support and in-classroom demonstrations and observations. The observations were really important: the teachers wanted me to watch them teach, then give them immediate feedback. Scheduling time for this was an invaluable part of the process, I think.

The weekly Wednesday afternoon meetings were an important part of the process. The Campus School tradition of sending the children home at noon so the teachers can work on curriculum development is a powerful tool for any school that wants to change. I've heard of public schools that do this, too. It is *not* a waste of time, as some parents and school board members might believe, providing the sessions are well-organized, purposeful, and designed to respond to the needs of the teachers and the school. The problem with in-services, from my point of view as a classroom teacher, is that the content is usually set without consulting with the teachers. Someone, somewhere, gets a bright idea, or a day is set and someone has to *come up with* an idea to fill in the time, and oftentimes it's not what the teachers really need or want. When a school, as a whole school, decides to undertake a project that will result in improving teaching and learning, there is motivation and interest in becoming involved. And as I think back over my years working with this system of curriculum development, I realize how valuable it is in building and maintaining the school culture. *We the teachers, together with the administrators,* are the builders and movers. We create the culture we want to live with, and it's a dynamic culture. It's in a state of continual change as we learn and as people in the school community come and go. It *can* change because we have that weekly time-slot set aside for dealing with our interests and concerns. Because we have a sense of empowerment, our weekly staff meetings are more dynamic and participatory. (In six years, I have never been bored in a staff meeting!) We don't gather just to be reported to and receive directives from someone on high; it is our right and we consider it our responsibility to critique those reports and decisions, to make suggestions for refinements, and to ask for change when we have justifiable reason. We are treated as—and feel like—professionals.

Something else the teachers appreciated that year was having a specific and detailed agenda each week that was decided upon at the end of the previous week's meeting, and clearly written out and distributed a couple of days before the next meeting. People knew what they were to be working on and thinking and reading about during the week and were ready to talk and problem-solve during the allotted time. Teachers need structure and direction as much as children, not because they are scatterbrained—they're absolutely *not* that—but because they are *so* busy all the time. Having someone to organize and lay out *their* agenda ahead of time made a big difference in the efficiency with which we used our precious time. We made a lot of progress that fall in getting kinks worked out and establishing understanding.

MARTHA: Right. And now the Wednesday agenda is outlined as a matter of course in our regular weekly bulletin. I had forgotten that it wasn't always that way!

MARGARET: But all this isn't to say it was smooth sailing. One problem I remember was that *Lessons from a Child* didn't work as a start-up guide for everyone. Tom, who was teaching sixth grade, found Calkins's presentation too "unreal" for his way of thinking. He was so frustrated at one point that he was ready to throw in the towel, if I remember. The book just didn't let him get a grasp on how to proceed on a practical basis. So on a Friday I gave him Donald Graves's book, *Writing: Teachers and Children at Work* (1983), and on Monday morning he was flying high. He needed that organized explicitness that Graves is so good at. Others had no problem extrapolating the "how to" from *Lessons*. And still others could use her ideas with the help of the list of techniques you pulled out of the book and handed out to everyone. And you were giving various articles to different teachers in response to their questions. From that point on, people weren't necessarily reading the same things. It came down to matching or adapting the resources and references to the individual teachers' personalities, just as we help children select materials based on their interests and styles.

MARTHA: Yes, it's only fair to talk about what didn't immediately fit into place. As anyone would guess in working with any group of teachers, being the perceptive and analytical people they are, there were those who weren't convinced that these were good pedagogical strategies—and still don't entirely agree even six years later. Some teachers incorporated new techniques into their own context, rejecting some of the philosophical base. Some of my strongest teachers cannot let go of control of the learning process. Yet they have a way of inspiring children with significant content and superb instructional skill; and they are very diagnostic in their teaching, aware and accommodating of individual needs. All of you, though, have been influenced by this exploration, and at least modified your teaching to some extent.

MARGARET: Absolutely. The last six years have been a tremendous growth period for me. Being surrounded by teachers who read widely, who are professionally very committed, and who always want the best learning atmosphere for their students has taught me there is no place for complacency in this business! But to add to your comments about teachers who aren't convinced easily, I think some people just need a lot of time to absorb the implications of an idea. A teacher in another school resisted having her children write anything that wasn't in perfect standard form for five years after the school first initiated a move toward process writing. Then she decided to give it a try and became an instant convert! It was taking that initial step that was so hard.

MARTHA: So where are we now in our evolution?

MARGARET: I think we could summarize the starting conditions that began evolution into whole language in *our* situation as a) an existing school community (including parents) that was favorable to change *as long as it wasn't just change for change's sake;* b) a period in our school history when improvements were needed; c) an individual who had become inspired by the whole language philosophy and was willing to commit to trying it out; d) a consultant who had some knowledge of *and practice with* whole language and process writing theory and practice; e) an administration that was willing to provide extensive support in the form of resources, guidance, and structured release time (Wednesday afternoons).

MARTHA: Those were certainly the major contributing factors to our getting started. But I wouldn't want to suggest to others that all of those factors are prerequisites for every school trying to break into whole language. I'm sure each school could identify its own enabling conditions, some of which might coincide with ours.

MARGARET: Good point. In another school where I worked, the impetus came from three inspired teachers, two of whom were the resource teachers, and a principal who supported us. There was peripheral interest and curiosity from two or three other teachers, but the majority were happy with the status quo. Sometimes it's sheer energy and commitment on the part of a single person that makes the difference. In a small rural school I know of, it was the drive of the teaching principal who single-handedly coached her teachers and parents into an understanding of whole language principles and practices.

MARTHA: So, we've gotten started. We should review the next stages of our evolution. But I must say, as we discuss this, it reminds me of how analogous change at a school is to the process of writing a long piece. As we describe the change, we are tempted to see it as chronological, linear, and outward, with some distinct starting point. But, in fact, who we are, all of our background experiences and beliefs, become part of the stage that precedes and then underlies observable change.

MARGARET: True. It's getting harder to stick to a time frame. It's almost impossible to sort out cause and effect. But I do know that midyear, when a grade-one teacher resigned, you and Ray convinced me to take the position. You did enough juggling of my duties, and gave me an aide, so that I could continue my studies at the same time.

MARTHA: That's right. It was disappointing at first because I had really enjoyed having a colleague with whom I could share ideas and strategies. It was team administration at its best. But I think being back in the classroom gave you the opportunity to continue to develop and refine your thinking about whole language, and this became a stronger base for your consulting and graduate work, don't you think?

MARGARET: There's no doubt about it. It confirmed what I had been suspecting for some time—that for me to truly understand theory well, I need to move back and forth between study and practice, between reading/listening/observing and *doing*. What was interesting was that the formal consulting position I was in at the school put me in an intermediary spot between theory and practice. I had to explain to others both theory and practice together. Many times *my* practice didn't fit *another's* style, and I had to go back to the theory-into-practice drawing board to find a way that would work for that particular individual. I had to recognize that different teachers had different tolerance levels, for example, when it came to noise or movement, and that that was okay. When I went back into the classroom, I was more relaxed with myself, more flexible and tolerant. As my mother used to say, I realized there was more than one way to skin a cat . . .

MARTHA: Margaret!

MARGARET: Hey! I *said* it was my *mother's* expression!

MARTHA: Hmm. Well, it only goes to reinforce what I was going to add—that you became a model for the rest of us. You demonstrated the thoughtfulness, flexibility, playfulness, and the joyful enthusiasm that inspired us all. By watching you, the staff learned how an environment can be created to stimulate language learning in all the right ways. It worked, and your teaching demonstrated this!

MARGARET: Well, thanks, but I have to admit I was pretty nervous. It was a put-your-money-where-your-mouth-is situation. And having your child in the class made me even more nervous! I mean, how would it look to others if the principal's son didn't read by the end of the year? But I had had enough time testing the theory in Nova Scotia to know it was strong and worthy, and I figured learners were learners (even in Massachusetts!) so Alex would learn, too.

MARTHA: That was trial by fire for you, wasn't it! Seriously, Alex even credits you still as the teacher who "made" him a writer. And you didn't get thrown out as a charlatan! In fact, at the end of that first year, you and I talked the teachers into presenting our learning experiences at a conference of the Independent School Association of Massachusetts. I think it was especially significant to the teachers that you and I presented, too. In putting that workshop together, we were all pushed to clarify our ideas. We saw how much we really did know (though we were already aware that we still had much to learn) and that we could articulate that knowledge to our colleagues in a way that was powerful. And then you and I designed a writing conference in which we hoped to entice our local public school to work with us to share ideas. We persuaded Smith to finance a guest speaker—Jane Hansen from the University of New Hampshire—and our own interested teachers prepared talks or demonstrations and led small discussion groups. Through these two events we learned again that the process of learning has only artificial or convenient endpoints. We were continually revising, reseeing, editing, and discovering new ideas.

MARGARET: For me as a teacher, those two points you just made are really important and have much to do with my own change process and, I think, ours as a school. The first is the importance of not just talking to others but *taking responsibility for what we say.* When we speak in public, we become authorities in some way, whether we want to or not. We feel a sense of accountability that we may not feel in a casual discussion in the staff room or at a Wednesday curriculum meeting. By speaking to an unknown audience, we have to really analyze what we know and don't know because teachers, parents, and administrators are a critical bunch. Those talks made us really carefully consolidate the knowledge we had gained to that point, with the result that we had a better understanding, as you said, of how far we had come, and of where we needed to go next.

The second point, about endpoints, reminds me that everything we do is social in both origin and nature. To me that means that nothing can ever be exactly the same because people and circumstances are always changing. A theme that is successful with one group can fall flat with another. If I have absorbed only one thing about teaching and learning out of all this, it is that I will never find "the answer"—in terms of methodology—to any aspect of my work, because the social dynamics will always be different from one year, one day, one moment to the next. The one thing I can count on is that every day will be a new, and in many ways, unpredictable adventure. It's the social dynamic that makes teaching such a creative profession.

MARTHA: That brings to mind that we have learned to not consider whole language *theory* the last and final "answer" either. A number of teachers and I have been significantly influenced by Al Rudnitsky, another member of the department, through his work with us on curriculum development. He talks about the importance of significant content, conceptually framed, and how we ought to avoid the oversimplifications that he feels appear in some of the whole language literature. His examination of cognitive theory has helped me see the deeper underpinnings of whole language as well as the intellectual climate in which it developed.

MARGARET: Agreed. For us as teachers, theories are useful as frameworks to guide our thinking, and they help keep us consistent in our ways of doing. But we have to stay open to the fact that as we learn more, and as cultural needs evolve, our theories will become refined or even radically changed. We may, eventually, come to some fairly reliable generalizations about how humans learn, but I think theories of *teaching* are culturally based to begin with. What and how we teach reflects what the culture needs and values in order to support a sense of well-being, social cohesion, and even social survival among its members.

To get back to our evolution, how would you characterize the period following that initial struggle to get under way?

MARTHA: Some of the intensity of that first year or two has calmed down (thank goodness!) and we have gone through a period of further building and consolidation. The two kindergarten teachers had pulled together a first draft of a curriculum guide during the first year and they revised and published that during the second year.

MARGARET: And we in grades one and two drafted ours during the second year. Susan pulled together the final draft as an independent study project during the third year. After our collaborative writing effort, she served as our final editor. I think writing down our ideas and practices was as helpful in consolidating our beliefs as the public speaking. An interesting addendum to this is that we are now ready to go through that process again. We have learned so much in the process of practice and continued study that we see how the guide needs to be improved. It goes back to that idea that the process of change and the building and maintenance of a school culture are dynamic processes.

MARTHA: Once the guide was well underway, we started to work on better parent communication and education. One of our projects was to invite parents to an evening in which teachers and I described the approach and addressed concerns.

MARGARET: I remember that! That was a challenge—lots of tough questions that night!

MARTHA: True, but personally I was pleased that the sticklers in our audience gave us a chance to address some of the most common concerns about whole language. They asked about phonics, you remember, and of course we have all been consistently amazed at how much of the sound-symbol patterns of written English children pick up through invented spelling alone. And there is so much direct contextual phonics instruction woven through the enlarged text lessons.

MARGARET: Not to mention from the reading and discussions about print conventions that *spontaneously* come out of our group language sessions!

MARTHA: Right. Another way we reach parents is by way of our progress reports. All levels continue to revise their reports so that they not only let parents know how their children are doing but serve to educate parents into the vocabulary and concepts that underlie the philosophy.

MARGARET: For me, coming previously from a system where report forms are standardized for the whole district, the practice at the Campus School of requiring that each level be responsible for developing its progress reporting systems is a major improvement. It allows us to make the reports relevant to what we are really doing. As far as content goes, we could conceivably rewrite it every year if we regularly changed our science themes, for example. The policy reflects the school's positive attitude toward teacher empowerment and supports the assumption that we can and should take responsibility for what we are doing. And you have made it easy for us by making it part of the secretaries' duties to type up the final drafts and run them off.

MARTHA: You've got it!

To go on with the story, we have developed new literature units across the grades, gradually moving away from the "basalization" of trade books.

MARGARET: Don't remind me! I remember when teachers were preparing lengthy "worksheets" to follow each chapter a child read! I did that once with *Casey the Impossible Horse* the first year I was there. What a disaster! It wasn't until I dropped the booklet and took the children up on their suggestion that they act out their favorite scenes that the book (and I) recovered!

MARTHA: That's what I was seeing in other classrooms, too. Children would read for twenty minutes and then write and write. Although the teachers' questions were thoughtful enough, the wonderful literature children were reading began to lose its wholeness. They were still seeing school reading as answering someone else's questions as they read. And connected to this was the issue of ability grouping. Actually it was one of the teachers I hired after we were involved in our curriculum revision who agreed to try my suggestion that she have heterogeneous literature groups. She had a personal interest in cooperative learning, so I approached the idea from that angle. We developed procedures for helping children choose books, then work together in small groups, making decisions themselves about the direction for discussion and written response. She was so excited about the way it worked, she sold the idea to others.

MARGARET: You've just touched on another important principle for making change. Just as we try to use a child's interest area as a means for facilitating certain learnings, you were using a teacher's interest to illustrate a principle you wanted her to try. Both her interest and yours were satisfied as a result. You got to me on the handwriting issue that way—by pointing out that issues of self-image and self-confidence were tied to the development of that skill. I'm afraid I didn't have much interest in the topic until then, but I *am* interested in children's psychological well-being.

MARTHA: Handwriting, yes. That's a biggie these days, and it's an area I think the whole language literature has neglected or dismissed. The preschool and primary teachers have reexamined the role of handwriting in the curriculum in light of two things. With the prodding of Sheila Kelly (our psychologist), we have been looking at the children who show significant handwriting disabilities by middle elementary age. Our process writing program was apparently increasing the problem because children were writing so much, long before they were given any specific support in how to hold a pencil or form a letter. We began to see some unusually dysfunctional grips and contorted and inefficient ways of making letters.

MARGARET: And the other view?

MARTHA: The other factor has been the new work on motor learning disabilities in what the occupational therapists call "sensory motor integration." Mary Benbow's research as an occupational therapist has been especially helpful. Both her consulting visits and her book, *Loops and Other Groups: A Kinesthetic Writing System* (1989), have helped me see handwriting not as a language art in its beginning stage but primarily as a motor skill that does, indeed, need routine and systematic strengthening.

MARGARET: How does it work?

MARTHA: First we work with the shoulder muscles, and eventually, through direct instruction and practice, we teach letter formation.

MARGARET: That's why Jan was doing all those large and fine motor activities five minutes a day this year with our first graders and having the children practice letter formation on a vertical surface. I was amazed, because they were having such a good time!

MARTHA: It's not as painful as *some* of you (ahem) have thought! But it's true that even I was taken aback by some of Mary's ideas. We wondered what happened to encouraging approximation. But we weren't recognizing the difference between reading or writing development—language processes—and motor development. We now see the need for a different approach to handwriting, but we are not sure how to mesh it with process writing. This may not be the place to elaborate, but suffice it to say that this is an area whole language researchers may want to consider.

MARGARET: It may turn out to be one of those areas where our theory needs more refining.

Before we wrap up, perhaps we should mention issues involving student teachers and new recruits on the staff when there's a changing of the guard?

MARTHA: Yes, I continually worry about what happens to a school culture when pivotal people move on. Losing your across-the-hall friend, Marlene Ducharme, last year, who is such an outstanding whole language teacher, and now you, next year, as you pursue your studies, affects all aspects of the system in some way. But it's part of the life of a school. We have worked hard in the recruitment process to find teachers with a holistic orientation that is not a superficial one. It's not easy, as you know, since you and the other teachers interview the candidates, too. It's an issue in need of further discussion because what passes in the field for whole language instruction, based now on a number of years interviewing and observing candidates teach, indicates to me that the training and supervision of whole language teachers hasn't yet caught up with theory and good practice. In any case, as new teachers have been hired, I have worked most intensively with them in language arts.

MARGARET: You know, Martha, as I look back over our conversation, it's clear that our school really does have the kind of environment that supports whole language practice. And I hope that if school board members or superintendents are reading this, they will take it from a teacher when she says the principal is an extremely important element in the change process. When I was a consultant, you gave me concrete direction, as you have with those who have succeeded me in that capacity; you freed us up as teachers so we could observe each other and attend professional conferences; you've been a proper whole language teacher by reading, writing, and presenting yourself, providing us with a model; you've done your homework and become thoroughly knowledgeable and articulate in theory and practice; you've problem-solved *with* us; you've brought the specialist teachers in so we can coordinate with them; you've been as self-questioning as you expect us to be; you share your readings and ideas with us; and, perhaps above all, you didn't make the mistake of setting up one teacher as the standard. This one's a big one, I think. By giving us time to read, write, talk, argue, and express doubts together, you let us find our own models among our fellow teachers. There's nothing more divisive, I think, than always saying, "Why don't you look at so-and-so? She's the one who has it all together." *None* of us has it *all* together, and we all have at least something to offer each other.

MARTHA: This is starting to look like a mutual admiration society! But I think it points out that collegiality among the people responsible for change *is* an important element in the whole mix. And I believe whole language may not be for everyone, not even for every excellent teacher. In any case, it just *cannot* be mandated.

MARGARET: It feels as though what we are really describing most here, as change and culture-building agents, are *attitudes,* or perhaps you could say *belief systems,* about how a school should operate. The nature of the school, as a teacher-training laboratory, demands that those at the helm keep up with current research in teaching and learning, which you and Ray have done. The teachers, because of their added role as teacher-trainers, feel they need to thoroughly understand theory in order to explain the teaching principles behind their actions. You and Ray see us as professionals, responsible for what we do, so you expect us to be involved in all the decision-making in the school that affects our teaching. We are "empowered," as the current jargon goes. You expect us to work together, to coordinate what we do with the other grade-level teacher, with the specialists and tutors, at the primary or intermediate level and at the school level, as appropriate. You keep us up to date on matters that affect us: salary negotiations with the college, progress on the playground reconstruction that we were all involved in planning, policies on multiculturalism . . . We are *treated* as a community and it is *assumed* that we will operate as a community.

MARTHA: And finally, when it came to the move into the whole language philosophy, if you look at the elements involved in our change, we used language-for-doing the same way it should be ideally used in a whole language classroom: we heard about ideas, we read, we talked, we read some more, we started to try out procedures suggested by the philosophy, the literature, and our observations of practicing experts (like Don Holdaway), we talked and read and did some more, we "published," in the sense that we made formal presentations and documents of our thinking to date and in that process, we drafted, revised, drafted some more, revised some more, produced "final" products, and, now, as we talk and read and continue to grow, we are ready to repeat the cycle. Our school process *is* the whole language process, a process of working, playing, reading, writing, talking, thinking, and doing—together.

MARGARET: And you know? If we hadn't talked together for this article, we might not have realized that. It was the process of collaborating with each other to describe our change—in writing—for a formal purpose, that revealed its nature more fully to us.

MARTHA: That reminds me of something Michael Fullen (1990) said about "the collaborative work culture."

MARGARET: Let's let him have the final word, then.

MARTHA: He said that "schools characterized by norms of collegiality and experimentation are much more likely to implement innovations successfully" (p. 12). We were able to build on the already positive aspects of the environment at a laboratory school to reframe and reignite teachers' thinking. I think by pushing the theory, the conceptual framework, we helped to ensure real change.

References

Benbow, Mary. 1989. *Loops and Other Groups: A Kinesthetic Writing System.* Instructor's Edition. Self-published.

Calkins, Lucy McCormick. 1983. *Lessons from a Child: On the Teaching and Learning of Writing.* Portsmouth, N.H.: Heinemann.

Durkin, Dolores. 1983. *Teaching Them to Read.* Boston: Allyn and Bacon. Originally published in 1970.

Fullen, Michael. 1990. Staff development, innovation, and institutional development. In *Changing School Culture Through Staff Development: 1990 Yearbook of the Association for Supervision and Curriculum Development.* Ed. B. Joyce. Alexandria, Va.: Association for Supervision and Curriculum Development.

Graves, Donald H. 1983. *Writing: Teachers and Children at Work.* Portsmouth, N.H.: Heinemann.

Holdaway, Don. 1984. *Stability and Change in Literacy Learning.* London, Ontario: University of Western Ontario. Available in the U.S. from Heinemann.

Hoskisson, Kenneth, and Gail E. Tompkins. 1987. *Language Arts: Content and Teaching Strategies.* Columbus, Ohio: Merrill.

8 | On Comfort, Culture, and Curriculum

Linda Henke

Drawing on both her experience and her research, Linda Henke describes how a whole language culture and curriculum developed at Clive Elementary School in West Des Moines, Iowa, where she was the director of curriculum. The process began when a district-level committee appointed to recommend a new basal reading series decided instead to recommend guidelines for a new curriculum that would allocate daily priority time to actual reading, encourage the use of trade books, and integrate reading with writing. Linda explains how she came to realize that traditional approaches to curriculum and staff development would not work in implementing their "Beyond the Basal" guidelines, which reflected whole language principles. Drawing upon Deal and Kennedy's *Corporate Cultures* (1982) and Lortie's (1975) concept of the "technical culture" in schools as an ideological framework, she describes in detail how the culture and shared belief system at Clive evolved, concluding with a discussion of this culture within the larger political context of the school system and the community.

LINDA HENKE is currently Assistant Superintendent for the School District of Clayton, in Clayton, Missouri. She has been involved in the study of literacy for the past fifteen years as a teacher, administrator, and consultant. Her work with teachers in the West Des Moines schools resulted in "Beyond the Basal," a project that moved the literacy program away from its heavy reliance on basal readers. The author of several articles, Linda is currently focusing her efforts on the exploration of curriculum as a cultural phenomenon.

* * *

Comfort
We think it is calm here
Or the storm is the right size.
WILLIAM STAFFORD

Clive Elementary School, set back from busy Seventy-third Street, was surrounded by towering oak and maple trees. Twice a day the shallow circular drive in front of the building became as heavy with traffic as the street it joined, as buses and cars steadily edged their way toward the red front doors to deposit or gather up children. A new addition completed in 1989 did little to change the face of the school. It remained a low, flat-roofed brick building, unobtrusive in the residential neighborhood. Because it was built on a hill, the back part of the building was two-storied and overlooked a large grassy play yard sloping down to a wooded creek bank.

Clive was one of eight elementary schools in West Des Moines, an affluent suburb of Iowa's capital city. The community earned high marks from several major corporations that had elected to locate offices there, and the suburb was growing rapidly. Because of the increased enrollment, the renovation of Clive had been necessary to add several classrooms, a new media center, and a computer laboratory and to reshape the administrative offices. With the remodeling completed, the building served its five hundred students well.

Wide, gray-carpeted hallways lined with lockers and children's art work and writing welcomed me as I returned to the building after several months' absence. It was January 1989, and I was beginning a formal research project at the school. In many ways I felt as if I was coming home. For the three previous years I had served as the director of curriculum in West Des Moines. The work had been both frustrating and exhilarating, and my thinking about schooling had continually been challenged as I worked with Clive and the other schools in the district to reshape our vision of literacy education. I resigned my position in the summer of 1988 to complete my doctoral work in school administration and went off to graduate school a hundred miles away. But I was drawn back to Clive and the teachers who worked there. Our efforts in West Des Moines to implement a program growing from a whole language philosophy had dramatically altered my understanding of curriculum, but much of that understanding I was unable to articulate, and I was left with many questions.

A Historical Perspective

The West Des Moines literacy curriculum began as a traditional basal reading adoption in the fall of 1985. I had just come to the district as director of curriculum and assembled a seventeen-member committee to begin the year-long process that was to lead us to a new basal series. Certainly I had no great desire to challenge the status quo during my first year in a new position. But in retrospect, I see that the process we designed for the study led us to do exactly that. The members of the committee spent a great deal of time that fall looking at ourselves as readers and writers, exploring the research on literacy learning, and examining our own classrooms as literate environments. This reflective stance allowed us to identify four major issues that we felt must be addressed by any new program:

1. *Reallocating time.* We wanted to ensure that daily priority time was given to the genuine tasks of reading and writing rather than to the drill and practice that were consuming well over half of our allotted block for teaching literacy.
2. *Expanding our reading options.* We worried about the excerpts and controlled vocabulary that were part of our reading program. We wanted our program built on real books written expressly for children to enjoy rather than to teach children to read.
3. *Changing attitudes about reading.* Issues of accountability had narrowed our vision of reading to success on criterion tests. When we surveyed our students, we found a large number of a-literates—children who could read but who chose not to. Additionally, we worried about what we labeled "low group syndrome." Far too many of our children in the bottom groups did not see themselves as readers and writers at all. We found children coming to kindergarten certain of their ability to read and write, who, after only a year or two in our well-intentioned program, became convinced that they would never be good at it at all.
4. *Integrating the language processes.* We believed that reading, writing, speaking, and listening were mutually supportive ways of making meaning but found that our practices simply did not support this relationship. Too often in reading class, writing and speaking seemed added on rather than woven throughout our curriculum.

These issues challenged us as a committee to acknowledge that adopting a new basal reader would not accomplish what children needed. As we reviewed the beautifully packaged reading programs that lined our conference room, we realized that a dramatic new approach to literacy was necessary. In January, after several long and emotional meetings, the committee voted to take to the teachers in the district a proposal that was quite different from what anyone had anticipated. We outlined a strategy that asked the district to:

1. Keep the current basal but scale back its use, making it optional for those teachers who wished to use alternative materials.
2. Develop a trade book program that would include multiple copies of selected books and skeleton teaching guides for each of the grade levels.
3. Give daily priority time to independent reading and build classroom libraries to support that emphasis.
4. Incorporate daily writing time into our reading/language block.
5. Provide intensive staff development to assist us in implementing the change.
6. Initiate a communication campaign to help parents understand the new program.

On January 29, after the committee had demonstrated some of the most intensive salesmanship I have ever seen, the district's teachers voted overwhelmingly to accept this new proposal to move "Beyond the Basal." The committee was ecstatic. And there I was, a brand new director of curriculum in a district where 185 teachers had just voted to make a radical change in literacy teaching. I looked out over the corn fields of Iowa toward all the other districts that seemed quite happy with a basal reader, and I thought of something my father used to say: "The first one out of a fox hole is not a hero. He's a casualty."

Conceptualizing Curriculum as Culture

What struck me almost immediately as we began developing and implementing "Beyond the Basal" was that traditional approaches to curriculum and staff development were absolutely inappropriate when it came to working with a whole language program. Bureaucratic practices that delivered curriculum to teachers to deliver to students stood in stark contrast to the whole language emphasis on individual meaning-making, interaction, and community-building. I noticed, however, that the reading I had been doing about culture seemed to fit very well with the kinds of change we were talking about. Deal and Kennedy's book *Corporate Cultures* (1982), for example, offered a critical perspective to the task we had forged for ourselves.

In their examination of sixty large companies, Deal and Kennedy found that the most successful were those they labeled "high culture." These companies gave priority to creating a culture that promoted collective efficacy by consciously giving attention to the articulation of shared values and beliefs. Every one of the top twenty companies focused on the importance of people. It was the people that had developed these organizations into successful ventures, and, we concluded, it would be people who would transform the literacy curriculum into something alive and functioning in our classrooms. This seemed such a logical idea, but my own background in education offered little to support such an effort.

I found myself juxtaposing Deal and Kennedy's examination of corporations with Lortie's classic study of schools, *Schoolteacher* (1975). Lortie's research suggested that teachers lacked what he described as "a technical culture," a shared system of values and beliefs to undergird their practice, a vocabulary for discussing their teaching, and a sense of connection to their peers, the very things Deal and Kennedy identified as critical to success in organizations. I began to see that a curriculum conceptualized as culture must address issues of personal and collective meaning-making that have been ignored in traditional views. As Devaney and Sykes comment, classrooms today "rest on concepts of learning as consumption and teaching as delivery of packaged knowledge which have formed a set of sociological features of schools that are as pervasive as chalk dust" (1988, p. 16). A cultural definition of curriculum required a paradigm shift, an organizational transformation that in West Des Moines and at Clive Elementary School stirred up a good-sized storm indeed.

Nurturing a Curriculum Culture

And so we embarked on an adventure in which curriculum and staff development became one and the same. Our curriculum document focused on articulating theory, suggesting possible teaching strategies, and most importantly, creating a vision of what an empowered

literate individual is able to do. But far more critical to our goal of
nurturing a technical culture to support the literacy program was the
series of organizational strategies we implemented to accomplish that
end. The greater share of our staff development budget was spent in
this endeavor.

Our first priority was to support teachers in developing shared
theory. We created professional literacy libraries at both the district
and building level that included multiple copies of key books;
designed staff development courses taught by our own teachers that
offered college credit; tailored monthly grade-level meetings so that
teachers could leave their classrooms to read, write, and discuss
together; and held fireside study, which gathered small groups of
teachers around a fireplace to discuss books they had read in common. Summer institutes, including the Iowa Writing Project, were
brought to the district and teachers were offered college credit for
these as well. Twice a year the entire district staff was released for an
afternoon to hear key speakers address issues in literacy education,
and then teachers were given time to discuss the implications for our
own classrooms.

We gave teachers control of their own teaching in ways we had
never done before. Moving away from basal domination was scary
for many, but we felt that it was essential to the development of our
new curriculum culture. Each teacher was given an individual budget
with which to buy trade books (we accessed the old workbook
account), and teachers as a group were given a good deal of freedom
in designing classroom strategies and selecting materials to support
literacy learning.

Because we believed that learning is both personal and social, we
designed strategies to foster reflective practice and collaboration.
Teachers and administrators alike were encouraged to keep professional journals, and these were used in many of our meetings. We
also talked a good deal about risk-taking, and in our workshops,
courses, and grade level gatherings we shared experiments, solved
problems, and celebrated together.

Lortie's comments about teacher isolation spurred us to cultivate
networks. Two advisory committees were established to help us keep
abreast of the program—one focused on the needs in individual
buildings, the other on the concerns and issues brought up at each
grade level. These committees met monthly and became powerful
analyzers of the culture. They noted the language that people were
using to describe their teaching, the attitudes that were expressed
formally in meetings and informally in lounges, indicators of stress
and frustration, the kinds of questions that were being asked, and so

on. This information helped us decide what should happen next in our unfolding curriculum. We also developed support groups in the buildings and across the district for people interested in exploring whole language theory and practice in this way.

Our curriculum culture focused on people, and so we celebrated heroes who exemplified the values that were part of our program. We encouraged teachers and administrators to become researchers of their own work, to write professionally, and to present at conferences and serve as resources for other districts. These individuals were recognized at school board meetings and in newsletters sent home to parents. National figures such as Don Graves and Ken Goodman, who came to West Des Moines to work with us, were another kind of hero, spokespeople for our cause. They walked through the halls, visited with teachers and children, and became a part of what we were trying to do. Their words in the books we read held special significance and tied us to a broader movement.

As we worked at Clive and other schools in West Des Moines, I realized that a cultural definition of curriculum, which focused on shared values and beliefs about teaching and learning, resulted in powerful change. Over a period of three years, teachers were provided with opportunities to meet, study, and discuss. In this collaborative environment, they began to construct new personal and collective meaning, and their perceptions of teaching and learning seemed to change. I returned to Clive in the middle of year four of "Beyond the Basal" to clarify those changes and to trace how they had come about and the effects they had elicited in individual teachers and in the institution.

Researching Clive's Curriculum Culture

During the 1988–89 school year, the year of my study, twenty classroom teachers worked at Clive. The building staff also included a half-time media specialist, a counselor, part-time art and music teachers, two special education teachers, and a reading resource teacher. This was a seasoned group of veterans, averaging twelve years of teaching at Clive; many had taught for several years before they joined the Clive staff. As the spring semester progressed, I conducted intensive interviews with all of them; developed case studies with three of the teachers; collected artifacts, such as newsletters, letters to the central office, memoranda, and reports to parents; and conducted observations throughout the school building. I also interviewed the building principal, Jerry Ellis, who was new to Clive that year, and Al Davis, who had served as the Clive principal for the preceding sixteen years.

What I found at Clive was a curriculum that functioned very differently from curriculum I had observed in the past. I was intrigued by how these teachers worked in their classrooms and with one another. The Clive literacy curriculum was a true technical culture, rich in language, ritual, roles, and patterns of behavior. In the remainder of this chapter, I will explore the major characteristics of the curriculum as I discovered it in the classrooms, hallways, and teachers' lounge of the school.

The Cultural Network

One of the most apparent characteristics of the technical culture at Clive was the strong sense among staff members that together they could make an important difference for children. Clive teachers relied on one another to support each other's teaching in a variety of ways; in discussions of their classrooms and their school, they demonstrated a confidence in what they were about. In the fall of 1989 I was in the midst of analyzing huge stacks of Clive data when I received a phone call from Charlene, a first-grade teacher who had resigned from the school because her husband had been transferred to another city. Charlene had just resumed her teaching in a new district and was having trouble adjusting to a different environment. "There's no shared vision here," she complained of her new school, "and they only meet once a month to talk about their literacy program. Can you believe that? How much good can that do?"

It was the first time I had heard a Clive teacher use the term "shared vision," yet a good deal of the teachers' talk, both formal and informal, suggested that such a vision existed and that it contributed to the teaching and learning that were accomplished at the school. While a broad range of classroom practice was evident, teachers believed they were united in important ways. As Susan, a first-grade teacher, commented, "There are so many different personalities, different approaches, yet there is consistency. We are all reaching for the same star."

Enhancing Professionalism

The confidence in their professional practice seemed to come from several sources. In part, it evolved from the study of the research that the teachers had done, both individually and collectively. Sandy, a second-grade teacher, explained how her professional study supported her practice:

Reading about the people like Donald Graves who really went into classrooms and documented what works and what doesn't . . . gives you a basis behind your own work. When you talk to parents and when you are in the classroom, it gives you some confidence that this is going to work. It's not just something we *hope* is going to work.

In interesting ways I had not anticipated, their professional reading seemed to help teachers like Sandy cope with the isolation of their classrooms. Through her reading, Sandy found the confidence to experiment in her teaching and to discuss her practice with colleagues and parents. She and her colleagues broadened their perceptions of professional community and felt part of a larger movement that was generating change across the country. In some ways, they saw themselves as missionaries in West Des Moines, suffering the criticism of those who did not read or study. Thus the reading became an important part of their group identity. As Jennifer remarked,

You have to be a learner in this program. I developed my own list for professional reading this year because we didn't get any support for that from the central office. You can't stop learning.

The Clive staff was committed to both individual and group study of the research on literacy learning. During the 1988–89 school year, as part of a project sponsored with district funds, all but four of the teachers participated in a building study of the use of the journal as a tool for learning. Louise, a fourth-grade teacher and a leader in the building, developed a plan for the study and organized teachers across the grades into small groups. The groups met regularly during the year, read Fulwiler's *The Journal Book*, experimented with using journals in their classrooms, and gathered as an entire staff to discuss their findings. The group seemed to allow teachers to build new networks within the building, as Kit, who taught third grade, commented:

Spending scheduled time talking to teachers at other grade levels allowed me to see common things we were doing that I didn't know were there. I think it made us feel closer in what we are doing.

Weaving Support Nets

These groups functioned in part as support nets for teachers as they experimented with new practices and tested their developing theory.

Jennifer, who taught kindergarten, found that her group helped her take the leap from teacher of writing to writer:

> I never perceived myself as a writer. But a personal experience I had with the nudging of others in my journaling group changed that. My group said, "Do you write?" I said, "No." They said, "You know you should write." But all I could remember was getting scores that said CREATIVITY—A, MECHANICS—B or C. So I never thought that I was a writer. But then I decided to write about a personal experience and share it with my group. I really wanted to share it with them; I didn't care how good it was. It was just because it was my story, and I wanted them to hear it. It still isn't done. If I would sit down and look at it again, I would change it again, but that's not threatening to me anymore.

As Jennifer's story demonstrates, the groups encouraged risk-taking. Within the safety of a small group of colleagues she was willing to write again. The fear of evaluation was gone. She wanted to share an experience with these teachers, and she was confident that they would receive her work with respect. This certainty that early drafts in thinking or writing would be accepted was an important part of the dynamics of the technical culture at Clive. The small group offered a comfortable place to try out new ideas and practices.

In addition to their professional study and discussion, the teachers at Clive also benefited from having Louise in their midst. Louise had been using the principles of whole language to guide her instructional decision-making for years before it was officially accepted by the district. She had done so quietly, keeping her door closed until the district decided to move away from basal readers. Louise's experience offered the new program roots—it wasn't just another trend passing through the district. She was also well read and able to articulate the theory that undergirded whole language practice. Deal and Kennedy (1982) would most likely have labeled Louise the culture's "priestess." She had been in the district for a quarter of a century and knew the history of the school as few others did. This, coupled with her understanding of whole language and her deep commitment to the school and to the teachers who worked there, made her an invaluable resource in connecting teachers to one another and to the evolving literacy program.

At Clive the teachers came to share an almost mystical belief in the power of the group. Although they themselves were not always able to articulate this belief, it was manifested in at least three important ways: a shared belief system, the framing of the teaching profession in terms of collaboration, and a strong commitment to the celebration of learning and teaching successes.

A Shared Belief System

Louise and Mae had been friends for a long time. They had shared professional books and articles about literacy and traveled to conferences together for many years. Mae's role as reading resource teacher put her in contact with every teacher at Clive School, and together she and Louise spent long hours over coffee at a local restaurant and on the phone at night discussing and analyzing the developing literacy program. In many ways, Mae was Clive's grandmother. Appropriately gray-haired and rounded, she worried over each of the teachers, was the first one they came to with problems, and took genuine delight in every child's and teacher's success.

Both Louise and Mae had grown into whole language through their years of reflective practice. Interestingly, both described whole language as much more of a world view than an approach or method, or even a philosophy of teaching. In her interaction log, which all case-study teachers kept to document discussion of the literacy program outside of the classroom, Louise described working with her new student teacher:

> I mentioned that whole language is not a flash-in-the-pan gimmicky fad. I emphasized that it is more than a way of teaching, but rather an approach to life and learning.

Mae echoed Louise's feelings:

> Too many teachers still see whole language as a series of activities and a set of materials. It's so much more than that. I think my beliefs that could be labeled "whole language" dictate a lot of the way I live my life.

Both teachers saw their teaching as evolutionary. Whole language for them was a part of that evolution, not the end product. For most of the other teachers at Clive, however, the movement toward whole language was much less gradual and represented less of an integration into a life view. When discussing whole language, they described specific changes in their teaching and the way they thought about schools. Most pointed to specific experiences that dramatically reshaped their vision. Nine of the teachers mentioned the Iowa Writing Project as an important turning point in their professional lives. Kit, for example, who taught third grade, noted, "I just couldn't imagine teaching without having taken the Writing Project. It changed so much of what I do in the classroom."

Al Davis, the former principal at Clive, agreed with Kit that the Project had had a significant impact on classrooms at Clive: "Two or three people really dragged their feet about the program until the Writing Project. Now they're some of the most excited people on the staff."

Peter was one of the reticent teachers Al was talking about. He described how the Writing Project influenced his work:

> I am kind of concrete sequential, and I needed things a little more clear-cut than it seemed like it was. The Iowa Writing Project really turned the corner for me. I can't imagine anyone teaching this way without having taken it. The year before, I was trying to do a little bit of both, trying to work my way into it and talking to different teachers around here trying to feel my way through it. I was very frustrated and kind of negative about it until after that workshop. Since then, I've sold my wife on it and teacher friends from other districts. I am very enthusiastic about it.

Peter's experience was illustrative of teachers' struggles as they began to experiment with whole language in their classrooms. Peter found the district literacy curriculum document vague and unhelpful in his initial attempts at working with new strategies. As he noted, he was "kind of concrete sequential" and "needed things a little more clear-cut." Certainly the former curriculum had been concrete and sequential. For teachers using the basal reader, the vast majority of teaching decisions had already been made. They needed only to follow the directions. The new literacy program, in contrast, was based on the idea that teachers would possess both a theory about how children learn to read and write and the practical knowledge necessary to shape materials, time, and space to facilitate that end.

Teachers such as Peter found themselves ill-equipped to work with such a program, and his frustration seemed reasonable. The new trade books were cumbersome and complicated to use when teachers were accustomed to the sleekness of basal reading programs and prescribed daily lessons. For the teacher who had taught language as daily lessons from the basal language book, developing a writing workshop required a great deal of new knowledge. Peter did his best.

He tried to "do a little bit of both" in his classroom, but the conflicting philosophies collided in his classroom. An isolated skill development orientation did not fit with a program calling for authentic reading and writing experiences. It was only when he took the Writing Project and began to develop his own practical theory that Peter once again became comfortable with his teaching. He was able to sort out which practices fit his beliefs and to adopt new strategies accordingly. Other teachers articulated a similar need for experiences and models that could help them visualize alternatives to traditional practice. As Penny, another teacher, noted, "Erasing the teacher in your head isn't easy."

Penny's powerful metaphor speaks eloquently to the complexities teachers faced as they were confronted with whole language. In many ways the philosophy did require erasing roles, expectations, and practices whose roots went as far back as childhood. Clive teachers had been teaching as they had been taught. Sandy explained, "I guess you need a chance to experience a different kind of model to counteract all the other things you've been exposed to in education— including when you were growing up."

The transformation Penny describes affected teachers differently. For over half of them, the rebirth signaled a new sense of professionalism and the beginning of a serious study of the art of teaching. They began to question practice and belief, struggling to articulate what had been tacit knowledge. These teachers were experimental and reflective in their stance toward teaching, continually developing hypotheses about teaching and learning, which they tested in their classrooms. For others, the rebirth focused on the changed surface features of the curriculum. In these teachers' classrooms, the literacy program appeared to be implemented and they were generally positive about their teaching. Yet they were often unable to explain why their practices looked the way they did. Just as they had worked their way through the basal reader, they now implemented writers' workshop and independent reading. The "whys" didn't seem terribly important. Despite this diversity, the technical culture of the school appeared to support and unite teachers as they taught and learned about literacy. It created an environment that connected individuals and supported risk-taking and experimentation.

Collaboration

A second dominant characteristic of the teaching environment at Clive was the value teachers placed on professional collaboration and consultation. This seemed to come at least in part from the processes that were used to develop and implement the curriculum, which served as a model for Clive in structuring formal and informal networks to support collaborative teaching.

Because teachers' schedules were highly structured, the teachers' lounge became an important place for discussions about literacy. Teachers reported that the lounge had always been a lively center of activity where teachers interacted freely, but now talk during lunch and before and after school invariably touched on the literacy program. Margie commented, "We talk in the lounge all the time about what kids are doing. It's real common for teachers to bring kids' writing in and pass it around or read it out loud."

In some ways, the lounge became the community well for the emerging technical culture, a place where news was passed along and problems and successes were discussed. Teachers congregated there early in the morning and found their way back for coffee and talk at the end of the day. Al Davis described the lounge's influence on the technical culture:

> Sometimes I'd get a little nervous or frustrated at Clive because the teachers were always in the lounge right up to the bell. But they shared a lot in the lounge. It wasn't just small talk. Louise did a lot of her work in the lounge in terms of helping people with the program.

Al seemed to recognize that the lounge was important to the sustenance of the technical culture. It was more than just a place for chatting or complaining, although those things were done there, too. The lounge was a place where teachers could learn and share their learning. It provided an essential forum for the work of Louise and Mae as they nurtured the teachers and their efforts at change.

Collaboration, whether in the hallways, in the lounge, or in organized study, contributed in important ways to the technical culture at Clive. As Karen explained, "If you are a whole language teacher, then you have to believe in talk as part of learning. You can't always learn by yourself. We need each other."

Celebration

Anecdotes about children's successes with reading and writing became one of the most common kinds of talk about the literacy program at Clive. Teachers told their stories in the lounge and the hallways, and these stories frequently made their way throughout the building, thanks to Mae. Often stories were told over and over in the lounge as teachers came in, and the telling was accompanied by laughter and sometimes clapping.

Examples of story-telling were woven throughout my interviews and informal discussions with teachers. Frequently the stories celebrated children's perceptions of the world as expressed in specific pieces they had written or comments they had made in class. At other times, the stories illustrated how well the program was working for children. Sometimes they even captured a turning point for an individual child, serving as a marker for the teacher that the child had joined the "literacy club." Collecting the stories seemed to reinforce the teachers' sense that they were doing the right thing for children.

A touching example of a celebratory story came during my interview with Peter, who was describing what happened in his classroom when things were going well:

> Yesterday was a good example. We have author share, and we had two funny stories and the kids enjoyed them. They were pretty good. And then a boy read a story about his sister who was diagnosed as having leukemia. I wasn't sure he would want to share because it's a very, very emotional piece. I had tears in my eyes both times that he read it to me, the different versions he'd been working on. But he was eager to share it. So he read. And you could hear a pin drop. And I was looking around with tears in my eyes after hearing this. There were other kids who had tears in their eyes, and everybody clapped when he finished. It was right at the end of the day and they were clapping when the bell rang. Things like that make it worthwhile.

Even as Peter retold the story, his eyes clouded with tears; and it was apparent that he was still deeply moved by the incident. Of the twenty classroom teachers I interviewed, all but three offered specific stories of children's successes in response to questions about how the program worked. These stories seemed to generate a good deal of enthusiasm in the telling. Teachers leaned forward, their faces animated. It was clear that this was the mode for discussing the program with which they were most comfortable.

Because Clive teachers were faced with a group of parents who were unhappy with the new literacy program, some of the stories centered on incidents that convinced parents of the program's merit. One morning in the teachers' lounge, Joann told the following story:

> Well, Chelsey's parents said they were learning quite a few things
> from her. On a car ride to Minnesota she asked her mother who her
> favorite author was. And her mother couldn't tell her, and she said,
> "Well, you're a lot older than I am, and you had better be thinking
> of a favorite author because I have a couple right now." She asked
> her father what books he was into right now, and he said he wasn't
> into books. He was into magazines. And she was quite shocked. She
> said, "Magazines are okay, but you need to be into books."

As Nancy Martin, a well-known author and language theorist,
has noted, "Stories are arguments, too." Certainly that was true at
Clive, where the celebratory story seemed a convincing argument for
a particular view of teaching and learning. The stories reinforced a
perception of active, self-confident learners who were able to function
successfully even on adult terms. The heroes of these stories were
children who felt in control of their own literacy learning.

Perhaps no one was as intent on the sharing of celebratory stories
as Mae, for whom story-telling had become one way of supporting
teachers. One afternoon, for example, I overheard her talking to two
second-grade teachers:

> Two second graders were coming past my desk the other day. I think
> they had just come down from PE, and I heard Karen say, "Now it's
> time for literature." One of the boys came past my desk on the way
> to the restroom, and he gave a little jump and shot his hand in the
> air and shouted, "Literature, oh boy!" If that doesn't make your day!

The second-grade teachers laughed and responded with apparent
pleasure to Mae's information. They were accustomed to her role as
chief storyteller at Clive, and they knew that she was also a willing
listener to their stories. Mae joined teachers in celebrating even the
smallest successes. The certainty that children's accomplishments
would be acknowledged seemed to contribute to the teachers' certainty that their own accomplishments were valued. As Sandy
pointed out, "No matter how good you feel about something that's
happened in the classroom, it helps to have someone to share it with."

The sharing of success stories was an art form at Clive. It served
as an essential feature of the technical culture, supporting the sense of
collective efficacy and rallying the spirits of teachers as they defended
the program against detractors. The stories appeared especially
important during 1988–89, as teachers felt the culture threatened by
parents and central office administrators.

The Technical Culture Within the Political Context

Although the focus of my study was the literacy program at Clive and the values, beliefs, and practices that supported and surrounded it, it is important to remember that the culture did not exist in isolation from the broader context of the West Des Moines schools and the West Des Moines community. The school people, the roles they played, the channels they selected for communication, all influenced how the teachers at Clive approached literacy education. Parental expectations and parents' willingness to vocally support or criticize the school's efforts were also important. At the same time, the literacy program itself became a powerful political force within the district. As it evolved, it reshaped roles, challenged accepted procedures, and revealed issues of power deeply embedded in the hierarchical curriculum process. While my research focused on the technical culture at Clive, the broader context had a major impact on what happened at the elementary school.

In 1985, when the reading committee began its work, it seemed to be functioning in relative isolation from the rest of the district. According to my journal notes, individual principals attended committee meetings only twice, and the executive director never attended. Periodically I gave brief reports on the committee's progress at administrative meetings, but they generated little discussion. Even when the committee recommended purchasing trade books instead of a new basal series, the discussion engendered little controversy. Attention, however, remained focused on the materials to be adopted. Reviewing and buying new texts was a familiar procedure in the district. Although the trade books provided a new twist, administrators were comfortable allowing teachers to choose.

What did not occur to anyone at the time, including me, was that the switch from basal to nonbasal reading involved issues of power and control that went far beyond simply deciding what texts children would read. The West Des Moines schools had for many years relied on the basal reading and language programs to provide almost all curricular linkage in the area of literacy education. Teachers had been dependent upon the basal texts to determine what would happen in their classrooms. The texts prescribed skills, strategies, materials, and use of time. The basal control of teachers and classrooms provided parents, teachers, and administrators with a sense of confidence that literacy learning was occurring consistently across the district. Teachers periodically sent to the central office evidence of the end-of-level tests children had taken in the basal, and standardized test scores remained high. As long as the materials controlled teacher decision-making, the bureaucratic curriculum model operated smoothly, and people were comfortable.

The creation of our "Beyond the Basal" program, however, made the use of the basal reading program optional. The new program's guidelines mandated time for reading and writing, but they did not limit teachers to particular materials. And while the guidelines suggested strategies such as thematic webs of trade books and writing workshop, teachers were given flexibility to adapt these to their own classrooms. For the first time, teachers were confronted with large blocks of time that had previously been filled by reading and writing textbooks, and the responsibility for the use of that time now fell squarely on their shoulders. Curriculum was no longer controlled in a linear top-down fashion, and power was transferred away from upper levels of the hierarchy to teachers.

In addition, the district's staff development component committed funds as it had never done before to curriculum change. Courses, speakers, visits to other districts, and conferences were suddenly available to teachers, along with materials for professional reading and time to read. In a fairly short amount of time—three years—the district found itself with a group of teachers who were increasingly confident in their curricular expertise. In many ways it was a series of coincidences that created this force, but the result, nonetheless, was that a large number of teachers began to demand a stronger voice in the organizational decisions affecting their classrooms. During the 1988–89 school year, teacher protests to the central office expressed concern about standardized testing, budget cuts for the literacy program, and the reporting of pupil progress. All of these could be traced in some way to the literacy program and the empowerment of teachers it seemed to nurture. Louise described the changes this way:

> The whole literacy program got started because somebody would be a leader but didn't lead us by the nose. Rather, we were involved in fashioning the program, learning as we were growing. We had the feeling that we were part of the program and we were important in developing it. There was nothing set from on high that says "thou shalt." There was involvement all the way. There are still things we need to change. After our meeting last night [an area-wide whole language support group meeting], I think there's a nucleus of people who probably won't be pushed around. These teachers will play the game we want to play despite their [central office] rules.

Louise's description of the development of the "Beyond the Basal" program certainly speaks to teacher empowerment. From her perspective, the program was shaped by teachers. Once teachers took control over their classrooms, they would not abdicate it without a struggle. She also acknowledged that whole language activists were "a nucleus," perhaps not representing the majority of teachers in the district. As a group, however, they were willing to challenge the central office as necessary.

Such challenges appeared to affect the relationship of many building-level and central office administrators to the literacy program. Clive teachers voiced concern, for example, that the executive director wanted to get rid of the program and was using a variety of techniques to do so. The program was made especially vulnerable during the 1988–89 school year. I had resigned. As a key player in the program's development, I had been a strong voice of support for it at the upper levels of the bureaucracy. The woman who replaced me resigned after only a month on the job. Although she did not leave the district until the end of the first semester, she did not meet with the reading advisory board, the reading resource teachers, or other groups of teachers concerned with the literacy program after her resignation. The district administration had also decided to reassign building principals that fall, and so teachers were confronted with new administrators in their buildings.

Finally, scores on the Iowa Tests of Basic Skills had dropped by three to four months at several grade levels the previous spring. The newspaper published a series of articles describing the "plummet" and quoted two teachers from one of the schools in the district who blamed the whole language program for the problem. In response to the lower scores, a group of parents in the district organized in order to persuade the school board to abandon the program.

When I established my study in January, I found a group of angry teachers at Clive who accused central office administrators of a lack of leadership, an unwillingness to listen, and a failure to understand the whole language program. Their anger reflected district concern. A letter explaining their concerns and signed by well over half the teachers in West Des Moines had been sent to the school board.

The letter, dated January 12, stated in part:

At the present time, the teachers are deeply concerned about the problems that must be addressed if we are going to maintain quality education and educators. It is imperative that the three elements of leadership (educators, administrators, and School Board) sit down together and openly communicate as equals. This communication must be characterized by respect and a true desire to understand. It must be conducted openly, in a nonthreatening atmosphere, free from the "patronizing tone" so prevalent in the past. Respectful, intelligent dialogue can develop trust. Trust is an inherent ingredient for risk-taking and risk-taking is essential for meeting the goals of the district. . . .

The West Des Moines Community School District is growing: more students . . . new programs. Do we have the courage to explore our definition of excellence? Is it higher test scores? Is it an authoritarian atmosphere which emphasizes one right way to accomplish a task? Is it ever-increasing class size with little regard for student well-being? A strong leadership achieved through a cooperative facilitative approach is mandatory. This is impossible unless all leadership elements communicate as equals to redefine excellence to meet classroom needs. If we do not accept this challenge, we may become LEADERS IN LEAVING.

The letter contained important elements of the whole language philosophy transplanted from the classroom into the political arena. The rhetoric of whole language used in developing and implementing "Beyond the Basal" was woven throughout the piece: "communication characterized by respect and a true desire to understand," "nonthreatening atmosphere," "respectful dialogue," "risk-taking," "facilitative approach." All of these terms were used repeatedly as "Beyond the Basal" became part of the district's curriculum. But now the language was no longer challenging the authoritarian classroom; instead it was attacking other power relationships within the hierarchy.

The issues addressed in the letter can also be traced to the whole language program. Concern about the view that there is only one right way to accomplish a task and about standardized testing, for example, most likely arose from the whole language program's presence within a traditional curriculum context. Precedent in West Des Moines prior to "Beyond the Basal" had certainly supported these features; however, teachers currently did not want standardized testing or a narrowly defined curriculum to dictate their teaching. The final line plays on the logo of the school district, "Leaders in Learning." Anger and frustration were communicated vividly in the capitalized "LEADERS IN LEAVING." The threat was hardly subtle.

The political furor that surrounded the whole language program emphasized the contrast between a linear model of curriculum and a transactive model built on interaction among all participants and contextualized decision-making. The "Beyond the Basal" program was designed to support teachers and students in negotiating literacy needs and goals, but it became apparent that whole language in West Des Moines was much more than a way to teach reading. It touched the core processes and relationships of the bureaucracy and it dramatized the social context of a transactive curriculum. Questions of power and control clearly became curriculum issues.

The Future

The future of the Clive whole language culture is uncertain. School bureaucracies have demonstrated little tolerance for idiosyncratic ways of doing. In settings such as Clive Elementary, successful schooling comes from uniqueness. The culture at Clive cannot be replicated; it is generated from individual and collective understandings that arise as teachers are granted time, access to one another and to professional literature, and safety to experiment in their classrooms.

Whether or not the bureaucracy finds ways to understand and support such a culture remains to be seen. The continued evolution of this culture depends in part on the hospitality of the larger institution, its tolerance for diversity, and its willingness to view curriculum as a perpetually unfolding social phenomenon. Such support places a heavy burden on the institution because it challenges ways of doing and knowing that are deeply ingrained in public education. Support of a curriculum culture must also face political demands for accountability, which currently allow asocial, technical processes to place serious constraints on the teacher and the learner.

In addition, the culture must confront threats from within. Soon Louise and Mae will retire, and Clive teachers will lose powerful advocates and nurturers. How the group deals with these changes will greatly influence the shape of the culture in the future.

There remains, as well, the question of teachers' willingness to exert the necessary effort to hold institutional norms in abeyance. The energy of this whole language curriculum comes from a view of teaching that is both liberating and demanding. Teachers at Clive work very hard at what they do. They see their practice as evolutionary, their theory as speculative. Such a professional perspective is energizing but it is also exhausting. It would be easy to settle for a little less challenge, a little more comfort, to allow literacy teaching to be driven by formula. The culture will evolve only if teachers are willing to continue to challenge themselves, their students, and their organization. In the end, perhaps, the future of Clive's technical culture will depend on these teachers' willingness and ability to generate the right size storm.

References

Deal, Terrence E., and Allan A. Kennedy. 1982. *Corporate Cultures: The Rites and Rituals of Corporate Life.* Reading, Mass.: Addison-Wesley.

Devaney, Kathleen, and Gary Sykes. 1988. Making the case for professionalism. In *Building a Professional Culture in Schools,* ed. Ann Lieberman. New York: Teachers College Press.

Fulwiler, Toby, ed. 1987. *The Journal Book.* Portsmouth, N.H.: Boynton/Cook.

Lortie, Dan C. 1975. *Schoolteacher: A Sociological Study.* Chicago, Ill.: University of Chicago Press.

Martin, Nancy. April, 1990. Workshop on literacy. Cedar Rapids, Iowa.

9 | Uncovering the Power and Vulnerability of Whole Language

Heidi Mills, with Patricia Diederich and Sally Hale

With the collaboration of Patricia Diederich and Sally Hale, Heidi Mills documents how whole language came to be the driving force of Child Development Centers in Grand Rapids, Michigan. Mills describes how collaboration among administrators and teachers gave rise to this new emphasis within the Centers, demonstrates the power of whole language learning, and explains how the teachers' belief system was modified as they learned not only from each other, but most crucially from the children. As the title suggests, however, whole language teaching is vulnerable when administrators operating from a different belief system come into power, which is what happened in Grand Rapids. Thus, Mills describes the demise of whole language as the empowering philosophy within the Child Development Centers, and offers concluding lessons for teachers and administrators.

HEIDI MILLS is an assistant professor in elementary education at the University of South Carolina. She established a whole language curriculum for the Child Development Centers while working for the Grand Rapids Public School System in Grand Rapids, Michigan. Her major publications include *Portraits of Whole Language Classrooms: Learning for All Ages,* coedited with Jean Anne Clyde (Heinemann, 1990), *Living and Learning Mathematics: Stories and Strategies for Supporting Mathematical Literacy,* coauthored with David Whitin and Timothy O'Keefe (Heinemann, 1990), and *Uncovering the Role of Phonics in One Whole Language Classroom* with Timothy O'Keefe and Diane Stephens (NCTE, forthcoming).

PATRICIA DIEDERICH is currently a marketing representative for Integrated Learning Systems for Computer Curriculum Corporation. She established the Child Development Centers while working as Assistant Director of

Elementary Schools in Grand Rapids, Michigan. She worked for the Grand
Rapids Public Schools for fourteen years and moved through the ranks as
a teacher, principal, and supervisor of principals and programs.

SALLY HALE is an elementary principal and special education supervisor for the
Grand Rapids Public Schools, Grand Rapids, Michigan. During the time
described in the article, Sally served as the coordinator of the Child
Development Centers. She also worked for several years as an adjunct
professor for Grand Valley State University and Western Michigan University. She is currently a member of the Task Force for Strategic Planning of
School Improvement and Least Restrictive Environment.

* * *

In recent years, whole language has gained increasing popularity as a
legitimate philosophy that supports sound literacy instruction. Many
whole language educators are having a difficult time responding to
the large number of requests for courses, workshops, and in-services
on whole language theory and practice. As the calls come in, I am
filled with mixed feelings of promise and anxiety. I am pleased that
educators recognize the potential of this very powerful way of thinking, yet I am convinced that many do not truly understand the implications of the curricular shifts that must take place to ensure its
success. Through my own experiences as a public school teacher and
teacher-educator, I have come to realize that the complexity reaches
far beyond the classroom walls to the district office, local community,
and oftentimes the state legislature.

Whole Language: It's About Possibilities

Educators are dreamers. We dream of possibilities for our children,
our curriculum, and ourselves. And our dreams often come true in a
fairy-tale-like manner. While we realize that there are strong heroes
and heroines, we also recognize the fact that conflict is inevitable and
that there might be some characters in the story who are working
hard to undermine our success. Yet we believe that good prevails.

Unfortunately, fairy tales represent only one genre in life, as in
literature. My initial experience with whole language in a public
school setting began like a fairy tale, but it did not end happily ever
after. Yet like all good literature, our experiences in the Child Development Centers offer important lessons. I came to appreciate both the
power and vulnerability of whole language. My colleagues and I had

tremendous successes and devised many important strategies to support and maintain the growth of whole language. We also had some
difficulties that were equally revealing. It is my hope that our story
will assist others who are interested in supporting whole language.

Once Upon a Time

It was a cool spring day in Grand Rapids, Michigan. I had just completed my undergraduate degree at Indiana University and was interviewing with Patricia Diederich, the assistant director of elementary
programs, for an internship in the Alternative Schools Teacher Education Program through Indiana University. As soon as we began the
interview, it became clear that she was an accomplished and competent administrator who had developed many innovative educational programs. She described several, but I was most intrigued with
the Child Development Centers. They sounded better than ideal.
Being interested in the development of alternative schools, I asked Pat
to describe how they got started. She responded:

> My best ideas seem to come to me in the shower. I have choreo-
> graphed dances, conducted meetings, performed song and dance
> routines before spellbound audiences, and juggled budgets to
> achieve purchases most people thought impossible—all in the
> shower. Of course moving from the shower to the real world is a
> transition my ideas have not always made successfully. I am happy
> to report that the Child Development Centers made the transition. It
> was rough at times but well worth it.
>
> Soon after my appointment as Early Childhood Coordinator, I
> realized that there was some controversy among teachers and
> administrators about the delivery of early childhood education.
> After a great deal of thought, in and out of the shower, I decided to
> seek out a colleague, Sally Hale, to help me build my background in
> early childhood education and develop a model program for the
> district. We talked a lot about theory but had difficulty conceptualiz-
> ing how to make it happen. I knew we had new money; I wasn't
> sure how to spend it.
>
> Call it fate or guidance or whatever but somehow I happened
> across a book by Margaret Skutch. She had started her own center
> for young children. I read the book in one evening. The next morn-
> ing's shower brought CDC into view. I could see it all clearly as the
> water beat upon my head. But when the water stopped, I had to step
> back into the real world. That's when Sally and I began passing the

book around to some teachers we thought might like it. We all loved
it. We all talked and talked. I wanted the staff to have ownership if
we were going to develop a new program, so the group picked six
representatives and off they went to Connecticut to *experience*
Skutch's center. It really was what we wanted. And so the proposal
was written and approved.

I absolutely had to visit these sites. Pat said she would be happy to
give me a tour, but she did not have outside funding for an internship
position in the Child Development Centers.

When we entered the Roosevelt Child Development Center, I
could tell it was better than I dreamed it would be. In fact, it was
better than anything I had read about or seen on video in my education courses. I was impressed with the organization of the center, the
diverse range of experiences that were available to the children, and
the ways in which the teachers collaborated to create the curriculum.
As we toured the room, Pat reminded me that she had gathered her
strongest teachers together and invited them to create a model program reflecting their beliefs. I was intrigued by Pat's admiration, trust,
and respect for classroom teachers. She considered it her responsibility to support rather than direct their efforts.

The center had distinct curriculum areas set off by different colors
of carpeting. As we journeyed from the mathematics/cognitive area to
the language area, Pat paused. After thinking for a moment, she
remarked, "The language area is our only real concern because it
seems inconsistent with the other areas. We would like something
like 'language experience,' but we are not sure exactly what we are
looking for." I immediately began sharing what I knew about whole
language. I had recently taken three undergraduate language arts and
reading courses with Jerome Harste and so had developed a solid
belief system based on whole language assumptions.

Pat asked perceptive questions and made insightful observations.
She made frequent connections between the theory underpinning
whole language and the other curriculum areas. We talked briefly
with the teachers and then hurried across town to visit the Straight
Child Development Center.

Pat enthusiastically introduced me to the Straight staff and then
recommended that I explore the center by myself. I found the Straight
center as intriguing and educationally sound as Roosevelt. Both were
based on the same philosophy, but there were some differences
between them that helped me to realize they were much more than
programs of learning. At the same time, I agreed with Pat's observation

about the language area. Some of its activities seemed to focus on language skills in isolation.

The teachers in the centers were vibrant, supportive of the children, concerned about providing quality experiences, and above all, collaborative. I had never seen professionals work together so effectively. I am not sure how long I browsed through the various areas, but I remember Pat inviting me to talk to the teachers about whole language. They listened and, like Pat, responded from a solid understanding of the learning process. They seemed to think it made sense. They were familiar with the language experience approach but wanted more.

Pat and I returned to the central office to discuss internship positions. I vividly remember waiting for the elevator. I felt that Pat was a friend and colleague already. Much to my happy surprise, she asked if I would be interested in working with the teachers in the Child Development Centers to create a whole language curriculum. She said it would probably be best if I spent two-and-a-half days each week at both schools. I would also be responsible for helping teachers develop a knowledge base for whole language theory and practice. I was delighted. She and the teachers had decided that she should create a position for me to implement whole language in the centers. It was exactly what they had all been searching for. It was exactly what I had been searching for. And so the story of whole language in the Child Development Centers began.

The First Year

The First Staff Development Meeting

Pat devoted one of the initial in-service days to whole language and asked me to orchestrate the session. I conducted a sharing session in which we looked at what the children already knew about language as evidenced by writing samples I had collected during student teaching. As the teachers made observations, I attempted to connect them to the literature. Our discussion was grounded in research but informed by their insights about literacy growth. Most of the teachers and aides were very excited about the ideas they were considering. They had been making intuitive observations about how children learn for years. Now they were simply looking at literacy learning in light of what they knew about learning in general and making their beliefs explicit.

Several teachers still seemed skeptical, and they asked legitimate questions:

- How can children learn to read if they don't know their letters?
- What do you say when they ask you how to spell a word?
- How will parents respond when they see children using invented spelling?

I do not think I fully resolved their doubt during our initial session. It was the children who were most convincing.

The Children Arrived

We all worked together to create an inviting learning environment in both centers. Although we did share resources, teachers concentrated on their own curriculum areas. I created a reading center with predictable books and familiar children's literature and a writing and listening center, and provided writing folders.

As soon as the children arrived, I invited them to read and write and then provided opportunities for them to engage in the process. Some children balked initially, but it did not take long to convince them that they simply needed to use what they knew about written language to grow as readers and writers. It also became apparent right away that the children could learn from each other. They began making connections about letter-sound relationships by reading each other's names.

The children responded positively to their initial literacy experiences. It was common to find several children reading books together; writing a message, a story, or a class book; or listening to their favorite books on tape. They all had writing folders that housed their written pieces and my observations about their growth. As they demonstrated what they knew about language, the teachers began making comments that reflected their own growth. I remember one teacher, who was hesitant in the beginning, commenting, "I discovered that Kristina can read and she doesn't even know all of her letters yet!" Insights like this were shared during the daily "coaching" meetings, when one of the teachers or aides would reflect on his or her observations of colleagues at work with children. Coaching allowed us to learn from each other. We looked at what the children knew and then devised strategies to build the curriculum from there. We also began to focus on ways in which reading and writing could be integrated into other curriculum areas. My colleagues began working with children to make number books, books about field trips, and science books related to thematic units.

Parents also responded to their children's love for reading and writing in positive ways. Although many were unsure of the unconventional writing at first, they soon appreciated the logical, systematic, and rule-governed nature of the children's thinking. We held individual parent conferences to share the children's writing folders and describe the progress their children were making. We also published class newsletters that demonstrated what early writing looks like. The newsletters provided the children an authentic audience and helped parents track their children's growth over time. Additionally, the centers had monthly potluck dinners attended by hundreds of family members. Sometimes children read predictable books or stories they had written. At other times, they made patterns or graphs and shared them with their parents. The most informative sessions seemed to be those in which the parents would play shadow to their child and actually engage in the same experiences the children did each day. The parents developed a realistic appreciation of the learning potential of the center's curriculum during such meetings. They realized how complicated it was to put a puzzle together, to author a book, and to run through an obstacle course.

The Evolution of Our Belief System

To truly appreciate the essence of whole language in the centers, it is necessary to examine the evolution of the beliefs that underpinned daily instruction. There were several key assumptions that initially drove our thinking:

- Children learn to read and write in the same ways they learn to speak and listen.
- Children learn to read and write by reading and writing.
- It is important to understand and value the process, since the product may not show us what the children know or how they come to know.
- Children learn from demonstrations and engagement in the process.
- Form develops through functional use.

These beliefs were grounded in early literacy research (Baghban 1984; Bissex 1980; Calkins 1986; Clyde 1986; DeFord 1980; Harste,

Woodward, and Burke 1984; Goodman and Goodman 1979; Graves 1983; Halliday 1975; Heath 1983; King 1982; Lindfors 1987; Taylor 1983; Watson 1980) and our own observations of children in the centers. We were careful to carve out a curriculum that reflected our beliefs, yet we understood the importance of remaining open to changes that would emerge from new insights about the learning process.

Initially, we transformed our theoretical notions about literacy into an immersion curriculum. We devoted most of our energy to the development of a print-rich curriculum that was functional in nature. In addition to well-stocked reading and writing centers, we capitalized on opportunities to integrate reading and writing into all facets of the program. The housekeeping area provided many literacy-based materials, such as phone books, note pads, and empty food containers. As soon as one of our students began playing "restaurant" in the area, we added menus and tickets. We also developed a realistic version of the corner grocery store. We labeled the entire center using the children's language. We encouraged them to write or dictate stories about pictures they painted in art or patterns they made in the math area. We extended literacy to the general movement room by labeling the obstacle courses and inviting children to compose stories to correspond to the block structures they created.

We knew children learned to talk by talking and wanted to provide them with opportunities to engage in open-ended literacy experiences for the same reason. The children's responses far exceeded our expectations. Most of them seemed to find their strides as readers and writers early on. Their folders housed at least one writing sample a week. For months, we marveled at their growth and were content with our curricular decisions. We certainly did not stop creating new reading and writing opportunities, but we did not do much more than that. We believed that if we immersed our students in print they would grow.

Well, they did grow. As Frank Smith (1988) says, we can't stop learning; it is as natural as breathing. However, I think we took the emphasis on *learning naturally* too literally. We were hesitant to provide information about language because we did not want to inhibit risk-taking. Our hesitation came to an abrupt end when we began noticing how much the children were teaching each other while engaging in the process. Then we began talking about language just as the children did. To do this in authentic ways, we began reading and writing with the children. As we composed our own texts or read for our own purposes we simply began commenting on our thinking about the print. We took Donald Graves's (1983) advice and only highlighted one primary feature at a time to ensure a focus on meaning. The children responded with interest. Soon they began adding their own comments. As we wrote messages for the message board, we would highlight various concepts we felt would benefit the children. We could be heard saying:

- "I am leaving spaces between my words so it will be easier for you to read my message."
- "I am using a capital "S" for *Shamika* because we always begin names with capital letters."
- "I think I will change this word because I use it too often. What is another word I could use for *exciting*?"

Reflecting on our successes with highlighting "skills in context" in our own writing, we transferred this strategy to the children's work. We did so by capitalizing on children's insights about language and formally sharing them with the class. We also used children's literature to help our students focus on the various features and functions of print. Although we had not yet heard of "mini-lessons" (Atwell 1987; Calkins 1986), we basically devised our own version of this strategy.

By the end of the first year, we truly realized the importance of "kid-watching" (Y. Goodman 1978). Although we were impressed with our students' growth, the closer we looked, the more we could see. We saw the value of making instructional decisions based on our observations of learning in progress. As we carefully reflected on our students' strategies, we began to create specific strategy lessons for individuals and small groups. The strategy lessons were intended to help children expand or refine their current reading and writing strategies.

Although our beliefs originated in the professional literature, it was our children who pushed us to revise these beliefs and with them our curricular decisions. As we watched our students and carefully reflected on the meaning of their actions, we saw the benefits and limitations of an immersion curriculum. In the end, the environment was still "littered with print" (Harste, Woodward, and Burke 1984), but we had grown to understand that there was much more to an effective literacy curriculum. By the second year, our beliefs had undergone significant revision. Some of our original notions still seemed to hold true, yet we had learned so much through our teaching that our beliefs were transformed. We believed that:

- Language is a meaning-based system in which all cue systems (syntax, graphophonics, and semantics) operate in concert to support the meaning-making process.
- Learning to read and write is as natural as learning to talk and is accomplished through engagement and demonstrations.
- Literacy is multimodal (involving alternative sign systems such as art, music, drama, and mathematics).
- Literacy involves being strategic, that is, using what we know in new and inventive ways.
- Strategic thinkers use language to reflect upon, organize, manipulate, share, and extend their experiences.
- Miscues are often signs of growth.
- Writing growth is not a linear process; what is learned is a function of the child's experiences, needs, and interests at the time.

During this time we added a third center in the district, Shawnee Park Child Development Center. A description of a typical day in one of the centers during our second year is provided in *Portraits of Whole Language Classrooms* (Mills and Clyde 1990). It details these and other core beliefs that guided our practice for the remaining time that whole language was central to our curriculum.

The Importance of Collaboration

We expanded and refined our beliefs for three years. The more we worked together, the more we learned from each other. One of the teachers who was most reluctant in the beginning turned out to be a strong whole language advocate who created very interesting invitations to reading and writing, and an appealing and well-organized reading and writing center. Once we had a chance to share our beliefs and test our hypotheses about children's literacy learning we all grew together daily.

Coaching opportunities helped tremendously. Teachers were observed by their colleagues on a daily basis. The observer was called the "coach." This role was shared by all staff members on a rotating basis. The coach carefully watched his or her colleagues interact with the children, and after school the staff met to share their observations. The coaching observations always followed a "three pluses and a wish" format: the coach highlighted three positive features of the experience and then added a wish or a goal for the child, teacher, or lesson. In this way, the teachers continually learned from one another by recognizing supportive teaching strategies, asking questions, telling stories of success, and considering various ways to teach concepts or demonstrate strategies.

The administrators built in a half day of planning time for all the teachers every week. On Wednesdays the staff met to discuss the children, their growth, and their needs. We also planned upcoming curricular experiences. The opportunity to meet together every week to discuss the children and the curriculum was critical to our success. We shared strategies that worked and problems we had encountered, and we made attempts to provide continuity within and across curriculum areas. Sally Hale, the center director, was always in attendance. She played a key role in facilitating the development of the curriculum. She supported us in the same ways that we were attempting to support children's growth. She listened to our needs, made positive observations, nudged us to consider new ideas, and provided necessary resources. I think Sally helped most by showing us that she was a learner too. Just as we were learning from the children, she made sincere efforts to learn about whole language from us. Although she was an administrator, she spent a great deal of time in the classroom and made connections between whole language and her background in early childhood and special education. Like Pat, Sally empowered the teachers as curricular decision-makers, but in the process she learned as much as she could about whole language so that she could effectively support its growth.

The centers made many of their curricular decisions independently. This made sense in light of the fact that we were developing specific activities based on children's needs and interests. It would have been a violation of the centers' philosophy for all three centers to look exactly alike. They were united instead by a common philosophy but were allowed to apply it in their own ways.

All three centers did collaborate to create formal descriptions of the program and to make decisions that would affect each site. Most of the group endeavors were quite productive, and it was helpful to get a variety of perspectives on topics of mutual interest. One exception occurred when the district purchased computers for the centers. The computers were intended to help us with record-keeping and to provide the office of curriculum and evaluation with information to compare growth in our program with that in Montessori programs and in traditional kindergartens. Although it sounded good in the beginning, as soon as we were required to develop a set of behavioral objectives to match our curriculum, things began to deteriorate. To begin with, it was impossible to devise behavioral objectives that were theoretically consistent with a process-based curriculum. We tried and we tried. Although I think we did a good job, considering the constraints under which we were operating, the objectives had a negative effect on our work with children. Suddenly, we began to focus more on the items on the list and less on the learning or the learners. We spent a lot of time simply determining whether or not a child had accomplished an objective. This meant less time to spend on teaching and observing authentic learning. Once the data was collected, it were stored in the computer. It soon became apparent that we were spending an incredible amount of time gathering the information and then logging it into the computer. Unfortunately, the computer that was supposed to help make record-keeping more efficient and informative simply told us what we already knew. As always, we took our concerns to Pat and Sally. Pat reflected on our dilemma and made a recommendation. She had used a significant amount of money from her budget to purchase the computers and train the teachers and aides. She had also made a commitment to her colleagues to provide evidence that the children were learning in the centers. Consequently, she needed to think strategically about her decision. Pat's character and devotion to the center came through once again when she shared her plan with the staff. She recommended that we donate the computers to the gifted and talented school for the children's use and suggested that we make our own decisions about record-keeping.

What Made the Difference

For three years whole language thrived in the centers. In fact, Jerry Harste still writes about the program. He believes we were addressing issues years ago that other sites have not yet considered. Our success was not incidental. Teachers, parents, and administrators played complementary roles in thoughtful ways.

Several threads interweave throughout our story. While the fabric of the curriculum was constantly shaped and reshaped by the participants, there were elements that remained constant, and the success of the program was due in large part to their existence. One of the most critical features of the curriculum was the fact that the *belief system* emerged directly from the teachers and administrators. Of course it was grounded in current research and successful programs elsewhere, but the centers were unique. We made the theory our own. We were empowered as curricular decision-makers. The visit to Margaret Skutch's classroom had a tremendous influence on our thinking and subsequent actions. Yet, the centers were far from templates of hers. The same was true for whole language. We did not attempt to adopt a formulaic view of whole language or adjust the program to fit it. Instead, whole language theory meshed naturally with our general philosophy, and it emerged with the curriculum in general. In fact, over time whole language became the driving theoretical force, informing much more than just the language arts curriculum. We soon came to realize that our interest in whole language really served as an avenue to help us better understand the learning process in general.

Collaboration among all staff members, teachers, aides, and administrators was also critical to the evolution of our belief system. We all had a common vision and were committed to it without compromise. This was possible because of the "hand picked" staff and the time built into the daily life of the classroom for collaboration. We were given time to plan, reflect, share insights and strategies, and develop instructional materials.

The collaboration went far beyond adult interactions. The teachers planned *with*, not simply *for*, children. We followed the children's lead when making curricular decisions. This stance on curricular decision-making evolved from a focus on learners and learning. We strove to support rather than direct learning. During long-term planning meetings, daily lesson planning sessions, coaching meetings, and work time with the children, the emphasis was always what was best for the children, not what might be easiest or most convenient for the staff. Although it took a tremendous amount of planning, the centers operated with ease. We frequently stepped back during the day and marveled at the functional nature of the curriculum and the responsible ways in which the children were responding to instructional invitations.

The strong *parent involvement* component of the curriculum also made a difference. The parents were much more than well informed about the philosophy underlying the curriculum. They actually took part in curricular experiences when possible and were visited at home at least twice a year. Because the parents were respected and valued, they were invited to be co-collaborators in their children's education. Activities like the monthly potluck dinners and monthly family days led to the creation of a parent group that was comfortable with the program and intensely involved in it. We often hear teachers say that they cannot implement whole language because of the parents. But we received tremendous support from parents. They were delighted to see how we were building on the knowledge the children brought from home, attending to what their children knew rather than what they did not know. They appreciated the fact that we could always articulate what, how, and most importantly *why* we were making various curricular decisions. They reacted with interest and joy when we pulled out their children's writing folders to explain how we were tracking their growth and making future plans based on our observations. We found parents to be among our greatest advocates. Though the first two centers were housed in low- to middle-income areas of the city, it did not take long for parents in the more affluent locations to begin requesting access to the Child Development Centers. Hence, the creation of Shawnee Park Child Development Center.

Another essential component of the curriculum was an *informed and supportive administration.* Unlike many situations in which teachers must devise whole language curricula independent of their administrators, the administrators in the Child Development Centers gave birth to the curriculum and nourished it continually. They worked with the teachers in the same ways the teachers worked with the children. They supported rather than directed the program. They trusted the teachers as competent decision-makers and gave them the time and resources necessary to put their beliefs into operation. The administrators did not make decisions about the centers without teacher input. They worked together with teachers to determine what would be in the best interests of the children. Sally spent a great deal of time in the centers, so she was sensitive to the teachers' perspectives. She did not impose mandates that would not make sense. Instead, we all considered the district regulations and devised strategies for compliance in our own ways. We were responsible for helping children succeed on their end-of-the-year test and make a smooth transition to first grade, but we were not willing to compromise our curriculum throughout the year.

Each center devised strategies that would help children translate what they knew about how language and mathematics work in authentic situations to a contrived test. We also decided to devote the last two weeks of school to what we called a transition period. Those children who were being promoted to first grade were grouped together. We turned the general movement room into a classroom with tables and chairs. There, the children worked together on traditional school tasks. We also took the kindergarten children on tours of local first-grade classrooms to acquaint them with the rules, work, and structure they were likely to find there. Although many of the rooms were drastically different from what we considered to be sound learning environments, we wanted the children to be successful in them. We had intriguing discussions with them about the similarities and differences between how they worked in the centers and what their first-grade colleagues were doing. Their insights were validated and extended to best prepare them for the year ahead of them. We found this strategy to be extremely effective because it allowed us to remain true to our convictions throughout the year and yet provided the children the chance to envision and experience the more traditional schoolwork they would encounter in years to come. The administration wholeheartedly supported such strategies. When the issue of success in first grade arose, we were given the freedom to create our own alternatives. It was the administration that ensured continuous staff development. The ongoing opportunities to learn from each other directly contributed to the professional atmosphere that pervaded our lives.

Whole language gave the curriculum a focus. The general movement teachers began labeling the obstacle courses; the mathematics/cognitive area teachers encouraged children to use oral and written language to construct graphs and conduct surveys; the science/sensory area teachers had book-making sessions in which children published their own stories about the birds they had been studying or special art projects. Language was intricately woven into all of the curricular experiences. It was this feature of the curriculum that enabled connections to be made between and across experiences. Reading and writing became tools for learning. Most importantly, whole language became a lens through which we better understood the learning process in general.

This story would not be accurate without a tribute to the children. It was the diversity in age, culture, and economic background that made our classrooms interesting places to live and learn. The cross-age grouping naturally demonstrated the value of learning from each other. The large Hispanic population afforded us the opportunity to have rich bilingual experiences. Many children who came to us knowing very little English soon became experts when they were invited to teach us Spanish. There was a large American Indian population at one site, and we had the privilege of seeing their culture through their eyes. The whole language curriculum encouraged all voices to be heard, and it was the children's insights and ideas that gave the curriculum its power.

What Happened: The Downfall of Whole Language in the Child Development Centers

I wish I could conclude this story like a fairy tale, but unfortunately it did not have a happy ending. The programs are still in operation and they provide good experiences for children. But over time they have lost their spirit and commitment to whole language. In other words, the power of our shared belief system was short-lived.

After working for three years in the Child Development Centers, I decided to go back to Indiana University to pursue my doctorate with Jerry Harste and Carolyn Burke. I found my work with the teachers so intriguing that I wanted to move into teacher education. When I left the centers, whole language seemed to be in place. The staff had remained relatively stable and the teachers, aides, and administrators all had a solid working understanding of the theory.

The following year the district underwent drastic changes. In fact, the superintendent left, which made all of the alternative schools within the district vulnerable. Some programs were cut immediately, regardless of their successes. There was a new emphasis in the district: back to the basics. The Child Development Centers were spared but were significantly altered. Until then, the teachers were hired according to their qualifications for the position, which meant much more to us than a teaching certificate. We were concerned with the beliefs that lay behind their practices, their ability to collaborate, their understanding of the learning process. Once a new administration was in place, positions were filled based on seniority. This single move was the beginning of the end. Teachers and aides requesting transfers to the centers did not have a philosophical base consistent with the program.

The whole language curriculum began to crumble under a largely new staff that did not share the beliefs of the veteran teachers. The teachers who remained tried desperately to salvage our curriculum but soon found that it looked like a skills-based program with "whole language activities." The staff began thinking on the activity level. They continued to *do* message board, written conversation, book making, graphs, and so on, but the activities were ends in themselves rather than strategies for communication, reflection, and learning. The principles that initially made the strategies effective were lost. The same activities were used in different ways and for different purposes. As teachers' beliefs changed, so did classroom activities.

Other things also occurred that influenced the shift to an activity-level orientation. The adult-child ratio at the centers increased and the budget was cut. All of the kindergarten children in the district were required to complete workbooks and reading series in a very structured manner. Suddenly, the teachers were no longer empowered as curricular decision-makers. The central administration was dictating how, what, and when to teach and sending monitors around to make sure that teachers were covering the material at the appropriate rate. Pat became very discouraged and left the district. Sally was transferred to another school against her will. Teachers no longer had an advocate at the district level.

The workbook mandate was far too restrictive for even the "whole language dress up curriculum" (White 1990). In an attempt to maintain the integrity of the program, the centers stopped serving kindergarten children. It was a sad time, but they simply could not operate as they wanted with such rigid constraints.

Sally Hale, the Child Development Coordinator, details the specific events that transpired:

> A series of problems in the district began to emerge which led to changes in the original structure of the program. Money was a major factor. While the seventies and early eighties had seen a period of economic stability in Michigan, and thus rapid growth and expansion in public schools, especially large urban districts, it came to an end about 1983–84. Cutbacks included the loss of ancillary and consulting staffs and some of our new innovative teachers. In addition, some administrative changes altered the program significantly. Lost teachers and assistants were replaced according to union contract, which, of course, was based on seniority. Staff assignments were no longer based on the knowledge and expertise of child development or whole language.
>
> The increasing demand for accountability as measured through student outcomes based on standardized test scores was in direct conflict with our philosophy. Pressure was being brought about to "push" young children harder and faster into "academic" skills by utilizing a curriculum that was the same throughout the district (i.e., basal readers, etc.). District curriculum mandates were, at that time, defined by the textbooks.
>
> Because a number of original staff members were being replaced and because of the philosophical changes that were beginning to occur in the district, the other visionaries became disenchanted and began to matriculate out of the program.
>
> While three primary Child Development Centers still exist within the open space environment and many of the elements remain, the educational focus is quite different, particularly as it relates to whole language. Reading and writing, while not totally changed,

are much more focused on isolated skill development rather than the holistic approach integrating reading, writing, and language naturally, using the child's language to build upon. Fortunately, however, there is a great resurgence in the writing process and our district is examining that very closely. Unfortunately, the approach is still materials- and companies-driven rather than child-driven, so again this represents a splintered approach to language and communication.

In all fairness, the program is still a wonderful educational option for children, but it lacks the framework under which the original curriculum was developed. We were subject to the fragilities of the system.

The Child Development Centers Today

Last year I was invited back to conduct a two-day in-service with the Child Development Center staffs. It had been several years since I left and I was not sure what I would see. I was deeply committed to the centers. I had learned more from the teachers and children there than from any other aspect of my career. I was excited yet very nervous, because I knew that the original teachers wanted me to come to help them reestablish whole language in the centers, and it was clear that there was a diverse range of philosophical positions among the new faculty.

Sally had a lovely gathering for me the evening I arrived. Although many of the teachers and aides had left the centers, some still remained. We told stories about the "good old days." We all seemed to feel as if our time together during that brief three-year period was truly magical. We had been in what Evelyn Hannsen calls "curricular heaven." We had power, commitment, and support. We were learners, and we developed authentically collaborative relationships with our colleagues, parents, children, and administrators. To this day, we all agree that we have never again experienced the satisfaction that came with our positions during that time.

It was an eerie feeling to walk into the centers again. They looked wonderful! The children were not there, so they did not have the sense of life that I remembered so fondly, yet the centers did look very consistent with the original design. But . . . it soon became apparent that though they were alike on the surface level, our philosophy had been lost through district mandates and personnel changes. The staff seemed to be operating on the "activity level." They still did "whole language activities," but that was the extent of the curriculum. As I spoke with individual teachers, it was clear that many of the veterans still held on to the essence of the belief system. My heart sank as we shared the writing samples of some of students at the centers to discuss how children learn to write. Years earlier in that same place the teachers were pushing me to see more in our children's thinking, and now we were struggling with basic issues like the value of invented spelling and correcting children's grammar. I was stunned when a teacher proclaimed that we would be encouraging children to make mistakes if we did not provide immediate feedback and correction. Oh no, how could this be?

This tale is sad but true. I doubt very seriously whether my brief workshop had much impact on the curriculum. How could it? It took us years to create the optimal program. We had ownership, time, and the support necessary to understand, develop, and put into operation a whole language belief system. And it was the children who made the critical difference. How could these teachers appreciate what I was telling them? They needed to see for themselves, just as we had. But in order to learn from our children we must allow them opportunities to show us what they know and build the curriculum from there. How could these teachers experience the power of the philosophy, track the children's literacy growth over time, and celebrate their accomplishments without opening up the curriculum enough to allow children to show them how to teach?

Insights into the Change Process

Change is at the heart of whole language. And while we often focus on changes that occur inside our classrooms, we do not operate in isolation. Through telling my own story, I have come to realize the significance of the process that either supports or restricts the growth of whole language. Just as we must understand the learning process and learners to create supportive whole language curricula, we must also consider the process that shapes and reshapes our teaching.

- Change is not unidirectional: it both reflects and stimulates modifications in our beliefs. Sometimes a new insight leads to informed instructional practice. At other times we might need to implement a strategy lesson and watch our learners carefully to appreciate fully the theoretical implications of the experience.
- The change process is ongoing. There is no one way to begin whole language or to develop it. Because we are continually

learning from our teaching, we encounter new beginnings frequently. Many of our experiences connect with what we currently know, but those that are anomalous push us to outgrow
our current thinking and revise our instructional invitations. A
new group of children, a new insight, or a new strategy all hold
possibilities for the development of a deeper understanding of the
teaching-learning process.

- Whole language cannot be mandated. Since our actions reflect
  our beliefs, teachers must own the philosophy in their hearts and
  minds. Whole language will flourish when we support teachers'
  growth in the same ways we expect them to support the growth
  of learners. Whole language classrooms are democratic in nature
  and professional decisions must also be made democratically to
  avoid violating the key assumptions that shape the philosophy.
- Collaboration among all participants is crucial to the establishment of a community of learners. Parents, teachers, administrators, and children all play key roles in the process. All facets of the
  support system must attempt to operate in concert to realize the
  potential of this philosophy. Traditional public school power
  structures dissolve in truly collaborative relationships. It is absolutely essential that different perspectives be heard and valued.
- Just as reflection leads to strategic learning in our classrooms,
  reflection also leads to strategic teaching. Teachers need time to
  reflect and plan. We urge teachers to make time for things they
  value in the curriculum. We need to do the same for them. Significant blocks of time need to be built into the daily life of our
  schools so that teachers can share success stories, pose questions,
  swap resources, or consider the underlying meaning of a particular child's response to an experience. Teachers also need time to
  think and plan independently in an environment free of distrac-
  tions. We provide such rights for our students; we teachers also
  benefit from such working environments. In addition, ongoing
  staff development strategies like "coaching" contribute to teacher
  growth. There is a great deal we can learn from each other if we
  devise ways to collaborate formally and informally.
- If outside forces mandate specific instructional objectives, teachers need the freedom, respect, and support to devise strategies to
  "uncover" rather than cover the curriculum. We all work under
  diverse conditions. Each context conveys a set of possibilities as
  well as constraints. Too often teachers are required to compromise their own beliefs and accept the beliefs of those in power.

And too often those beliefs are grounded in concerns about testing and management. Teachers must act each day. We cannot afford to wait for the tests or textbooks to improve or the legislature to become enlightened. We must encourage teachers to respond to constraints in their own ways. We undercut their professionalism when we impose specific teaching and testing strategies on them.

- Teachers who work in whole language schools must be considered in light of their expertise and interest in learning rather than their years of seniority. Although teachers are continuously growing and may be at different places in their understanding of whole language, there are characteristics that unite these teachers and allow them to move forward. Teachers must trust children as learners and must trust themselves as curricular decision-makers. Only then will they learn to trust the process. Teachers who hold a model that privileges teaching over learning will find it very difficult to open up the curriculum enough to allow the children to show them how they learn. It is this shared belief system that gives whole language power, and teachers in a whole language school must share and shape its potential.

- Administrators must support the development of a shared belief system among teachers, but it is not enough to relinquish all responsibility for curriculum. Although we believe it is essential for curriculum to be in the hands of the teachers and students, administrators play a key role in the success of the process. Administrators who share the whole language belief system, or who are at least willing to learn from and with teachers, will make the critical difference. When administrators function as learners and share authority with teachers, entire schools can be transformed.

Reliving the Fairy Tale

Good literature touches our hearts and minds. And after we finish a good book, it lives on and influences our thinking for years to come. So too with my teaching experiences in Grand Rapids. Although it has been years since I left, I learned lessons there that still influence my living and learning. It was there that I learned how to understand and interpret children's growth, how to plan for children's needs and interests, how to collaborate with colleagues, and how to grow as a teacher. In this way, the fairy tale lives on.

References

Atwell, Nancie. 1987. *In the Middle: Writing, Reading, and Learning with Adolescents.* Portsmouth, N.H.: Boynton/Cook.

Baghban, Marcia J. 1984. *Our Daughter Learns to Read and Write: A Case Study from Birth to Three.* Newark, Del.: International Reading Association.

Bissex, Glenda. 1980. *GNYS AT WRK: A Child Learns to Read and Write.* Cambridge, Mass.: Harvard University Press.

Calkins, Lucy McCormick. 1986. *The Art of Teaching Writing.* Portsmouth, N.H.: Heinemann.

Clyde, Jean Anne. 1986. Talking on paper: Exploring the potential for a quality language experience. *Forum in Reading and Language Education* 2:1–10.

DeFord, Diane E. 1980. Young children and their writing. *Theory into Practice* 19:157–62.

Goodman, Kenneth S., and Yetta M. Goodman. 1979. Learning to read is natural. In *Theory and Practice of Early Reading.* Vol. 2. Edited by L. B. Resnick and P. A. Weaver. Hillsdale, N.J.: Erlbaum.

Goodman, Yetta M. June 1978. Kid watching: An alternative to testing. *National Elementary School Principal* 57: 41–45.

Graves, Donald H. 1983. *Writing: Teachers and Children at Work.* Portsmouth, N.H.: Heinemann.

Halliday, Michael A. K. 1975. *Learning How to Mean: Explorations in the Development of Language.* London: Edward Arnold.

Harste, Jerome C., Virginia A. Woodward, and Carolyn L. Burke. 1984. *Language Stories and Literacy Lessons.* Portsmouth, N.H.: Heinemann.

Heath, Shirley B. 1983. *Ways with Words.* Cambridge: Cambridge University Press.

King, Martha L. 1982. Language foundations for writing: A research perspective. Speech given at the Language in Education Conference, Ohio State University.

Lindfors, Judith W. 1987. Perspectives on language acquisition. In *Children's Language and Learning.* 2nd ed. Englewood Cliffs, N.J.: Prentice-Hall.

Mills, Heidi, and Jean Anne Clyde, eds. 1990. *Portraits of Whole Language Classrooms: Learning for All Ages.* Portsmouth, N.H.: Heinemann.

Smith, Frank. 1988. *Joining the Literacy Club: Further Essays into Education.* Portsmouth, N.H.: Heinemann.

Taylor, Denny. 1983. *Family Literacy: Young Children Learning to Read and Write.* Portsmouth, N.H.: Heinemann.

Watson, Dorothy J. 1980. Whole language for whole children. Paper presented at the Third Annual Reading Conference, Columbia, Mo.

White, Connie. 1990. *Jenon Doesn't Sit at the Back Anymore.* New York: Scholastic.

10 | The Bureaucratic Undoing of a Whole Language School

Jane Doe

In this article, Jane Doe documents the rise, fall, and eventual restoration of whole language at East Meadow School. When East Meadow was officially declared a whole language bilingual school in 1980, the parents, teachers, and principal acted upon the whole language tenet of shared responsibility and decision-making, forming a coalition to work together to improve education for the school's children and their families. All of their successes were undermined, however, by a new principal whose actions reflected a traditional belief in the power of his office, not in the power of shared authority. The author describes in heart rending detail how matters went from bad to worse with yet another principal—until he was replaced by a principal willing to listen to and learn from the teachers. As the story of East Meadow demonstrates, the principal's commitment to collaboration and the sharing of power and authority among all members of the school community is critical to the success of whole language.

NOTE: The events described in this chapter are true. But to protect those involved, all proper names have been changed to pseudonyms, including all place names and the name of the author.

* * *

Fundamental to whole language is the teacher professionalism it engenders. It redefines the role of teachers both inside and outside the classroom. Whole language teachers throw off the shackles of textbooks and management systems; they reject the inauthentic assessment of standardized tests. Drawing on their understanding of language and learning, of curriculum and pedagogy, they engage in classroom inquiry, taking their instructional and curricular cues from their students. Learning experiences arise not from the pages of textbooks or from programmed curricula but from the needs and interests of the students.

Another primary feature of whole language is collaboration between home and school. As Ken Goodman (1991) writes, "parents and teachers work together to expand on the home culture and to extend the learning horizons of all members of the school community." Parents play a central role in helping to shape the curriculum and the policies of a whole language school.

But the process is not always painless. As school faculties adopt new ways, they often encounter opposition from those with power and influence who resist change, particularly change in the belief system that accords them their power. The resulting conflict can easily damage the developing whole language culture. Serious damage of this nature occurred at East Meadow School, where I worked as a whole language consultant in the late eighties. My purpose in this chapter is to examine the East Meadow conflict and consider what teachers and administrators can learn from it.

Up from Failure

Housed in a sprawling, salmon pink stucco building resembling a cigar factory, East Meadow School is surrounded by pitted asphalt and a littered playing field. Dilapidated apartment buildings line the streets across from the school, their balconies obscured by piles of clothes and other belongings that won't fit inside the small, cramped apartments. East Meadow is the poorest school in the area, a working-class community in a metropolitan area. East Meadow parents are largely Hispanic, monolingual Spanish-speakers who are recent immigrants from war-torn El Salvador and Nicaragua or economic refugees from Mexico. Many have never had access to schools; some cannot read or write. Their children initially mirror this lack of formal education. Some of the older children entering East Meadow have never attended school, and virtually none of the students have had any kind of educational head start.

In the mid-seventies, such students seemed frustratingly hard to reach. At East Meadow, the traditional instructional fare of basals and textbooks produced poor results. Test scores placed the students three to four years below grade level. In the spring of 1975, the State Department of Education, alarmed by the low scores, sent a team to investigate, initiating several years of soul-searching on the part of the teachers. Elaine Johnson, the former resource teacher, read *Dark Ghetto* by Kenneth Clark (1965) and found in it "proof that schools in much worse situations than ours could be successful." She began to guide the faculty toward ideas and practices that eventually coalesced into whole language.

Led by Johnson, the teachers read professional literature, consulted with educational experts, and searched for more appropriate instructional strategies and curriculum. In 1978, inspired by a visit to Marie Shroyer's psycholinguistic reading program in a nearby school, East Meadow teachers opened a psycholinguistic reading room for fourth, fifth, and sixth graders. Students were invited to choose their reading from a range of high quality children's and adolescent literature. Faculty hopes rose as reading test scores increased dramatically, and with the help of outside consultants the school moved to adopt whole language and bilingualism schoolwide. The support of Superintendent Edmund H. Stone and a sensitive and informed school board president, Joan Hendrick, coupled with a generous grant from ChemTech, a neighborhood corporation, made their dream a reality: in 1980, East Meadow was officially declared a whole language bilingual school.

Johnson recalls this as a most exciting time. Teachers gladly gave up their Saturdays to attend workshops, they made trips to book distributors and began to build their classroom libraries, they filled the teachers' room with energetic discussions about the growth they were seeing in their students and in themselves. In addition to the changes that were taking place in the classrooms, positive, exciting changes were also occurring outside, in the school community. Under the guidance of Manuel Garcia, the father of five and a janitor at Glendale, East Meadow's sister school, parents, teachers, and the principal, Tim Elliot, formed a strong coalition and began to discuss how they could work together in their effort to change conditions at East Meadow. The group felt that many of the problems students encountered in school were related to their parents' lack of formal education. In an attempt to meet the challenge of parent education, an ambitious program, Project Family Learning, was launched. Parents and their children attended classes at East Meadow twice a week; babysitters were provided for the little ones, so that for two hours, parents and their older children could devote their time to learning English and developing their literacy skills.

While the teachers were building this thriving whole language culture, they were becoming empowered professionals. They worked hard at exploring their own personal literacy and expanding their understanding of language and learning theory. They published chapters and articles in professional books and journals. They pursued master's degrees, participated in summer courses and workshops, conducted workshops themselves on the local, state, and national level, and often assumed a leadership role in the school district. In 1989, they were featured in a nationally telecast PBS documentary about successful school programs.

Principal Tim Elliot not only supported the teachers' developing professionalism, he also encouraged it, inviting them to assume leadership roles in the school and community. Elaine Johnson suggested that he meet with Marie Shroyer, a teacher in a neighboring school who had abandoned basals in favor of quality children's literature, which formed the heart of her reading curriculum. After his meeting with Shroyer, Elliot agreed that a similar change would work well at East Meadow. He helped the teachers organize a parent meeting, invited Johnson to present the proposal to the parents, and then, working through a translator, asked the parents to share their thoughts and feelings about the adoption of children's literature. Every step of the way, he used his authority to invite others into the decision-making process. He recognized Johnson's visionary leadership and encouraged her to guide the school toward a student-centered pedagogy. He also recognized the critical need for professional development and worked hard to provide both the time and the funds for intensive in-service workshops. And as an open, committed learner himself, he was an active participant in all the in-service sessions.

This parent-teacher-administrator coalition, coupled with a deep commitment to whole language, brought notable changes to the school. Johnson interviewed Delphine Wilder, the first teacher to staff the reading room, and gives this account of the students' positive response:

> Kids loved coming to the reading room. They came at P.E. time, during recess, and even during classroom parties and school dances. They came after school and wanted to borrow books to take home. The first year and a half we lost hundreds of books—and Delphine was delighted. No one had ever taken a basal reader home to keep.

A final note on this rise to success: it was not accomplished by a completely harmonious faculty. As in any human institution, unforeseen problems arose. A schism developed between whole language and bilingualism that nearly brought the school down. Teachers who were ardent supporters of bilingual education mistakenly viewed whole language as a threat to bilingualism and boycotted in-service sessions that were devoted to furthering the faculty's understanding of whole language. Other teachers failed to understand the active, creative role of a whole language educator and functioned as passive observers in their own classrooms, short-circuiting their students' development. These problems were openly discussed and debated, and as time passed they diminished.

Administrative Trouble

More serious because they did not diminish but increased with time were the problems involving two principals who worked successively at East Meadow after Tim Elliot moved to the district office in 1983. (Elaine Johnson and I have written to them inviting them to contribute their views to this chapter, but they have not responded.)

Soon after the first principal, George Beal, arrived at East Meadow, he began to emphasize the traditional authority of his office and to wage a covert power struggle with Johnson and other whole language teachers. The conflict often manifested itself in petty ways. Johnson compiled a bibliography of professional whole language books to hand out to the many educators who visited the school; Beal transferred the bibliography to his computer files and deleted her name. This was only the first of several incidents in which he claimed teacher-authored contributions as his own. Johnson listed the strengths and weaknesses of the school's commitment to whole language and developed a detailed action plan for strengthening that commitment; Beal complimented her efforts and then buried the plan. Although the superintendent had agreed that Johnson and the East Meadow faculty should be involved in the hiring of new teachers as a way to assure a continued commitment to whole language, Beal ignored this agreement and on his own, during summer vacation when teachers were away, hired new teachers who did not share the faculty's commitment to whole language and professional learning.

Again and again Principal Beal undermined or blocked the teachers' attempts to critique and improve the school's implementation of whole language. Clearly, he was not able to embrace the evolving East Meadow whole language ethos in which responsibility, decision-making, and authority were to be shared by all members of the educational community. The resultant unspoken power struggle made little sense, given the professional nature of the faculty and the frightening problems facing the school.

A low-income housing project, built next to the school in 1987, brought drug dealers and a dramatic increase in crime. The impact was immediate and shocking. Children arriving at school in the morning would find used needles from drug parties held on the school grounds the night before and bullet holes in their classroom walls from the increasingly violent rampages of local thugs. Drug dealers threatened the children of parents who tried to take a stand against them. One morning, a mother who had spoken out repeatedly against the drug dealers ran onto the school grounds screaming, "Where is my son?" She had just received an anonymous phone call informing her (falsely) that her nine-year-old son had been killed. For reasons such as these, both the sheriff and the child protective services were regular visitors to the school campus. Poverty and crime afflicted the school and consumed the principal. With so many life-threatening problems at hand, he simply lacked the time or the resources to serve as the school's curricular and instructional leader.

Sadly, his strict adherence to traditional patterns of power and authority prevented him from creating collegial relationships with Johnson and the other whole language teachers, who were ready and willing to push the continual learning needed to keep whole language strong and growing at East Meadow. These teachers did not want to usurp the principal's authority, nor did they want to control him or anyone else. They simply wanted to serve as advocates for the school and community and to work in directions that would strengthen and benefit everyone.

Authoritarianism was replaced by complete ineffectuality when, in 1988, the district installed yet another principal at East Meadow. Principal Joe Alvarez had been characterized by a high-level district administrator as "incompetent." Unfortunately, even when administrators were recognized as ineffectual, it was no easy matter to fire them. The attempted solution was often reassignment, moving them from one position to another in hopes that they would function more effectively. Alvarez had failed at a district position and as principal of another elementary school. Still, for reasons that remain unknown to the faculty, the superintendent was reluctant to fire him. The superintendent apparently hoped that, as a Spanish-speaker, Alvarez would be effective in the Hispanic East Meadow community. Faculty frustration gave way to anger and outrage, however, as the new principal revealed an astonishing inability to relate to students, teachers, or parents.

One day, when an irate and unstable parent with a history of family violence burst into the school office, threatening to kill his child's teacher, Alvarez hid in his office, forcing Johnson to face the parent. In a calm but forceful manner, she told the man, easily twice her size, that he had no business threatening East Meadow teachers and that he would stop immediately or she would call the police. Fortunately, the man complied and a potentially violent incident was averted, but not without great personal risk to both Johnson and the teacher who had been threatened. Later, when a signature was required on a sheriff's statement explaining the incident, Alvarez refused to sign, fearing reprisal from the parent. Once again, it was Johnson and the teacher who took the risk; they signed the document.

Almost daily confrontations with Principal Alvarez left the teachers frustrated and demoralized, with little recourse but to go public with their grievances. Their letters to the district went unanswered, and so as a next step, they arranged to meet with the superintendent. He referred them to the assistant superintendent. Fifth-grade teacher Arlene Androtti, in an interview with Johnson, explains what happened:

> We felt that we were so organized, so clear about the problems, but presenting it to [the assistant superintendent], we again got the feeling that we were slightly incompetent women appealing to "daddy" for help. There was much talk about compromise and making the best of it. In our extreme frustration, some of us got quite emotional, and then we felt like we had blown it because we did get emotional and women always do that. They didn't acknowledge our pain and our concern, and it felt as if they didn't recognize what we knew, or at least didn't care. We felt more and more as if our strength of feeling was viewed as a weakness.

While the teachers' demand that the principal be removed seemed to go unheard, district officials did hear their pleas for more support for East Meadow students, so many of whom were at risk physically, emotionally, and academically. The superintendent suggested that the teachers draw up a plan for using the school's available funds in ways that would best protect and support the children. In response, teachers worked day and night drafting a remarkable "Community Plan" that would not only bolster East Meadow's commitment to whole language, but would reestablish East Meadow's connection to the parents and make the school a viable part of the community, supporting both the children and their families. Arlene Androtti recalls the "euphoria" they experienced as the plan took shape. "It very nearly wrote itself. We brainstormed ideas and there was near unanimity on each point."

The East Meadow Community Plan

Goals for Our School

We envision the school as the heart of the community, providing a center for social events, community classes, neighborhood clubs, sports events, and so on. The community feels ownership of the school. Parents feel free to use the school, and the school helps them become aware of the power that they have. Strong home-school bonds exist. We want to help parents become advocates for their children and for other members of our school and community. We want to work to provide social services to the community and parent orientations at each grade level, with special emphasis for the parents of entering kindergartners. We want to sponsor a school-wide family literacy program. We will provide the necessary education to help parents understand literacy development and what they can do to best support their children's development. Our ultimate goal is that all members of our school community—teachers, students and parents—take pride in East Meadow as a unique and personally/socially valuable part of their lives.

Goals for Our Students

We want our students to be:

- Competent, confident, conscious language users.
- Prepared for the real world, empowered people who know their rights.
- Fully and joyfully literate.
- Independent learners who know how to learn, who know what they want to learn, and who can take responsibility for their own learning.

We want our students to have:

- High expectations, to have goals that they consciously and actively strive to achieve.
- A belief in themselves as first-class citizens who can participate in a democratic society.
- A global worldview, to feel responsible for the quality of life for all humanity.

Solutions

We will use existing funds and write proposals to fund the following:

- A *community organizer* who will organize the school as a community center providing:
  - An after-school program for the children of working parents.
  - Adult classes.
  - Counseling groups.
  - Sports events.

- A free clinic.
- Enrichment classes drawing on people from the community.
- Library and study center.
- Parenting classes.
- Tutoring services.
- Legal aid services.
- Childcare.
- A full-time, on-site trained bilingual *social worker* who will do parent outreach and organize counseling groups for children.
- A full-time *"Reading Club" teacher* who will train and work with two strongly bilingual aides. Together they will work with at-risk readers and provide one-on-one instruction.
- *Creative staffing* to reduce class size to 16 to 18 students for a core of reading/writing/research/math, and at the same time, provide better instruction in PE, hands-on science, art, music, radio, drama, and computer science.
- *Summer school* focusing on language use, with small classes of 12 to 16 students.
- *Preschool.*
- *Parent education.*
- *Kindergarten orientation.*
- *Schoolwide parent/child literacy program.*

Continuing Conflict

Instead of embracing the plan and congratulating the teachers for a job well done, Principal Alvarez refused to accept it, largely on the grounds that he would lose Johnson as his administrative assistant (the plan called for her to head the Reading Club). In many ways, it was Johnson who kept the school functioning; Alvarez fully realized the ramifications of losing her constant support and guidance. As he stated over and over again, "I need an assistant. I can't run this school on my own; I can't run this office on my own." He tried to negotiate with Johnson, suggesting that she serve as his assistant four days a week, and head the Reading Club one day. This, of course, was unacceptable to both Johnson and the faculty.

The faculty voted unanimously on three separate occasions to adopt the Community Plan; Alvarez vetoed it each time. The teachers, he declared, had not involved parents in the planning. Immediately the teachers translated the plan into Spanish and called for a meeting with parents. On the day parents were scheduled to meet with the teachers, Alvarez suddenly announced that he had an appointment with the interior decorator of his apartment; teachers would have to cancel the meeting. Third-grade teacher Debbie Hayes spent an entire afternoon trying to notify parents about the cancellation.

In spite of the principal's opposition, teachers and parents did manage to meet at night once a week for several months. Parents stood by the teachers. They liked the Community Plan and exhorted Principal Alvarez to accept it. At the last meeting, which included East Meadow teachers, parents, and district administrators, Manuel Garcia stood up and addressed Alvarez. *"Le ruego, le pido del corazon que apoya a los maestros de la escuela"* ("I am pleading with you, I am begging you to support the teachers"). Alvarez sat with his arms folded across his chest and said only, "I am entitled to my opinion." District administrators rolled their eyes, but only one, the bilingual director, spoke on behalf of the plan. It was to no avail. The meeting ended; nothing was resolved. In a recent interview with Hayes, Garcia recalled that night: *"Yo nunca he asistido una junta donde se presento un plan para ayudarles a los ninos, para que nejor aprenden y que el director lo rechaza asi. 'Queria preguntarle si vino a apoyarnos o a destruirnos?' "* ("I have never in my life been to a meeting where a project was presented to help the children learn, to give them a better advantage, and have a principal completely reject it. I felt like asking him, 'Have you come to help us, or come to destroy us?' ").

Parents were puzzled, teachers were devastated, and the school machinery ground to a halt. What followed was a debilitating year for teachers, parents, and students as they struggled to work with a principal who apparently could not and would not see or listen to his school community, and with a district office that was not providing the support the school so desperately needed. In Arlene Androtti's words, the district responded to a "very human problem in a very bureaucratic way." East Meadow teachers were told by district officials that the Community Plan was unacceptable because they had not developed it according to the prescribed procedures.

The district bureaucracy not only failed East Meadow teachers, it failed East Meadow parents. The parents were asked to meet and were told how crucial their input was, that they had decision-making power and were valued members of the school community. Yet the meetings were mired in bureaucratic red tape and talk that ultimately stripped the parents of any real power they had. As Androtti explains,

> There was an excessive amount of paper read to them detailing how the Council must be run. The superintendent, school board members,

district office personnel came to "in-service" them. Everything was worded in bureaucratic terms that were confusing at best and boring at worst. One parent complained privately that she was embarrassed to ask any more of her friends to attend Council meetings because those who had, found them pointless.

The parents wanted to support the Community Plan the teachers had developed but were told they couldn't because the plan had not come from them. And their attempts to create a new plan were effectively blocked by the bureaucracy.

What Went Wrong

East Meadow teachers and parents reacted with resentment, even bitterness. How, they asked, could such things happen here? The school district has long enjoyed a reputation as innovative and forward-looking, dedicated to humane and quality education for all its students, many of whom are poor and minority. Over the years, it has actively supported, through funding and professional development, bilingualism, cooperative learning, and whole language. Concepts like "site-based management" and "shared decision-making" were part of the district lexicon long before they appeared on the mainstream public school agenda. Yet, after a decade of struggling to implement whole language, a struggle that more often than not pitted teachers and parents against the principal and district administrators, East Meadow teachers were demoralized. Several teachers talked of leaving. Garcia, declaring that he had been "deceived," resigned as leader of the parent group and withdrew from the school.

At the end of 1989, in an attempt to ascertain what had gone wrong and why, Johnson wrote a letter to Superintendent Edmund Stone. She reminded him of the courage and commitment of the teachers who had spearheaded whole language at East Meadow:

> Part of the uniqueness of East Meadow is that it was entirely created by teachers. Everything we have, everything that has won us attention across the country . . . happened because of teachers and in spite of administrators. Principals have had little to do with the advances we have made and much to do with the problems. It is the teachers who meet to discuss curriculum, it is the teachers who demand in-service and training, and it is the teachers who had the courage to abandon skill-based pedagogy and curriculum and try to change things for the better for their students.

Stone did not respond to Johnson's letter. A year later, Johnson wrote him again explaining that I was working on this article, and asking him to provide me with his interpretation of the events at East Meadow. Within the week, his response arrived in the mail. He chose not to focus on individuals or even to write much about the past. Instead, he outlined what he would do "if I had to do it over again."

Drawing on the work of Henry Levin and the "accelerated school" movement, Stone listed five essentials needed to restructure schools successfully:

* Using developmentally appropriate learning approaches.
* Establishing an ongoing evaluation system.
* Instituting school-based management.
* Developing partnerships with parents and community.
* Having adequate staff, facilities, and resources.

Stone explained how these essentials relate to East Meadow:

> Equal credence must be given to each essential in developing a foundation for a school-wide change effort. At East Meadow, we addressed some of these essentials but some were not addressed at all. In the process of change there should be methods developed for maintaining good communication; seeking out problems and solving them; resolving conflicts; and making decisions. I don't think we established a reliable governance mechanism that addressed those imperatives.

From the teachers' and parents' perspective, these essentials *were* addressed, but the principals, for one reason or another, chose to ignore them and ultimately destroyed them. Johnson's efforts to involve the faculty in careful evaluation of the East Meadow whole language program were buried on the principal's desk, and a strong parent partnership was shattered. When Principal Tim Elliot left, Garcia recalls, *"Yo sabia, como padre de familia, que los maestros no tenian el apoyo que antes tenian"* ("I could even tell as a parent that teachers didn't have support they had once had"). Parents also got little support. Principal George Beal allowed the parents to continue their meetings at the school but never participated or talked to the parents. Garcia remembers that the principal would open the door for them and then leave. *"Esperabamos que dijera algo"* ("We kept waiting for him to say something, but he never did"). Garcia shook his head sadly as he recalled, *"Nos sentimos abandonados"* ("We felt abandoned").

Unlike Tim Elliot, who had made home visits and worked hard to communicate with parents even though he had to rely on a translator, George Beal did not seem to feel comfortable with the East Meadow parents. By the time I was hired as a whole language consultant in 1987, parent participation had declined dramatically. Unaware of the history of East Meadow, I noted that a weak link in the whole language program was a lack of parent involvement. Principal Beal agreed, but explained that these parents were too busy trying to keep food on the table to attend school functions. In fact, despite daily battles against poverty, the East Meadow parents, like most parents everywhere, did care and had spent hours working with teachers to implement whole language; their interest waned only when Beal failed to continue the administrative support and the open lines of communication that Elliot had worked so hard to establish. While parent involvement was severely undermined by Principal Beal, Principal Alvarez destroyed it. Garcia describes him as a man of "intelligence." *"Porque,"* he adds, *"un director que trabaja solo para el no sirue, porque para manejar una escuela, se tiene que formar un equipo entre los maestros, los padres de familia y la direccion"* ("But a principal who works only for himself doesn't work, because in order to run a school, you've got to have teamwork").

The Principal's Role: A Legacy of Sexism

East Meadow teachers certainly agree with Garcia that the necessary teamwork between teachers and the administration was missing. The root cause, they believe, was sexism. Johnson recalls a conversation with Alvarez in which he told her that at the school where he had previously worked as principal, the women teachers were "happy to do things for me," and that the East Meadow teachers "should be too."

An inquiry into the historical origins of the principal's role reveals that it was essentially nonexistent when teachers were almost exclusively male. During the latter part of the nineteenth century, women began to replace men, particularly in the elementary schools. The feminization of the teaching force and the bureaucratization of schools (more formal control of credentialing, curricula, and pedagogy) led to the creation of a manager—a principal—who was almost always male. As Apple (1986) notes, once teaching became "women's work," the very nature of the job changed. Male teachers, fairly autonomous in their own classrooms, were replaced by females who were deemed in need of administrative control and management. David Tyack concurs. "Hierarchical organization of schools and the male chauvinism of the larger society fit as hand to glove. The system required subordination; women were generally subordinate to men; the employment of women as teachers thus augmented the authority of the largely male administrative leadership" (1974, p. 60).

All but one of the East Meadow teachers were women, and an underlying current of sexism does seem evident in the administrators' treatment of them. Inherent differences in the way men and women view and use power may also have contributed to the conflict. David McClelland found that men equate power with "assertion and aggression," while women cite "acts of nurturance as acts of strength" (reported in Gilligan 1982, pp. 167–68). In our efforts to restructure schools in more positive and humane ways, perhaps we should begin with a far-reaching analysis of power. What *is* power? How should power be used in school settings? To accomplish what ends?

Johnson addressed the issue of power in her 1989 letter to Superintendent Stone. She explained that, through their commitment to whole language, East Meadow teachers had become strong, professional educators, and that their strength ultimately led to their undoing, as they experienced one power clash after another with administrators:

> Whole language and our study of it empowered us, taught us how children learn, and gave us the right to work together as a strong, visionary faculty to create a better place for our kids. We have done this in spite of many difficulties and much discomfort. Those of us who know how this feels cannot go back to being submissive and subservient to a management system that believes in control by fear, coercion, and threats.

A Whole Language Principal

Finally, responding to two years of teacher dissent and parent dissatisfaction, the district administrators asked Principal Alvarez to leave his administrative position and return to teaching. He chose to leave the district altogether and look for work elsewhere. Thanks to the determined efforts of the school board president, Joan Hendrick, a new principal, Jim Stimson, arrived in August 1990 and immediately began working twelve-hour days. He did not stay behind his desk but reached out to the community, meeting with parents and responding to their needs. New to whole language, he proved willing to listen, willing to let teachers take the lead, willing to learn. Third-grade teacher Karen Hunt explains the difference he has made for her:

> He really cares about us, about the community, about the children, and has already implemented several changes. We had a pep rally but it was meaningful. It was the first time the children were shown that we are proud of our school. Jim is an advocate for our school; we can trust him to do the best for all of us. He finds a way to do what needs to be done. As teachers we should be able to rely on the administrator. Now we can. It's an incredible feeling to know that I can go back to becoming the teacher I know I can be, and somebody else will be looking out for the school.

These eloquent words glow with new hope for East Meadow.

In reviewing the history of East Meadow administrators from Tim Elliot to Jim Stimson, I have come to believe that a true whole language principal possesses the following qualities:

1. Hardworking manager of the school. The principal manages the myriad mundane but critical details that are a necessary part of creating a productive and efficient school. He or she works with teachers and students to establish a safe and comfortable learning environment and, in so doing, enables teachers to attend to their primary business—teaching.
2. School advocate. The principal uses power to achieve ends for the school, not to control people. He or she strives to create what Richard DuFour terms a "culture of pride" (1987, p. 65) in the school, working with faculty to define the school's values and then promoting and celebrating them at every opportunity.
3. Honest learner. The principal doesn't know all the answers and doesn't need to pretend he or she does. He or she is willing to let teachers take the lead and to learn from them. Together they read professional literature and research and consult with outside authorities as they all work together to further their understanding of language, learning, curricula, and pedagogy. The principal is not threatened by strong teachers but welcomes them as the best assest in building a strong, effective school. The principal and teachers work in concert as colleagues.

4. Instructional leader. DuFour writes, "Even those studies in which instructional leadership was identified as coming from a source other than the principal—a central office administrator or a group of teachers—[it was] acknowledged that the principal provided the cooperation and support that made the leadership of others possible" (p. 79). Leadership entails understanding the research, establishing clear goals and high expectations, carefully monitoring student progress through authentic means, providing time for in-service and teacher self-reflection and evaluation, and in all ways, carefully attending to, critiquing, and revising as needed the school's overarching philosophy and practices.

The Wider Culture

And what do whole language schools such as East Meadow need from district administrators? Most important, I believe, is open-minded, supportive attention—certainly not destructive indifference rooted in unspoken, perhaps largely unconscious, prejudice. What administrators should avoid is summed up by Ian Cumming, a member of the East Meadow community. "The district's response," he comments, was skewed by "sexism, racism, and class bias against the teachers, students, and community."

For whole language to fully realize its great promise in America, changes must be effected not only in schools and districts but in society as a whole. Change lies at the heart of whole language: change from skill-based classrooms to student-centered, meaning-focused ones; change from teachers-as-technicians bound to textbook scripts to teachers as learners, mediators, initiators, and liberators (Goodman 1991); change from schools as protectors and perpetuators of the status quo to schools as political catalysts of a more humane and equitable society. Change like this is not possible within a traditional school bureaucracy in which some have a voice and some do not. We cannot create lasting changes in our classrooms that empower children if we do not also work to effect changes within the structure of schools that empower teachers. "We need revalued teachers," Ken Goodman (1991) writes, "to achieve revalued students." And likewise, the liberating changes that teachers and students experience through whole language will have no lasting impact if, beyond the classroom and the school, we do not concern ourselves with greater social change that will help *all* members of our society realize the promises of our democracy. As Michael Apple (1991) has written:

> For all its meritorious goals, the whole language movement cannot insure that its own goals and methods will have a lasting and widespread impact unless it is willing to act not only within the school, but outside it as well. Its proponents need to join with others in the wider social movements that aim at democratizing our economy, politics, and culture, and that act against a society that is so unequal in gender, race, and class terms. (p. 416)

This remains the guiding vision of the East Meadow teachers and parents as they work with their new principal to rebuild their whole language school.

References

Apple, Michael. 1986. *Teachers and Texts*. New York: Routledge and Kegan Paul.

———. 1991. Teachers, politics, and whole language instruction. In *The Whole Language Catalog*. Ed. Kenneth S. Goodman, Lois Bridges Bird, and Yetta M. Goodman. Santa Rosa, Calif.: American School Publishers.

Clark, Kenneth. 1965. *The Dark Ghetto*. New York: Harper and Row.

DuFour, Richard. 1987. *Fulfilling the Promise of Excellence*. Westbury, N.Y.: J. L. Wilkerson.

Gilligan, Carol. 1982. *In a Different Voice*. Cambridge, Mass.: Harvard University Press.

Goodman, Kenneth S. 1991. Whole language teachers. In *The Whole Language Catalog*. Ed. Kenneth S. Goodman, Lois Bridges Bird, and Yetta M. Goodman. Santa Rosa, Calif.: American School Publishers.

Tyack, David B. 1974. *The One Best System: A History of Urban Education*. Cambridge, Mass.: Harvard University Press.

11 Nurturing a Change in Belief Systems: Building a Culture that Prevents Polarization and Supports Change

Michele M. Pahl and Robert J. Monson

Drawing upon their experiences in the Westwood, Massachusetts, public schools, Michele Pahl and Robert Monson raise the provocative question, Can you mandate a belief system? And more specifically, Can you mandate whole language? They suggest that educational change must reconcile the "top-down" needs of the organization, the decision-makers, and the innovation itself with the "bottom-up" needs of the individuals from whom change is expected. The model for change that emerged from their own experience suggests that significant educational change cannot be effected by mandate alone, but it can be facilitated by an administration sensitive to and supportive of teachers' needs. They conclude that although administrators cannot simply mandate the kind of shift in a school's belief system that whole language requires, they can help to bring it about.

MICHELE M. PAHL is currently a doctoral student at Harvard University and an adjunct faculty member at Lesley College in Cambridge and at Wheelock College in Boston. At the time this chapter was written, she was a reading specialist and staff developer in the Westwood Public Schools. She remains involved in Westwood's ongoing transition to whole language as a consultant to the program and participates in several whole language networking groups. Her research interests center on the reflective practitioner as a catalyst for reform in literacy education.

ROBERT J. MONSON is currently Superintendent of the Westwood Public Schools and an adjunct faculty member at Lesley College in Cambridge. Drawing on his past experiences as an administrator, consultant, and teacher, he has been an active facilitator of the transition to whole language in the elementary schools of Westwood. His research interests include the emerging role of the administrator in an era of reform and the leadership factors that influence educational change. Together, he and Pahl have published an article in *Educational Leadership* (March 1991) on the paradigm shift required by whole language and a forthcoming article in the *Journal of Reading* (April 1992) on the transformations in curriculum and instruction that whole language inspires.

* * *

Mention the words "whole language" in the context of a faculty meeting and be prepared to observe an interesting phenomenon. The whole language philosophy, and the myths surrounding whole language practice, inspire the kind of passionate debate that often results in intense staff polarization in many school districts. Because whole language challenges our assumptions about the nature of teaching and the nature of learning, staff conflict around the issue is as understandable as it is difficult to resolve. In our experience, polarization becomes most extreme when administrators attempt to mandate a change in teachers' belief systems; and yet, a major redirection such as whole language requires that teachers focus on changing their classroom behavior while at the same time addressing the impact of these new practices on their belief systems.

Decision-makers would be wise to ask themselves some difficult questions before they begin to explore their existing practices and consider alternative approaches. Can whole language be addressed in a way that will avoid the innovative "false starts" we witnessed, and survived, in the sixties and seventies? If so, should a school or district mandate the implementation of whole language for all teachers? And if a community moves in this direction, can decision-makers avoid polarization while supporting meaningful changes in beliefs and behavior? In this chapter, we attempt to answer these questions on the basis of our own experiences and to share their philosophical and organizational implications from the combined perspectives of the individual teacher and the larger community.

Establishing a Perspective on the Process of Change

Before an administrator, faculty committee, or school board decides to move in a new philosophical direction and make changes in instructional practice, serious reflection and dialogue about the implications of these changes for those most likely to be affected by the outcome are necessary. In any school district, it is the individual teacher who will be asked to take substantial risks in the classroom in order to respond effectively to a new direction in organizational philosophy. A recent study by the Northeast Regional Laboratory (Huberman and Miles 1982) found that in the sixties and seventies school districts spent too little time and allocated too few resources to helping teachers acquire the skills that educational innovation required. In other words, decision-makers considered new organizational directions but failed to build the support structures that would allow individuals to achieve meaningful change. Despite the integrity of the original idea, the ultimate result for many progressive reform efforts was failure. What have we learned from these unsuccessful attempts to implement change? Did these innovations fail because teachers did not know what to do, or because teachers did not believe in the philosophy? Or was it a combination of both these factors, along with others? What are the implications for a district considering the "implementation" of whole language?

As we know, the term "whole language" represents a philosophy (see Chapter 1 in this volume). It is a model supported by theory and implemented in practice. But for many teachers and for many school systems, this model pushes against the parameters and boundaries of an existing belief system. The traditional paradigm, a filter for interpreting new information, is challenged and stretched. In our district, the initial impetus for change came from a small group of teachers who had been exploring the implications of a whole language philosophy by experimenting in their classrooms, examining the research and professional literature, and attending conferences. This group acted as a catalyst for a systemwide review of literacy instruction, which was conducted by a committee of teachers, specialists, and administrators representing all the schools in the district. Empowered to make decisions and faced with the obvious option of adopting a new basal reading series, the members of this group asked some critical questions that resulted in a new interpretation of the parameters. Instead of asking which basal series was best suited to the purposes of the district, they asked why basals were being used at all! Over an eighteen-month period, the committee redefined the direction of the school system by examining their assumptions about reading, writing, and learning. In the end, rather than revise the existing curriculum, they chose to begin anew. Although this may seem straightforward, in a district where success as defined by traditional measures had always been achieved through traditional means, it represented the first brave step on a long road to paradigm revolution.

Change—at both the individual and organizational levels—requires a complex paradigm shift (Monson and Pahl 1991). Yet as history has demonstrated, this is no easy feat.

Thomas Kuhn's (1970) analysis of paradigm transformations in science offers important insights for an educational community engaged in the process of change. Throughout history, scientists have resisted innovation because preconceived paradigms blocked their ability to accept new models. Indeed, if the experiences of Copernicus, Newton, Galileo, and Darwin are any indication, "old paradigms do not retire gracefully, and the avatars of new ones are often scorned and savaged" (Finn 1990, p. 589). As one might expect, our district is no different than any other district faced with philosophical upheaval. Once teachers decided to adopt whole language as the *district* philosophy and to align classroom practice with this purpose, there was bound to be trouble! Initial resistance to the idea, although expected, was dramatic and vociferous. Because district leadership—namely the school board and administration—firmly supported the decision made by the staff committee, some viewed "whole language" as a district mandate. The challenge, therefore, was to simultaneously support the decision *and* the staff throughout the transition. How could such a challenge be met? Through historical analysis, Kuhn builds a powerful case in support of the notion that "the transfer of allegiance from paradigm to paradigm is a conversion experience that cannot be forced." He suggests, however, that change can be "induced" when the old paradigm is perceived as being "in crisis" (1970, pp. 151–53).

Can You Mandate a Belief System?

Can a belief system be mandated? Long before sitting down to write this chapter, we faced each other over this very question from the perspective of both practitioner and administrator. Perhaps it comes as no surprise that one of us responded in the negative and one of us in the affirmative. Yet we realized that in doing so, we were trying to balance organizational and individual needs in very different ways. Through our collaboration and discussion, we settled on a response that more adequately represents the complexity of the issue.

Let's assume that you have a "good idea": as an individual, you've embraced the philosophical tenets of a new approach to washing windows. In fact, you believe so strongly in the power of the idea that you try to influence others to view it as you do. You build a rationale for cleaner windows in the community, and you identify some of the problems inherent in the old window washing approach. You meet initial resistance to the idea in a myriad of forms—the approach is ignored, rejected, modified, or accepted on a variety of different levels—and find that community response falls into three basic categories: those who enthusiastically adopt the new technique, those who oppose any new method, and those who are willing to try the new technique but aren't sure where to begin. How do you proceed?

In weighing your options, you consider two possibilities. If you mandate the new approach, you risk polarization. You will undoubtedly alienate certain members of the community while engendering the support of others. You will encounter pockets of passive resistance, overt denial, and open hostility. Some people will tell you that they have already washed their windows, some will claim that their windows are clean enough, and some will refuse to wash their windows just to spite you. In some cases, external compliance with the mandate may result in the superficial implementation of window washing behavior; although the window washers may be using the correct tools, they may not be washing windows in the spirit of the new approach. This would be a crushing blow to the integrity and value of your original idea.

You could, of course, rely on the evolution of grassroots support to promote a change in attitudes about washing windows, but this takes time, energy, and unlimited patience. In most communities, these commodities are in short supply. Certain skeptics may begin to express the opinion that, given all the support in the world, those in opposition and those who are on the fence may *never* come around to a new way of washing windows without external motivation to do so. Meanwhile, those who are behind the idea grow impatient, frustrated by the disequilibrium of the community and the dirty windows of their neighbors. They are losing their enthusiasm and their support is waning. Given the strength of the idea, can you afford *not* to force the issue and raise the question within the community?

Since we believe that whole language *is* a "good idea," we are willing to be its advocates. If the professional literature is any indication, the old paradigm is "in crisis" (see Adams 1990; Carbo 1988; Chall 1967 and 1989; Shannon 1990; Taylor 1989), and this may be the ideal moment to explore the question and consider alternatives. Whole language is not an easy answer to a difficult question. It represents a fundamental shift in our thinking about teaching and learning.

An effective transition to a whole language philosophy requires an awareness of the complexities of this change and the issues faced by a school community engaged in the process. We feel that a comprehensive shift of this magnitude can only be "induced" through an unusual combination of top-down facilitation and bottom-up commitment—a symbiotic blending of administrative and grassroots involvement. (See Figure 11–1.) Support for this position can be found in the literature on effective change, which suggests that decision-makers must attend to the needs of the people being asked to change in addition to the needs of the innovation itself (Huberman

FIGURE 11–1 *Responding to Interests and Effecting Change*

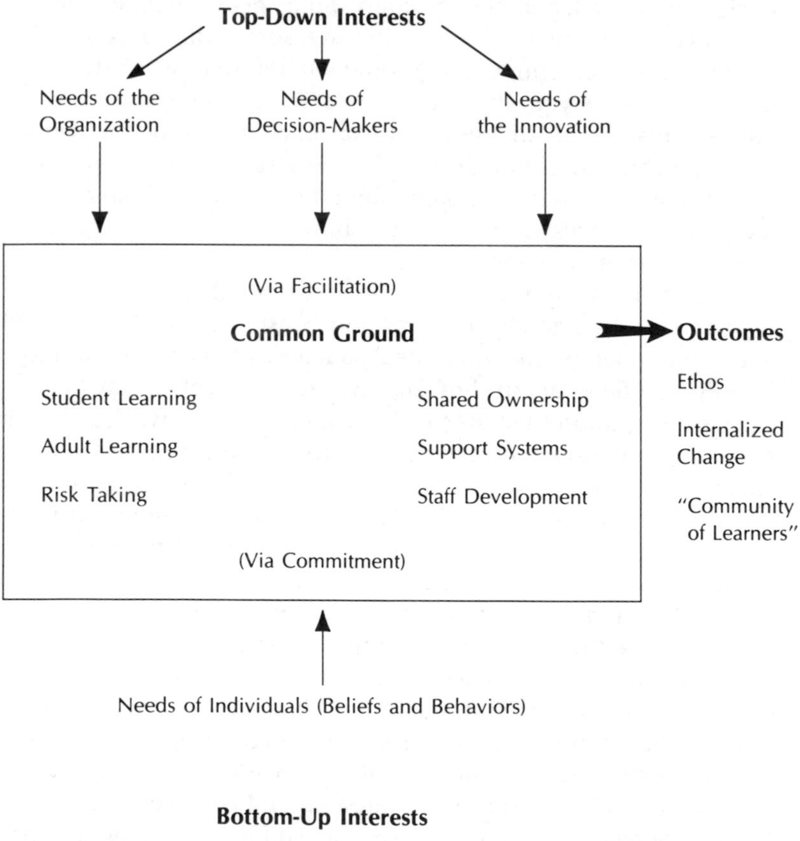

and Miles 1982). We believe that staff polarization can only be prevented and sustained change can only be achieved when both top-down and bottom-up interests are addressed. In this way, we hope to be able to nurture a comprehensive paradigm shift and in the process establish common ground between administrators and practitioners.

Top-Down Interests

Top-down interests include the needs of the organization, the needs of decision-makers, and the needs inherent in the innovation itself.

Needs of the Organization

Traditionally, educational institutions have not been supportive of innovation and change, nor are elementary and secondary schools considered to be communities for adult learning. Administrative practices and hierarchical structures often act as constraints to the adult learning process in these settings. At the same time, regardless of whether these restrictions actually exist, individuals within a community may perceive an absence of vision, autonomy, intellectualism, or democratic decision-making within the institutional context and thus not feel empowered to take risks in pursuit of their own learning. Nancy Lester and Cynthia Onore (1990) conclude, "there is nothing that blocks change as effectively as the *perception* that the reins of power are in the hands of others."

In contrast, an organizational culture that supports change rests upon a strong foundation of professional trust and shared values. Jon Saphier and Matthew King have identified twelve norms of school culture that promote the success of new innovations (Saphier and King 1985). Of these, we have found tangible support, experimentation, collegiality, and involvement in decision-making to be the most influential in our own efforts to a nurture a paradigm shift at the school system level. Although all of these factors are imbedded in our discussion here, they each deserve additional mention from an organizational perspective.

Tangible organizational support should take the form of an articulated vision, action plan, incentives, resources, and staff development. When one of these components is missing, the organization may be perceived as unsupportive. The organization must be responsible for establishing a context in which collective change can occur. In our own district, a staff committee articulated a vision for language arts instruction that required all members of the community to become comfortable with whole language philosophy and practice. This same committee is continuing to make decisions that shape the implementation of an action plan aligned with this vision. Over a five-year period, all teachers will be engaged in the process of "becoming" whole language teachers. The kinds of incentives that support our teachers in this process are both *internal*—the enthusiasm of students, the growth of literacy, the challenge of working with other teachers—and *external*—the administrative expectation that change will occur and release time for staff development activities. By providing *resources,* things such as classroom literature, writing materials, and the support of parent volunteers, and *ideas* through staff development, our organization sets up conditions in which teachers are encouraged to experiment.

Once established as a norm, experimentation acts to minimize the effects of institutional stasis by combining the energy of individuals and creating a dynamic community of learners. As Lester and Onore note:

> When experimentation begins to occur in many isolated classrooms and when experimentation begins to reveal the impossibility of reconciling institutional demands with individual goals and to exaggerate the inadequacies and contradictions . . . then the individual teacher's decisions or choices simultaneously begin conditioning the larger school community. Collective action and change on the level of teachers' worldviews can come to influence the institution. Rather than having a teacher's choices controlled by the institutional practice, the institutional practice can come to reflect the collective beliefs and practices of teachers. (1990, p. 191)

The collegial norm, often developed through increased experimentation, also supports the development of a community of learners in that it breaks down the polarizing effects of isolation. Without opportunities for collegial interaction, teachers become, as Judith Warren Little describes it, "caught up in the immediacies of the classroom and isolated from comparative practice or theory" (1990, p. 526). As a result, they often "take strong stands against practices different from their own and rely on personal experience to defend what they do" (Fieman-Nemser and Floden 1986, p. 512). As Little adds, "to the extent that successful decision making requires informed consideration of alternatives, teachers' general isolation places them at a disadvantage" (p. 527). Therefore, an organizational context that supports collegiality will also enhance an individual's contribution to the decision-making process.

Needs of Decision-Makers

An initiative of the magnitude of whole language carries with it expectations from all those who are affected by it, particularly the decision-makers responsible for initiating the exploration. Whether this takes the form of financial support, additional staffing, staff development, or the encouragement of risk-taking, the probability of achieving a successful transition will go up in proportion to the level of active facilitation on the part of decision-makers. Once a decision to implement whole language has been made, those responsible should play a direct role in nurturing the change they have inaugurated.

If it can be assumed that the "decision-makers" in this context are either administrators, parents, staff, or school board members, these people will have a vested interest in the outcome. In short, they will want to see positive growth in the ability of students to use language for authentic purposes. Knowing that the impact on student learning will be evaluated in the larger context of public opinion, those who made the decision have an interest in finding common ground with those who will be expected to use this approach in the classroom. Decision-makers must feel confident in promoting understanding in the external community, in negotiating differences of opinion, and in demonstrating an understanding of the implications of their decision.

What has this meant for the decision-making group in our community, the staff committee that moved the district in the direction of whole language? When faced with the conclusions of this representative committee, the educational community responded along a continuum that ranged from enthusiasm to resistance and included elements of suspicion, concern, and denial. Regardless of the nature of the endeavor, history has demonstrated that pioneers tend to endure hardship for the sake of their vision; to be successful, they must possess a quality that in Japanese culture is called *gambare*. It means "to persevere; to do one's best; to be persistent; to stick to one's purposes; to never give up until the job is done and done well" (Sergiovanni 1990). At some point in the implementation process, however, decision-makers must undergo a role transformation and become facilitators of change. Perseverance and esprit de corps just aren't enough to carry them through. What levels of awareness and skill development are needed to enable decision-makers to play an active role in change facilitation?

Although we can't pretend to have the answer to this question, we are certainly closer to finding one than we were earlier in the process. We believe that decision-makers need to demonstrate respect for the change process by anticipating conflict and viewing it as a natural, healthy opportunity for growth. Understanding how organizations and individuals respond to change is the first step.

The CBAM (Concerns-Based Adoption Model) (Hord et al. 1987) has been a useful framework for addressing the needs of the decision-makers. In Westwood, the decision-making staff committee is currently participating in a series of ongoing sessions in order to learn about and use the CBAM concept. Based upon the assumption that change is a personal process, the CBAM framework outlines the "stages of concern" that teachers may pass through on the way to becoming comfortable with the philosophy and practices of whole language. These stages are oriented around concern for self, concern for the tasks involved in implementing the change, and concern for the impact of the change on teaching and learning.

After receiving a general orientation to change theory and practicing conferring techniques designed to assess teachers' levels of concern about whole language use, committee members felt better able to assess the "pulse" of the faculty in relation to this innovation. Through our growing awareness of the stages of concern individuals pass through during the transition, we have enhanced our understanding of the challenges faced by all staff members in our district. In view of our developing awareness, we are in the process of improving our skills in assessing the level of concern among staff members and in identifying interventions appropriate to each level. As a result of this training, the decision-making group is in a better position to address the needs of individuals, reduce the level of staff polarization, and live up to the tremendous responsibility of initiating change. Participatory decision-making can be effective if teachers not only have knowledge of the innovation (whole language content in this case), but also understand how people will react to the process.

Needs Inherent in the Innovation

When an innovation such as whole language takes on a life of its own and usage becomes widespread, it is important that the requirements of the innovation are met. What does this mean?

Whole language practice implies a set of philosophical and behavioral assumptions (see Chapter 1). Whole language theory may mean nothing if teachers do not implement it within an acceptable level of variance at the classroom level. How much variance from the original intent will be allowed in practice within a school or district? How much can the concept be changed and still be called whole language?

These questions reflect what we term the "interests of the innovation" and ought to be discussed at the outset and monitored throughout the process of implementation. Because whole language does not exist as a prepackaged curriculum, the range of teacher interpretation of the philosophy and teacher practice might be quite diverse. Teachers who gain an understanding of whole language practices and internalize whole language beliefs will demonstrate a strong theoretical base in their classroom approach to literacy instruction and in the articulation of their own philosophies. The process through which the community interprets whole language rests in part on the informed and reflective practice of the teachers implementing the philosophy. Teachers must develop a strong awareness of their role in the process and the need to remain in philosophical alignment with the intent of the innovation.

These needs really speak to the issue of teacher and school site autonomy, a touchy subject in most school districts. The wider the variance in the staff's belief systems and instructional behaviors, the more problems will be encountered in addressing this issue and, more importantly, in trying to agree on what is considered an acceptable level of classroom use. Addressing the needs of the innovation is a challenge, but ignoring them compounds problems for all those involved.

In an effort to meet this challenge in Westwood, we have tried to provide a comprehensive program of staff development in which all staff members participate. Staff development provides a forum in which teachers consider evidence that the traditional paradigm is in crisis and in which to consider research in support of alternative approaches. Throughout the school year, teachers are released for one afternoon every other week in order to attend presentations on the essential elements of whole language philosophy and practice. In this way, we are developing a shared body of theoretical knowledge and common expectations about whole language practice. Once these foundations have been established, small group sessions are held to discuss particular implications at each grade level, and voluntary opportunities are provided to explore specific issues in greater depth.

Bottom-Up Interests: Needs of Individuals

Bottom-up interests consist of the needs of individuals involved in the change process. How does one go about addressing the needs of teachers? In the case of whole language, we feel that it is important to focus on two needs in particular. First, any teacher engaged in the process must feel confident that the transition to whole language is the right thing to do. Questioning the integrity of the idea is an indication that the teacher's philosophical conscience is active. This "conscience" is really the belief system that serves as a foundation for professional behavior. While a majority of teachers may express an interest in only learning "how to use the whole language approach," at some point their consciences are going to demand a strong philosophical rationale and substantial theoretical support. Sustained change is more likely to occur if the teacher believes that whole language is better for children. To understand the potential of whole language, teachers need to have opportunities for continued reflection. Providing teachers with only isolated, cookbook-style in-service sessions decreases the possibility that they will ever internalize a whole language philosophy.

Second, we must acknowledge that any teacher trying to change instructional practices will feel a certain level of anxiety about not being successful. A teacher must feel confident that his or her classroom practice is effective. This demands the acquisition of a substantial body of new knowledge, but it also requires new skills, which take time to develop even with guided practice and coaching. A teacher's first attempts to explore whole language will probably fall short of his or her own expectations. These feelings must be legitimized and acknowledged by those involved in the program's implementation.

Change is an incremental and personal process, not an isolated event (Hord et al. 1987). When the organizational context reflects this understanding, a learning community forms and participants in the environment come to accept diversity. Whole language is often acquired in unique and idiosyncratic ways by teachers engaged in the change process. While some teachers may internalize the philosophy almost immediately, others need to be given time to see the worth of the philosophy through observation and reflective practice.

In many cases, "the most significant changes in teacher attitudes and beliefs come *after* they begin using a new practice successfully and see changes in student learning" (Guskey 1985, p. 57). Staff members who make a transition to whole language in this way may initially appear to be applying the "techniques" they associate with whole language, but in effect, they are acting like whole language teachers without thinking like whole language teachers. For these individuals, the transformational process takes time. They must discover and witness the link between rationale, behavior, and outcome on a personal level. For many teacher-learners, seeing is believing. With organizational support and a cultural expectation for change, teachers often begin to explore and experiment in ways they might otherwise not attempt on their own.

One paradox we have observed is the impatience that some teachers, those who are more comfortable with the philosophy, express toward their peers who are undergoing a slower transition. While certainly understandable, this phenomenon is disturbing to witness, contributes to staff polarization, and seems to run counter to the belief system that supports whole language. In large part, to be a whole language practitioner is to acknowledge that language acquisition is developmental and to subscribe to a philosophy of natural learning. Whole language teachers take their cues from where the children are, immerse them in authentic experience, provide demonstrations, structure opportunities for experimentation, and celebrate approximations. We believe that adult learners have needs analogous to those of young learners, that people learn in different ways, and that there are many paths to the same conceptual destination.

One of our goals in Westwood is to establish a climate in which *all* efforts to grow are supported, recognized, and celebrated. In addition, the cultural expectation that growth *will* occur is strong. The resulting tension between top-down facilitation and bottom-up commitment is something we believe will produce sustained results on an organizational level and present meaningful possibilities for the individuals involved in the process.

A Common Ground: Facilitation and Commitment

Common ground is established when top-down and bottom-up interests are addressed simultaneously.

Shared Ownership

The thoughtful implementation of a whole language philosophy and whole language practice relies on the collaborative articulation of the vision of teaching and learning that is valued by the educational community. Because the process of strategic planning "uses the expertise of the school community in the development of methods to achieve mutually supported goals" (Nebgen 1990, p. 28), it can provide a forum for establishing common ground among the various stakeholder groups—school board members, administrators, teachers, parents, and students—who will eventually be affected by the implementation of whole language. This process involves communicating the rationale for planning; selecting a core planning group; developing a mission statement; completing an environmental assessment; formulating objectives; selecting strategies; developing action plans; and implementing and evaluating the program (Nebgen 1990).

Because initial districtwide exploration of whole language often takes place as the result of a "grassroots movement" on the part of classroom teachers, other members of the educational community must be involved early in the process in order to foster a sense of ownership and engender support. Strategic planning is one way of identifying common goals and building a foundation of support for new initiatives. Since whole language represents such a complex shift in beliefs and behavior, external support for experimentation is essential for successful implementation. For example, does the school board value risk-taking? Do administrators understand and support the changing role of the classroom teacher? Are teachers supportive of the professional growth of their peers? Are parents comfortable with the goals and objectives of the initiative? These questions and many others should be addressed as part of the strategic planning process.

Staff Development

Once shared values have been articulated and common goals established, staff development efforts should promote a "reaching out to the knowledge base" (Saphier and King 1985) if changes in beliefs and behavior are to take hold. A natural outgrowth of the strategic planning process would be to involve staff in the collaborative shaping of the knowledge base around whole language. From a philosophical viewpoint, this can be extremely problematic; after all, "whole language is not a program to be defined and mandated but a belief system that is in a constant process of evolution and implementation" (Newman and Church 1990, p. 24). We feel, however, that this lack of definition is one of the root causes of staff polarization.

We are not suggesting that whole language be reduced to a formula or a methodology. But a lack of understanding of what constitutes "whole language" can inspire anxiety, misconceptions, and dichotomized thinking. What we are suggesting is that staff members become engaged in the process of identifying what the educational community believes to be true about whole language and what areas community members feel must be explored further through staff development. By articulating in a tangible way the beliefs and behaviors that reflect the community's interpretation of whole language, the knowledge base can be addressed in a manner that respects the individuals involved in the process.

Our staff development effort, for example, is focused on a transition guide developed by teachers. The guide, and therefore the knowledge base, centers on process orientation (reading process and writing process), contexts for learning (reading workshop and writing workshop), and the role of the classroom teacher (modeling, assessing, direct instruction, conferring, facilitating, encouraging, and sharing). (See Figure 11–2.) Our goal is to broaden the repertoire of all teachers by having them participate in demonstrations of whole language practice and in discussions of the supporting belief system; our knowledge base, therefore, is composed of the "hows" and the "whys" of whole language practice and theory. The transition guide is a temporary expression of our direction and purpose.

Support Systems

Regardless of the planning and involvement that goes into whole language staff development, once the process of change is initiated staff members begin to respond to the innovation. The instances and degree of staff polarization might actually increase at this point if the district leadership is not prepared to understand and support the staff through this transition.

As a school or district begins to implement whole language, all participants need increased opportunities, beyond formalized staff development sessions, to continue the process of reflection and personal exploration. As individuals responding to change in unique ways, they need to arrive at their own decisions about "how" whole language beliefs will become embedded in practice and "why" certain practices reflect whole language beliefs. It is essential that teachers continue to engage in dialogue about the interaction between what they *believe* and what they *do*.

There are several designs for learning (Levine and Broude 1989) that seem to support the professional growth of teachers as they

FIGURE 11–2 *Model of Whole Language (from "A Transition Guide for Whole Language Implementation," 1990)*

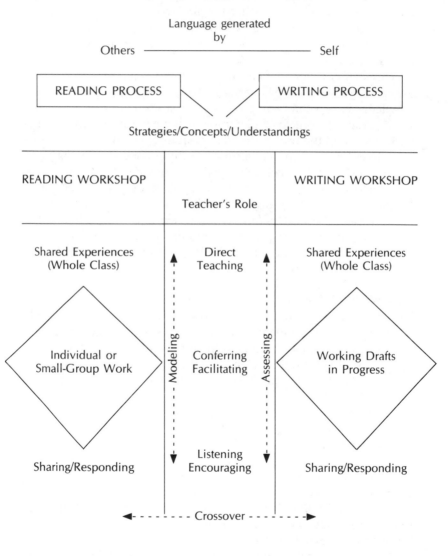

WHOLE LANGUAGE

Language generated
by
Others ——————————————— Self

| READING PROCESS | | WRITING PROCESS |

Strategies/Concepts/Understandings

READING WORKSHOP		WRITING WORKSHOP
	Teacher's Role	
Shared Experiences (Whole Class)	Direct Teaching	Shared Experiences (Whole Class)
Individual or Small-Group Work	Modeling Conferring Facilitating Assessing	Working Drafts in Progress
Sharing/Responding	Listening Encouraging	Sharing/Responding

◄- - - - - - - Crossover - - - - - - - ►

Parent Communication and Involvement

take the first steps toward whole language and to sustain teachers who have been more deeply involved with the philosophy. Whole language staff development programs can be responsive to diversified needs by providing experiences that foster increased collaboration and inclusivity.

• *Support Groups*
Through voluntary participation and an informal structure, support groups alleviate feelings of isolation by providing a forum for sharing advice, perspectives, and resources (see Chapter 6). Individual participants benefit from the collective expertise of the group. By encouraging participants to establish their own agendas, members can focus on relevant issues through a process of discussion, clarification, and problem-solving. In our district, support groups meet at the primary and intermediate levels on a monthly basis. These groups have addressed issues ranging from the theoretical to the practical. Some of the questions that drive group meetings include: How do I integrate instruction? What is the fit between whole language and developmental philosophy? How can I use response journals effectively? How can the public library be a resource for teaching and learning?

• *Coaching*
Coaching provides an important link between a theoretical orientation and the expression of this orientation in a classroom setting; it "acknowledges the complexity of transferring learning to practice" (Levine and Broude 1989, p. 74). By emphasizing observation and practice, coaching encourages the acquisition of new kinds of behavior. Peer coaching is often an outgrowth of support group meetings; teachers who are engaged in discussion about aspects of practice may want to formalize this relationship by observing in each other's classrooms and providing feedback. We find that this is best handled on a casual, voluntary basis.

• *Networking*
Networking opportunities expand staff development efforts by bringing in fresh perspectives from the external environment. We have encouraged administrators and teachers to interact with professionals from other districts, supported site visitations, and hosted whole language professional meetings in our own district in order to draw on the expertise of the larger community.

Summary

Can whole language be successfully implemented in a school system by a top-down mandate alone? We think not. Although it would seem that superficial behavior can be legislated to a certain extent, beliefs are personal constructs that resist mandate. Decision-makers who attempt to impose whole language on an unwilling staff run the risk of achieving a Pyrrhic victory. In the end, grudging compliance is not the same as informed conviction. Mandated practice may look like "whole language" on the surface, but the danger is that the resemblance will end there. Changing behavior alone, decontextualized from a teacher's belief system, increases the probability that whole language will go the way of the failed innovations of the sixties and seventies.

On the other hand, we feel that grassroots interest in whole language must be cultivated by the organization. The thoughtful and effective implementation of *any* belief system requires frequent opportunities for experimentation, training, and collegial exchange; the development of a *shared* belief system requires community participation in these experiences within the organizational context. By establishing a culture in which these individual and organizational needs are addressed, decision-makers can nurture a change in belief systems. Behavior and belief are the warp and woof of the whole language fabric; it takes time, commitment, and encouragement to weave these threads into something strong and durable.

The active facilitation of grassroots interest in whole language may eventually lead to the creation of a new learning paradigm (Monson and Pahl 1991) and the establishment of a community of learners. Polarization can only be prevented if people work at it, and common ground can only be found if people look for it. District administration should support teachers in their professional development by working with them to articulate a clear commitment to shared goals and by identifying a common purpose. Administrators must reach out to teachers and provide the resources, training, and collaborative structures that will make change possible. Through this process, teachers will understand that the organization encourages risk-taking, tolerates approximations, acknowledges hard work, and supports the need for change. The potential benefits of working together far outweigh the costs. At the very least, the school community engaged in such a process and committed to such an endeavor may discover within themselves one of the most elusive characteristics of the effective educational environment—"ethos."

References

Adams, Marilyn. 1990. *Beginning to Read: Thinking and Learning About Print.* Cambridge, Mass.: MIT Press.

Carbo, Marie. November 1988. Debunking the great phonics myth, *Phi Delta Kappan* 70(3): 226–40.

Chall, Jeanne. 1967. *Learning to Read: The Great Debate.* New York: McGraw-Hill.

———. 1989. Learning to read: The great debate—twenty years later. *Phi Delta Kappan* 70(7): 521–38.

Feiman-Nemser, Sharon, and Robert Floden. 1986. The cultures of teaching. In *Handbook on Research on Teaching.* 3rd ed. Ed. Merlin C. Wittrock. New York: Macmillan.

Finn, Chester. 1990. The biggest reform of all. *Phi Delta Kappan* 71(8): 505–26.

Guskey, Thomas. 1985. Staff development and teacher change. *Educational Leadership* 42: 57–60.

Hord, Shirley, William Rutherford, Leslie Huling-Austin, and Gene Hall. 1987. *Taking Charge of Change.* Alexandria, Va.: Association for Supervision and Curriculum Development.

Huberman, A. Michael, and Matthew B. Miles. 1982. *Innovation Up Close: A Field Study in Twelve School Settings.* Andover, Mass.: The Network.

Kuhn, Thomas. 1970. *The Structures of Scientific Revolutions.* Chicago: University of Chicago Press.

Lester, Nancy, and Cynthia Onore. 1990. *Learning Change: One School District Meets Language Across the Curriculum.* Portsmouth, N.H.: Boynton/Cook.

Levine, Sarah, and Nancy Broude. 1989. Designs for learning. In *Staff Development: A Handbook of Effective Practices.* Ed. Sarah Caldwell. Oxford, Ohio: National Staff Development Council.

Little, Judith Warren. 1990. The persistance of privacy: Autonomy and initiative in teachers' professional relationships. *Teachers College Record* 91(4): 509–36.

Monson, Robert, and Michele Pahl. 1991. Charting a new course with whole language. *Educational Leadership* 48(6): 51–53.

Nebgen, Mary. 1990. Strategic planning: Achieving the goals of organization development. *Journal of Staff Development* 11(1): 28–33.

Newman, Judith, and Susan Church. 1990. The myths of whole language. *The Reading Teacher* 44(1): 20–26.

Saphier, Jon, and Matthew King. 1985. Good seeds grow in strong cultures. *Educational Leadership* 42(6): 67–74.

Sergiovanni, Thomas. 1990. *Value-Added Leadership: How to Get Extraordinary Performance in Schools.* San Diego: Harcourt Brace Jovanovich.

Shannon, Patrick. 1990. *The Struggle to Continue: Progressive Reading Instruction in the United States*. Portsmouth, N.H.: Heinemann.

Taylor, Denny. 1989. Towards a unified theory of literacy learning and instructional practice. *Phi Delta Kappan* 71(3): 185–93.

Westwood Public Schools. 1990. A transition guide for whole language implementation. Westwood, Mass.: Westwood Public Schools.

12 | Should a Superintendent Advocate One Set of Educational Beliefs?

Peter Krause

From his position as Director General (Superintendent) of the Lakeshore School
Board in the Montreal area, Peter Krause argues that superintendents
should not settle for defining good education as high test scores but rather
should promote education that instills in students a passion for learning,
the challenge to dream their own dreams, the ability to think critically and
independently, and a desire to compete against their own personal best.
Such an education, he claims, is much better fostered by a whole language philosophy of learning than by the reductionist philosophy of education that has traditionally characterized our schools. As he recounts his
personal experience with the Lakeshore School District, Peter makes clear
his belief that superintendents have a responsibility to seek out the best in
educational theories and to promote these appropriately, not to settle for
popular but insufficiently examined notions of successful education or
good teaching.

PETER KRAUSE first became interested in the whole language movement in
1984 and has vigorously pursued that interest since then, through studying
the available literature on the subject and attending numerous whole
language seminars and workshops. He took part in three ten-day whole
language seminars at the University of Arizona in Tucson, both as a
student and as a presenter. He belongs to a whole language support group
(TAWL) in Montreal and has given many workshops and seminars over the
last six years to both teachers and administrators in Canada and the United
States. He received the Administrator's Award from the C.E.L. (Child-
Centered Experience-based Learning) Group in Winnipeg, Manitoba, for
continued efforts to improve the quality of education and for encouraging
and supporting teachers in their quest for excellence in the classroom.

* * *

When I first became Director General (Superintendent) of the Lakeshore School Board, I had no specific philosophical stance regarding education. I simply wanted to ensure the best possible education for the children of the district. During the previous three years, we had implemented the "Madeline Hunter Model of Instruction" (Instructional Theory Into Practice—ITIP). I saw this model as providing teachers with the skills they needed to do a "good job" of teaching. In fact, the administrators who brought the model to the board did so on the grounds that we, the Lakeshore School Board, needed to do something to improve "instruction" in the classroom— that is, the delivery of the curriculum that had been created by our school district and for which we had built up quite a reputation in Quebec and Canada. The common remark that one could hear over and over again was that enough time had been spent on developing curriculum: it was now time to start developing good teaching.

As the new Director General, I began by reading all I could about Madeline Hunter and by attending a number of week-long Madeline Hunter institutes, even though I had a number of personal reservations about what we were doing. For one thing, our language arts curriculum, created largely by teachers, was whole language based; our math curriculum, created largely by teachers, was activity based (manipulatives in math); and our other curriculum areas, also largely created by teachers, were also whole language based. For another thing, the manner in which this process of teacher change was being implemented seemed to me to suggest criticism of what many teachers had been doing with children in the classroom. Also, the top-down manner in which the process was being implemented caused strong resentment among the teachers. Both the instructional model itself and the manner of its implementation seemed contrary to much of what had given our school district its reputation for excellence.

By the spring of 1985, my disequilibrium in trying to reconcile our curriculum and its whole language philosophical base with the direct hierarchical teaching techniques advocated by the Madeline Hunterites was reaching disturbing proportions. As Director General, I had seen my role in this teacher re-education plan as peripheral. Until then, Director Generals in the Lakeshore School Board had very little if anything to do with the pedagogical side of the organization. I had already broken the mold by attending the Madeline Hunter institutes, which was unheard of up to that point.

Within the district there were ongoing debates regarding appropriate methods of instruction, but I didn't feel knowledgeable enough to participate fully. I decided I had to get to know as much about whole language as I knew about Madeline Hunter's technology of instruction. What little I did know about whole language teachers was that they did not use Madeline Hunter's techniques but that the children in their classrooms were really turned on to learning. So I joined the Montreal Reading Council and the local whole language teacher support group. I also read many books and articles about whole language. I invited a local university professor to my office to explain the contradictions between Madeline Hunter and whole language; and I attended a number of seminars, both long and short, to hear the experts.

It soon became clear to me that we had a serious problem in our district and that if it continued all hell would break loose. At this point, I was not convinced that the whole language philosophy was the one that provided the best education for children, but I had decided that I had to come to grips with the Madeline Hunter–whole language dilemma. Through this experience, I came to realize that, yes, a superintendent has to adopt an educational philosophy and that whatever he or she does must reflect that philosophy.

I now realize that a superintendent buys into *some* educational philosophy, whether aware of it or not. If the superintendent unthinkingly accepts test scores as a measure of education, for example, then he or she has also bought into a learning theory according to which knowledge and complex processes can be broken down into bits and pieces, taught, rehearsed, and tested. As long as this philosophy remains unconscious, however, it is not likely to be examined. What I came to believe is that superintendents have a responsibility to consider alternative philosophies of education and the evidence for their success, then consciously adopt the most promising philosophy and draw upon that philosophy in guiding the development of the district.

Toward a Characterization of the "Best Education"

I believe that my foremost responsibility as superintendent is to ensure that the best education possible is provided to the children of our district. I also believe just as strongly, based on my reading of the research and observation of many classrooms, that the whole language philosophy ensures that that will happen. I know that many educators and scholars will argue with me on that point. However, I have yet to find one of them who can demonstrate that any other philosophy of education is as successful in promoting what I consider the best kind of education.

What Characterizes What the "Best Education" Is Not

Let me share with you what I do *not* believe constitutes the "best education." I do *not* buy into the premise that so many educators appear to be lulled into: that test results necessarily reflect good education. In fact, it has been shown time and time again that test results do one and only one thing well: determine which children are best able to regurgitate memorized knowledge or demonstrate the mastery of isolated and often useless "skills." In other words, they can correctly answer questions that someone else considers important. I don't wish at this point to get into a lengthy discussion of the nature and limitations of tests; I will merely ask two questions. First, of all the knowledge available in the world—which, by the way, according to experts (Ogden 1990) is doubling about every eighteen months— how can we have the audacity to determine an individual's entire future by the way in which that individual answers one, three, or twenty questions about a totally insignificant segment of all of that knowledge? Second, who has a right to decide that these particular pieces of knowledge on the test, both the questions and the answers, are important enough to either brighten or extinguish the curiosity of a young mind? There are so much more meaningful and valuing ways of assessing learners, ways that respect their dignity and build upon their self-esteem. Some of these are discussed later in this chapter.

One last comment about tests. Too often in education, administrators' insecurity causes them to be preoccupied (sometimes to the point of obsession) with "knowing" and "having a handle on" what is going on in every classroom. This leads them to constrain and constrict the possibilities of what *can* go on in the classroom, which in turn leads to artificially limited expectations of what students can actually accomplish and achieve. In effect, the administration imposes restrictions on students' learning, focusing instead on test expectations rather than on meaningful learning that would undoubtedly reach far beyond the narrow curriculum aimed at responding to the demands of the tests. I think it is time that we rid ourselves of our very tattered security blanket and the educational paradigm that it reflects.

Further, I do not believe that the best education is taking someone else's techniques or ideas and simply "doing" them in the classroom. It is such common practice in education to take teachers, give them a one- or two-week "how to" workshop on some new methods, and then expect instant success back in the classrooms. To believe that this technique would work at all is to sell teachers far short of being the professionals they are or certainly could be if given the opportunity. The most glaring example of this has already been discussed— namely, Madeline Hunter's ITIP "Instructional Theory into Practice" program or, as I prefer to call it, the "Instructional Technology into Practice" kit, a model that requires teachers to conform to standard behaviors. Supposedly all that teachers have to do to be good teachers is follow the lockstep prescriptions that get students to respond uniformly and on cue. I do not believe that this is good education.

Finally, I do not believe that the best education is treating students as little people who know nothing when they come into school and have to be "educated" or "filled up" with knowledge (some educators refer to this as the "banking model" of learning). This approach treats teachers as omnipotent sources of knowledge whose responsibility it is to "feed" the students knowledge in bite-sized pieces so as not to overwhelm them and ensure that they will know enough to pass the tests discussed earlier.

What Characterizes the "Best Education"?

So what is my definition of the "best education"? First and foremost I believe we must instill in our students a passion for learning. When they leave our school system, they must have a passion for learning that will stay with them for the rest of their lives. Is it not true that they originally come to us with this passion overflowing? Our responsibility is to ensure that we not only maintain this love of learning but enhance it. For this to happen these students must be taught by teachers who themselves are passionate about learning.

It is my experience that teachers who abide by a whole language philosophy are such individuals. They are first of all learners themselves. I invite administrators to join me at whole language teacher conferences to see for themselves. Publishers such as Irwin Books, Heinemann, Richard C. Owen, Scholastic, and others cannot keep up with teachers' demand for more and more professional literature. Teachers *are* reading professional books more than at any time in the past. Why? Because they want to know, and they want to become better and better teachers. They are reading these books because they are seeking their own answers to their own questions about learning and teaching, not questions imposed from outside by the system or the administration.

Exactly the same applies to the students whom these teachers teach. That is, the teachers try as much as possible to let their students pursue answers to their own questions, for inquiry is natural to all learners. It is only when learners begin to ask their own questions that real learning begins. Every member of the learning community moves in and around the center of the curriculum, taking on various appropriate roles—researcher, resource person, listener, support team member, advocate, presenter, or expert, but always inquirer (Watson, Burke, and Harste 1989). Whatever the curriculum area being pursued, unless the learners ask their own questions learning will lack depth and be difficult (Caine and Caine 1991). Why is it so difficult for us as educational administrators to see how much more powerful and meaningful learning is if students pursue answers to their own questions? That is the key to motivation. If I, as a learner, am seeking an answer to my own question, then I'm the stakeholder and will take full responsibility for whatever learning I have to do to attain the answer.

My second expectation is one that comes from Paulo Freire. He states that our task is not to impose our dreams on our pupils, but to challenge them to have their own dreams, to define their choices, not just to assume them uncritically (1985). To restate this in my own words, our responsibility as educators is to free our students to do their thing and get excited about their world in order to create their own realities and achievements.

A third expectation is that students become independent critical thinkers and in so doing become constructive forces in their own social context. In whole language classrooms the teacher not only encourages students but also creates opportunities for students to raise their inquiring voices, to challenge one another's assumptions, and to develop a respect for differences of opinion. Students are challenged to defend their positions by developing and articulating support for that position. Students are constantly encouraged to ask the difficult question and then given full support in taking the risk necessary to come up with the answer. The one certainty that students in whole language classrooms encounter is they will be encouraged to develop more questions for which answers are to be found. The powerful thing about such a process of inquiry is that it is student driven and therefore always student involving.

A fourth expectation is that students will compete against their own personal best rather than against their fellow classmates. So often in our educational system student competes against student. This is so destructive to a cohesive and positive learning environment.

In his book *No Contest: The Case Against Competition* (1986), Alfie Kohn makes perhaps the most powerful case against our ingrained tenacity for competition. One comment on the book from the *Publishers Weekly* review perhaps best summarizes this destructive force.

> Kohn . . . persuasively demonstrates how the ingrained American myth that competition is the only normal and desirable way of life—from Little Leagues to the presidency—is counterproductive, personally and for the national economy, and how psychologically it poisons relationships, fosters anxiety, and takes the fun out of work and play.

In contrast, whole language classrooms foster collaborative learning environments, where everyone is a co-learner, contributing to their own and each others' learning. Looking around our own communities, we see that wherever good is being accomplished, someone is helping someone else or they are working together for the common good. For whole language teachers and students, this is a natural, everyday occurrence. And for anyone who thinks this would never work in business, books by such authors as Tom Peters and John Naisbitt can be enlightening. John Goodlad (1984) demonstrates the same for the educational environment.

The question I often hear when sharing these expectations with my colleagues is "What about the content, the facts, the minimal knowledge base that every child needs in order to begin on the ladder of life?"

I begin my response by suggesting that before children ever come to school, they have already learned more than they probably will for the rest of their lives. Just think about it. They can walk, communicate, think, create, interact successfully with their environment, and do many other things. Yet up to this point no one has formally controlled their learning. No one has formally evaluated their learning or formally predetermined what that learning should be and in what sequence it should have been acquired. Surprise, surprise! The child has learned anyway. I find that as educators we sometimes take ourselves much too seriously and in so doing we actually prevent the child from learning. Surely this is not our intent.

As far as content of education is concerned, all of the aspects of a good education I have articulated cannot be attained unless they are surrounded by and intertwined with content. You cannot think unless you think about *something*. You research questions to find *information* that bears upon them. You argue and defend your position about something, using factual evidence in your support. Content is necessarily both the foundation and the by-product of an education focused upon process; the two are inextricable. But in whole language classrooms, the content is meaningful content, that which engages the curiosity of children and challenges them to ask even more difficult questions to which answers must be found. Whole language teachers respond to children's inquisitive minds by allowing them to make choices and take risks, by encouraging them when they stumble and gently taking their hand and helping them up again.

Caine and Caine (1991) suggest that there is no question that facts and specific knowledge are important aspects of learning but that schools have concentrated too heavily on the memorization of facts as the basis of a good education when in reality they should be emphasizing meaningful relationships in knowledge and how that knowledge relates to life, especially the students' own. They go on to say that specific knowledge is in fact much easier to learn in that type of context than memorizing unrelated and individual bits of information. It is my experience that children in whole language classrooms where that type of meaningful teaching is carried out not only learn the specific facts we want them to learn but also actually learn more and do so in a pleasant, positive atmosphere.

In sum, what I expect the "best education" to encourage in students is a passion for learning, an eagerness to dream their own dreams and to devise and accept their own challenges, the ability and inclination to think critically and independently, and the disposition to repeatedly exceed their own personal best, through collaboration rather than competition. These expectations are, in my opinion, best promoted by a whole language philosophy and paradigm of education.

Whole Language as an Educational Philosophy

What I began to understand as I started my investigation of whole language is that it originally developed from a theory of reading. From there, it evolved to encompass writing, listening, and talking, all elements of a good language arts program. Since its early beginnings in the late 1960s and early 1970s, whole language has taken on a much broader definition and scope. As Jerome Harste (1989) put it at a recent educational conference, whole language has become a theory of learning. Much has been written about that since, and one of the best presentations in book form can be found in Constance Weaver's

Understanding Whole Language: From Principles to Practice (1990). Nowadays, the principles of whole language philosophy embrace all aspects of learning and include all subject areas.

Whole Language as a Theory of Learning

Whole language rests upon the clearly established premise that in order for meaningful learning to take place, certain conditions must be satisfied.

First, the learning experiences must engage the learner. I use the word *engage* because, for me, it implies commitment and total immersion with the activity at hand. It suggests that learning is not an extrinsic activity, something that one is passively involved with, but rather an intrinsic activity that incorporates the learner's intellectual, physical, and emotional state. It totally absorbs the learner. There is never any trouble with short attention spans in this type of learning climate. Caine and Caine (1991) contend that learning engages the entire self.

Second, the learning must be meaningful to the learner. Learning begins by making connections between what is known and what is being learned. Jerome Harste (1989) says that no matter what you want to teach, children need to begin by making connections in terms of their own experience. Gordon Wells (1986) also states that children are active learners attempting to construe what is new in terms of what they already know. Frank Smith (1987) makes the observation that learning takes place only when something makes sense.

Third, whole language proponents advocate that all members of the classroom, including the teacher, must be learners in both thought and action. I cannot state strongly enough that if the teacher in the classroom, the principal in the school, and the superintendent in the head office are avid learners in thought and deed, so will all those who work with these people be learners. An eagerness to learn is contagious.

Fourth, whole language educators value all learners. This principle is the one that leads many whole language supporters to reject the notion of testing learners and ranking them one against the other. They find the idea repugnant and unacceptable. As Alfie Kohn (1986) would put it, the only competition should be with oneself, because that leads to true growth as a learner. The terms *self-esteem, self-worth, self-image,* and others have long been the topic of discussion in educational circles. In whole language classrooms, because of the fundamental principle of valuing each learner and accepting all learners where they are, these concepts easily become reality. It is next to impossible to find an insecure child in a whole language classroom.

From the Reductionist to the Constructivist Paradigm of Education

What happens in the classroom is obviously crucial to education. Traditionally our educational paradigm has promoted and supported the teacher as the dispenser of knowledge. Students were viewed as empty vessels to be filled by the teacher dispensing canonical knowledge. In fact, many classrooms that I visit today still employ this approach to learning. Often this method of teaching is referred to as the transmission model of instruction (Madeline Hunter Technology), or the reductionist theory of learning, where knowledge is broken down into its smallest elements and then delivered to the learners in boring bit by boring bit.

The whole language philosophy, on the other hand, approaches learning, the learner, and the teacher from a completely different premise. First, it reflects the constructivist theory of learning, which is the exact opposite of the reductionist theory. Second, it uses, almost entirely, a transactional model of instruction, which requires the learner to be actively engaged in exploring answers to questions that the learner has raised. In other words, learning activities fulfill the purposes of the learner. The teacher is not the dispenser of knowledge, with the pupils being the empty vessels; rather, the teacher becomes one of the learners in the classroom and acts as a full participant in the explorations and discoveries being made by the students. The teacher serves as mentor and guide to the pupils as well as being a co-learner. Such a constructivist paradigm of learning and teaching is most likely to promote the "best education." Constance Weaver, in the first chapter of this book (Figure 1–5) illustrates the differences between the transmission (reductionist) and the transactional (constructivist) paradigms of education. Note the similarities that exist between that analysis and the one found in Figure 12–1, from Caine and Caine's (1991) discussion of brain-based teaching.

FIGURE 12–1 *Comparison of Teaching Models (From Caine and Caine 1991)*

Elements of Orchestration	Traditional Teaching	Brain-Based Teaching
Source of information	Simple. Two-way, from teacher to book, worksheet, or film to student.	Complex. Social interactions, group discovery, individual search and reflection, role playing, integrated subject matter.
Classroom organization	Linear. Individual work or teacher directed.	Complex. Thematic, integrative, cooperative, workstations, individualized projects.
Classroom management	Hierarchical. Teacher controlled.	Complex. Designated status and responsibilities delegated to students and monitored by teacher.
Outcomes	Specified and convergent. Emphasis on memorized concepts, vocabulary, and skills.	Complex. Emphasis on reorganization of information in unique ways, with both predictable outcomes, divergent and convergent, increase in natural knowledge demonstrated through ability to use learned skills in variable contexts.

Assessment in and Evidence for Whole Language Education

Caine and Caine (1991) suggest that our methods of evaluation govern the way we teach and the freedom to learn. They go on to state that the result is precisely what we have: a majority of teachers teaching to simplistic tests, teaching for memorization, and thereby limiting what students can learn and the connections they can make.

They add that teachers must dramatically extend their range of observations of students. This would still include tests of all types, but
would relegate them to their appropriate place, namely a relatively
small part of the global assessment process. Frank Smith (1986) states
that the two major assumptions that underlie our obsession with
testing are that children will learn more and that teachers will teach
better. What in fact happens, he observes, is that children learn not to
learn and teachers learn not to teach. He suggests that we eliminate
testing altogether and simply allow children to learn to their potential
without our interference (Smith 1988).

As can be seen from the above and our own experience, the
testing dilemma is what is driving the educational community.
Because of our constant concern with evaluation, we tend often to
forget about the joys of learning and how very natural it is in the
proper setting. We don't seem to trust that children will learn without
having to be constantly tested.

At the Lakeshore School Board, in whole language classrooms,
the processes of assessment and evaluation are under constant review
and change. Marilyn Wray, our learning consultant for secondary
language arts, shared the following story with me concerning our
final English Literature examinations in our high schools:

> We believed that talk was essential to the clarification of thinking
> and hence an important element in the writing process. Our
> province also required that students write formal examinations for
> the High School Leaving Certificate. Putting talk together with
> examinations became quite a trick. We allowed several days (from
> five to eight) in regular classes for the initial responding to literature
> and planning to write, and then finished with revision and final
> draft of the writing during a three-hour examination period. That
> examination period was held in the gymnasium, where two hun-
> dred students were placed in groups of three, four, or five, the same
> as they were grouped normally in their classrooms. Instead of a
> horrendous noise, which we had feared, quiet, businesslike discus-
> sions prevailed. If we were pleased with the process, we were even
> more pleased with the results. What a pleasure the papers were to
> read. Both teachers and students were convinced that what they had
> accomplished was their very best work. Both were elated. The pro-
> cess, regardless of the formality of the setting, had worked.

As I stated earlier, this was *our* experience of what is called process exam writing. For us it had worked; we have been doing it now
for three years. The up-side of this initiative by a group of whole

language secondary English teachers is that similar processes are being explored by other teachers in different subject areas. It is a slow process but encouraging nonetheless. The down-side is that the Evaluation branch of the Department of Education of the Government of Quebec is upset that we have only a four to seven percent failure rate. This to them is much too low. According to their statistics it should be at least twenty percent. For me, four to seven percent is still too high. I believe that there should be no failures at all. The fact that we have reduced the rate from twenty to thirty percent to four to seven percent convinces me that it is possible to eliminate failures altogether.

Unfortunately, it will be a while before our secondary schools will change because it is there that I still find much evidence of the transmission model of teaching, where students listen and take notes while the teacher talks and does most of the learning. This reluctance to change can be attributed to what I have already referred to, namely, the teachers' preoccupation with the requirements of the Provincial exams that all high school seniors must write. Teachers often comment about their willingness to change, but unfortunately, they say, they have to prepare their students for these exams.

In our elementary schools things are changing much more quickly. Many more teachers have accepted the move toward whole language and as a result are changing their assessment and evaluation practices. I say "moving toward" whole language because I feel that you never "get there." There is always something new to learn and new questions to ask. If you ever think you have all the answers, it is time to retire and let others with more unanswered questions take your place.

The assessment and evaluation practices in our elementary schools are constantly being reviewed and revised as well. The premises that underlie these practices are best summarized in a paper by Lorraine Gillmeister-Krause (August 1991): She states that all assessment and evaluation are done in the course of ongoing classroom activities, that they focus on the strengths of the children, and that the teacher must be a constant "kid watcher" (Yetta Goodman's expression). For her, the challenge of assessment and evaluation is to help children find their strengths and the confidence to take the necessary risks to make literacy choices and enter into functional literacy events. She continues by stating that assessment must fulfill two requirements:

1. It must help the student and the teacher move forward in reading and writing and the understanding and creating of new knowledge—that is, assessment must help create curriculum.

2. Assessment must reflect the expectations communicated to the student in each day's writing and reading.

Further, she observes that whole language teachers are constant kid watchers:

> A teacher informally assesses a child's growth and development in reading and writing whenever the teacher:
>
> 1. watches a child write;
> 2. listens to a child's response to a book;
> 3. listens to a group of children discuss or plan together;
> 4. has a casual conversation with a child;
> 5. sees ways in which a child uses reading for learning across the curriculum;
> 6. notes when a child chooses to read silently for the first time or for sustained periods;
> 7. observes a child browsing or sharing a book (fiction or nonfiction) with others;
> 8. listens to a child read aloud;
> 9. becomes aware of the influence of a particular story or book in a child's drama play or in his or her writing;
> 10. sees evidence of a bilingual child using knowledge of reading in French, for example, to support learning to read in English;
> 11. and . . . the list is endless and unique for each child.
>
> These informal observations form our understanding of how and what children learn.
>
> To document all of the information, there are many many ways—each unique to each teacher.
>
> a. my kid watching binder is used daily;
> b. student teacher conferences;
> c. self-evaluation and peer evaluation.
>
> Writing assessments about children in narrative form is very important and powerful. It helps teachers analyze and evaluate the student's language development and learning opportunities.
>
> The most important form of evaluation is self-evaluation. Teachers continuously evaluate themselves and their teaching, and we must help pupils develop ways of evaluating their own development, of knowing when they are and when they are not successful in using language and learning through it. Whole language helps children value what they can do and not be defeated by what they can't do. Children learn to trust themselves and their linguistic intuitions, and they become self-reliant in the sense of what they are reading.

Assessment and evaluation in whole language are complex processes. They cannot be adequately dealt with in a single chapter such as this one. Figure 12–2 offers some references for further consideration

FIGURE 12–2 *Some References on Assessment and Evaluation*

Anthony, Robert, Terry Johnson, Norma Mickelson, and Alison Preece. 1991. *Evaluating Literacy: A Perspective for Change.* Portsmouth, N.H.: Heinemann.

Atwell, Nancie. 1987. *In the Middle: Writing, Reading, and Learning with Adolescents.* Portsmouth, N.H.: Boynton-Cook.

Baker, Ann, and Johnny Baker. 1990. *Mathematics in Process.* Portsmouth, N.H.: Heinemann.

Boomer, Garth. 1982. *Negotiating the Curriculum: A Teacher-Student Partnership.* Sydney, Australia: Ashton Scholastic.

Caine, Renate Nummela, and Geoffrey Caine. 1991. *Making Connections: Teaching and the Human Brain.* Alexandria, Va.: Association for Supervision and Curriculum Development.

Goodman, Kenneth S., Lois Bridges Bird, and Yetta M. Goodman, eds. 1991. *The Whole Language Catalogue.* Santa Rosa, Calif.: American School Publishers.

Goodman, Kenneth S., Yetta M. Goodman, and Wendy J. Hood, eds. 1989. *The Whole Language Evaluation Book.* Portsmouth, N.H.: Heinemann.

Goodman, Yetta M. June 1978. Kid watching: An alternative to testing. *National Elementary School Principal* 57:41–45.

Harp, Bill, ed. 1991. *Assessment and Evaluation in Whole Language Classrooms.* Norwood, Mass.. Christopher-Gordon.

Heald-Taylor, Gail. 1989. *The Administrator's Guide to Whole Language.* Katonah, N.Y.: Richard C. Owen.

Minnick-Santa, Carol, and Donna E. Alvermann. 1991. *Science Learning; Processes and Applications.* Newark, Del.: International Reading Association.

Stephens, Diane. 1992. *Research on Whole Language: Support for a New Curriculum.* Katonah, N.Y.: Richard C. Owen.

Stice, Carol F., and Nancy P. Bertrand. June 1990. *Whole Language and the Emergent Literacy of At Risk Children: A Two Year Comparative Study.* Center of Excellence: Basic Skills. Nashville, Tenn.: Tennessee State University.

Weaver, Constance. 1990. *Understanding Whole Language: From Principles to Practice.* Portsmouth, N.H.: Heinemann.

Whitin, David J., Heidi Mills, and Timothy O'Keefe. 1990. *Living and Learning Mathematics: Stories and Strategies for Supporting Mathematical Literacy.* Portsmouth, N.H.: Heinemann.

---

of ideas in holistic assessment. What I have tried to do here is simply to introduce some possibilities that can take us beyond our narrow testing focus and that add immeasurably to the learning dimensions of both teachers and students.

From Whole Language Principles to Practice

I am often asked how I got the administration of the Lakeshore School Board to reconsider the Madeline Hunter model of instruction. How did I get them to the point of adopting a set of beliefs about education that appear to be so compatible with the whole language philosophy? I don't believe that any one person played a singular role in the process, least of all me. Rather, a number of circumstances contributed and still contribute to change at the Lakeshore School Board.

I don't believe that it was a secret among my administrative colleagues that I had some real conflicts with the implementation of Madeline Hunter's technology and the whole language curriculum we were implementing in our schools, especially at the elementary level. Fortunately, there were a number of conditions and processes already in existence in the district that allowed certain things to happen quite naturally.

First, with the introduction of the Madeline Hunter model, we introduced a concept called "Dialogue on Learning." This concept was interpreted by many members of our educational community as being directly related to implementing Madeline Hunter's model. However, when *I* used the term "Dialogue on Learning" I always prefaced it with a brief definition. This definition stated simply that "Dialogue on Learning" meant educators talking to other educators about learning and encompassed all aspects of learning that were being discussed in our district. These included dialogues on whole language; manipulatives in math; constructivism in the sciences; discipline with dignity; reality therapy and control theory; second language learning; *l'approche intégrée* in our French schools; cooperative learning; negotiating the curriculum; mainstreaming; learning styles; and, of course, Madeline Hunter. As time passed and staffing changes occurred at the central office, less and less dialogue was going on about Madeline Hunter's model and more and more on the other topics mentioned above. The one constant principle that exists among the remaining items is the principle that the learner is the center of the learning process and as such is expected to take full responsibility for learning, behavior, and social interaction.

Because of my strong convictions about the whole language philosophy and the principles it represents, I have always approached the dialogue about the conflict between Madeline Hunter and whole language with a great deal of thought and openness. The principle of whole language I have consistently tried to apply was to value each learner in my community. Often it has been difficult, but always necessary. I am certain that even today we have some members of our educational community still applying Madeline Hunter's technology and some members struggling, as I did, with the inherent contradiction between the two. The thing I know for certain is that you cannot mandate the whole language philosophy. It must be adopted by each member of the educational community, one by one, as each works through the process of identifying what is the "best education" that can be provided to each student.

Second, many of my administrative colleagues held much the same view about learning and learners that I held and welcomed the opportunity to develop a statement of beliefs that corresponded to their innermost beliefs about learning. In fact we had, over a period of about four years, often discussed the necessity to do just that. We felt that everyone in the Lakeshore School Board had a right to know the basis upon which we decided major issues and directions for the district. So we, the senior administration, developed and adopted a set of beliefs about education that has been shared with everyone in the district. These beliefs state clearly what we as the district's senior administration value in the schools, what we see as the "best education," and what is required to offer such an education. Specifically, this belief statement characterizes the kind of school system we are, the things we believe about learning and learners, the kind of organization we run, and our conviction that we must all be learners for life. The belief statement reads as follows:

1.0 It is essential that our school system become an inclusive one that responds to the needs of all learners.
2.0 Our students are the central focus of our learning vision.
    2.1 Learning requires the active participation of the learner.
    2.2 People learn in a variety of ways and at different rates.
    2.3 Learning is both an individual and a social process.
3.0 Quality learning opportunities will:
    3.1 assist learners to see relationships and connections;
    3.2 be authentic, real, and meaningful to the learner;
    3.3 be gained from an integrated curriculum;
    3.4 come from within the learner.
    We believe that the above four points define holistic education.
4.0 It Is vital that all classrooms, schools, adult education centres, and offices in the Lakeshore School Board be humanistic (*people centered*) since such an environment will enhance learning and performance.
5.0 Learning is a lifelong process.

It took us, a group of twelve administrators, about two years to develop the statement. One objective was that we wanted to make certain that each of us clearly understood the meaning of the words in each belief in order to ensure that when we shared these beliefs with our colleagues in the district we were all speaking the same language.

Another objective that we set for ourselves was that we would not present these beliefs as a directive for everyone to adhere to. What we did was to invite the people of the Lakeshore School Board community to read our belief statement. We emphasized that these were *our* beliefs, not necessarily theirs. Everyone in the Lakeshore community could choose to buy into them individually or as a staff. Or they could choose to develop their own set of beliefs and share them with us so that if we wished to we could modify ours accordingly. In other words, the senior staff invited the people of the Lakeshore School Board community to engage in their own learning, drawing as they might or might not choose upon our demonstration. This process is similar to what occurs in whole language classrooms.

We initially presented our beliefs to the people of the Lakeshore school board a year ago. To date we have received many very positive comments from board members, administrators, teachers, and others, many of whom have adopted these beliefs themselves or advised us that they held these beliefs even before we published the statement.

Of course, there are many things occurring in our district that need to be worked on; we have not solved all our problems. However, as a whole language proponent I strongly believe that the walk speaks louder than the talk. I therefore continuously strive to influence, to persuade, to challenge, and to teach in much the same way as I expect teachers to work with our students in our classrooms: the whole language way. Eventually there will come a time when one may say that we have truly all adopted the whole language philosophy in our everyday actions at the school board. Whether this will come during my tenure at the school board or after is hard to say, but come it will. I am convinced.

In closing, I wish to share a quote from an article by Sam Crowell that appeared in the September 1989 issue of *Educational Leadership:*

> A word about the future: One of the most sensible explanations of the future that I have seen comes from Constantinos Doxiadis. . . . He viewed the future from four perspectives: (1) the constant past— such as mountains, rivers, oceans, continents—that will remain as part of our foreseeable future; (2) the declining past—such as institutions, buildings, traditions, values, ideas, even people; things that

may be in a state of decline but will continue to influence and affect our lives; (3) the continuing past—which includes each of us and our children, as well as the structures, ideas, and values that have been learned from the past yet adopted for the future; (4) the created future—the spontaneous acts of creativity that provide shape and direction for the world to come. The future, in other words, is rooted in the past yet is open to imagination and creative initiative.

As we help students explore their future, we will inevitably explore our own. We need to appreciate where we are and how we got here. The challenge of a new way of thinking is not a call to abandon cherished values that have provided meaning and direction. Rather it is a challenge to participate in creating a new vision of our role as humans and in educating students to achieve that potential.

I believe that the challenge is clear: we administrators must be learners with our teachers and our students. We must discard our old roles and replace them with new ones made like a quilt, with a delicate balance between patches of the old and patches of the new, but guided by a new vision of what education is all about and a new vision of us all as active, lifelong learners.

Whole language for me responds to that challenge in the best way I know. I leave you with a thought that I recently shared with some parents in my school district in a letter that I wrote to them about whole language:

I hope that the above has given you some insight into why I hold such strong biases toward whole language. After all, if you had a chance to choose between the best and everything else, what would you choose?

References

Anthony, Robert, Terry Johnson, Norma Michelson, and Alison Preece. 1991. *Evaluating Literacy: A Perspective for Change.* Portsmouth, N.H.: Heinemann.

Atwell, Nancie. 1987. *In the Middle: Writing, Reading, and Learning with Adolescents.* Portsmouth, N.H.: Boynton/Cook.

Baker, Ann, and Johnny Baker. 1990. *Mathematics in Process.* Portsmouth, N.H.: Heinemann.

Boomer, Garth. 1982. *Negotiating the Curriculum: A Teacher-Student Partnership.* Sydney, Australia: Ashton Scholastic.

Caine, Renate Nummela, and Geoffrey Caine. 1991. *Making Connections: Teaching and the Human Brain.* Alexandria, Va.: Association for Supervision and Curriculum Development.

Crowell, Sam. September 1989. A new way of thinking: The challenge of the future. *Educational Leadership* 47:60–63.

Freire, Paulo. January 1985. Reading the world and reading the word: An interview with Paulo Freire. *Language Arts* 62: 15–21.

Gillmeister-Krause, Lorraine. August 1991. Valuing children: Evaluation in whole language. Paper presented at the Second Whole Language Umbrella Conference, Phoenix, Az.

Goodlad, John I. 1984. *A Place Called School: Prospects for the Future.* New York: McGraw-Hill.

Goodman, Kenneth S., Lois Bridges Bird, and Yetta M. Goodman, eds. 1991. *The Whole Language Catalogue.* Santa Rosa, Calif.: American School Publishers.

Goodman, Kenneth S., Yetta M. Goodman, and Wendy J. Hood, eds. 1989. *The Whole Language Evaluation Book.* Portsmouth, N.H.: Heinemann.

Goodman, Yetta M. June 1978. Kid watching: An alternative to testing. *National Elementary School Principal* 57:41–45.

Harp, Bill, ed. 1991. *Assessment and Evaluation in Whole Language Classrooms.* Norwood, Mass.: Christopher-Gordon.

Harste, Jerome C. November 1989. A vision of curriculum for a democracy. Paper presented at the annual meeting of the National Council of Teachers of English, Baltimore, Md.

Heald-Taylor, Gail. 1989. *The Administrator's Guide to Whole Language.* Katonah, N.Y.: Richard C. Owen.

Hunter, Madeline. 1976. *RX Improved Instruction: Take 10 Staff Meetings as Directed.* El Segundo, Calif.: Theory Into Practice (TIP) Publications.

———. 1982. *Mastery Teaching.* El Segundo, Calif.: TIP Publications.

Kohn, Alfie. 1986. *No Contest: The Case Against Competition.* Boston, Mass.: Houghton Mifflin.

Minnick-Santa, Carol, and Donna E. Alvermann. 1991. *Science Learning: Processes and Applications.* Newark, Del.: International Reading Association.

Naisbitt, John. 1988. *Megatrends.* New York: Warner.

Naisbitt, John, and Patricia Aburdene. 1986. *Reinventing the Corporation.* New York: Warner.

Ogden, Frank (Dr. Tomorrow). 1990. Vivid visionary, Dr. Tomorrow is in business to describe the future today. *Canadian Magazine* (July): 23.

Peters, Thomas, and Robert H. Waterman, Jr. 1982. *In Search of Excellence: Lessons from America's Best Run Companies.* New York: Harper & Row.

Peters, Tom. 1987. *Thriving on Chaos.* New York: Alfred A. Knopf.

Peters, Tom, and Nancy Austin. 1985. *A Passion for Excellence: The Leadership Difference*. New York: Random House.

Peters, Tom, and Robert Townsend. 1986. *Excellence in the Organization*. Chicago: Nightingale-Conant.

Smith, Frank. 1986. *Insult to Intelligence: The Bureaucratic Invasion of Our Classrooms*. Portsmouth, N.H.: Heinemann.

———. 1987. *What the Brain Does Well*. Victoria, B.C.: Abel Press.

———. April 1988. How education backed the wrong horse. Paper presented at the Springboard Conference of the Quebec Reading Association, Montreal, Quebec.

Stephens, Diane. 1992. *Research on Whole Language: Support for a New Curriculum*. Katonah, N.Y.: Richard C. Owen.

Stice, Carol F., and Nancy P. Bertrand. 1990. *Whole Language and the Emergent Literacy of At Risk Children: A Two Year Comparative Study*. Center of Excellence: Basic Skills. Nashville, Tenn.: Tennessee State University.

Watson, Dorothy, Carolyn Burke, and Jerome Harste. 1989. *Whole Language: Inquiring Voices*. Richmond Hill, Ontario: Scholastic-TAB.

Weaver, Constance. 1990. *Understanding Whole Language: From Principles to Practice*. Portsmouth, N.H.: Heinemann.

Wells, Gordon. 1986. *The Meaning Makers: Children Learning Language and Using Language to Learn*. Portsmouth, N.H.: Heinemann.

Whitin, David J., Heidi Mills, and Timothy O'Keefe. 1990. *Living and Learning Mathematics: Stories and Strategies for Supporting Mathematical Literacy*. Portsmouth, N.H.: Heinemann.